enjoy!

GOOD GUYS WEAR WHITE HATS

SPONSORS

WANDA BASS

WILLIAM E. AND MARGARET H. DAVIS FAMILY FUND

KERR FOUNDATION

LOCAL OKLAHOMA BANK

JULIAN J. ROTHBAUM

SONIC CORPORATION

Good Guys WEAR White Hats

THE LIFE OF GEORGE NIGH

BY BOB BURKE

OKLAHOMA TRACKMAKER SERIES

SERIES EDITOR: Kenny A. Franks

ASSOCIATE EDITOR: Gini Moore Campbell

Printed in the United States of America

ISBN 1-885596-17-0

LC Number 00-104132

Designed by Carol Haralson

OTHER BOOKS BY BOB BURKE

From Oklahoma To Eternity: The Life of Wiley Post and the Winnie Mae
Lyle Boren: Rebel Congressman
These Be Thine Arms Forever
3,500 Years of Burkes
The Stories and Speeches of Lyle H. Boren
Corn, Cattle, and Moonshine
Like a Prairie Fire
Push Back the Darkness
The Irish Connection
Lyle H. Boren: The Eloquent Congressman
Dewey F. Bartlett: The Bartlett Legacy
Glen D. Johnson, Sr.: The Road to Washington
An American Jurist: The Life of Alfred P. Murrah
Mike Monroney: Oklahoma Liberal
Roscoe Dunjee: Champion of Civil Rights
Out From the Shadows: The Life of John J. Harden
Abe Lemons: Court Magician
Glory Days of Summer: The History of Baseball in Oklahoma
Alice Robertson: Oklahoma Congresswoman
Victor Wickersham: Your Best Friend
Historic Oklahoma: An Illustrated History
Bryce Harlow: Mr. Integrity

Oklahoma Heritage Association
201 Northwest Fourteenth Street
Oklahoma City, Oklahoma 73103

Unless otherwise noted all photographs are from the George and Donna Nigh family collection.

THIS BOOK IS DEDICATED
TO THE PEOPLE
OF OKLAHOMA

We are eternally grateful to the people of Oklahoma who have given us so many opportunities and have encouraged us each step along the way. The late United States Senator Thomas P. Gore expressed it best for us:

I love Oklahoma
I love every blade of her grass
I love every grain of her sand
I am proud of her past
and I am confident of her future.

—GEORGE AND DONNA NIGH

CONTENTS

The public service contributions of George and Donna Nigh were recognized in 1999 when the Oklahoma legislature funded the George and Donna Nigh Public Service Scholarships. The scholarships, wholeheartedly endorsed by Governor Frank Keating, the Board of Regents for Higher Education, and regents for the various colleges and universities, will be awarded annually to deserving students at all Oklahoma private and public institutions of higher learning. The George and Donna Nigh Public Service Scholarships were first awarded in 2000.

PREFACE

HONESTY is the most crucial ingredient of leadership. Without credibility, a leader cannot persuade others to follow. Loss of trust has forced leaders, including governors and one American president, to resign. Being dishonest has fatally wounded many political leaders since the founding of the Republic. A recent Associated Press poll showed that American voters chose honesty as the most important trait of a political candidate, ahead of compassion, leadership skills, and philosophy of government.

George Nigh's trademark was honesty. He was full of compassion and demonstrated extraordinary leadership acumen in 50 years of public service to Oklahoma. Even though opponents might question his decisions, no one questioned his integrity. If George Nigh told you something, you could go to the bank with it.

This is the story of an honest young man with an honest goal—to do his best for his native Oklahoma.

Along the way, a strong partnership was formed with his wife Donna. Together George and Donna Nigh made an indelible mark on the landscape of Oklahoma.

—BOB BURKE, 2000

ACKNOWLEDGMENTS

TELLING THE STORY of George and Donna Nigh was exciting and often overwhelming. George has been a moving force in Oklahoma since he was elected to the state legislature in 1950, a half century ago! Since 1963, Donna has stood beside George as they fulfilled the highest calling in Oklahoma public service any couple could have.

George's name appears in state newspapers more often than that of any other Oklahoman in history. For example, one can access the archives of *The Daily Oklahoman* on its website and find George mentioned in nearly 8,000 stories and that's just since 1981.

For those who might wonder, George acts no differently in retirement than he did in 50 years of public service. He speaks to strangers on elevators and is never too busy to discuss any topic with fellow patrons at restaurants or the grocery store. His genuine love for people is obvious to any observer.

Donna was gracious in opening her home to my perusal of family photo albums in the same gracious manner that she opened the governor's mansion for the people of Oklahoma.

Thousands of newspaper clippings and interviews with George, Donna, their son Mike Mashburn, their daughter, Georgeann Nigh Whitener, former staff members, and friends comprise the backbone of this biography. I was humbled by offers of help from so many people whose lives have been touched by George and Donna.

I owe much to many who helped make this book a reality. Carol Campbell, Mary Phillips, Melissa Hayer, Robin Davison, Billie Harry, and Linda Lynn at the archives of *The Daily Oklahoman*; Debbie Neill, Shelley Dabney, and Debi Engles who transcribed interviews; and Kitty Pittman, Adrienne Butler, Melecia Caruthers, Marilyn Miller, and Mary Hardin at the Oklahoma Department of Libraries (ODL), often dropped what they were doing to help me research. ODL Director Robert L. Clark provided enthusiastic encouragement. Scott Dowell, Delbert Amen, Rodger Harris, and Judith Michener at the Oklahoma Historical Society; Becky Rickard and April Tippens at Sonic Industries, Inc.; and Juanita Kidd assisted in research.

Judge Steven Taylor in McAlester spent days showing me George's old neighborhood and introducing me around Pittsburg County. Bill and Vickey Nigh, Mary Nigh Cargill, and Lorena Crockett Razook provided family stories and photographs. Information on George's rich McAlester heritage came from Mary Ann Gaberino and JoAnn Tiemann at the McAlester Building Foundation.

My editors, Dr. Kenny Franks and Gini Moore Campbell, were understanding and encouraging as the manuscript grew beyond original specifications. My administrative assistant, Eric Dabney, is unmatched in devotion and assistance on my book projects. Surely I have bored Eric and my lovely wife, Chimene, with my insistence on reading them my latest chapter.

I continue to marvel at the incredible talent of book designer Carol Haralson. From her transplanted-Okie post in Sedona, Arizona, Carol turns out masterpieces in book form.

I appreciate the Oklahoma Heritage Association, including its president Dr. Paul Lambert and chairman of the board Lee Allan Smith, for its commitment to preserving Oklahoma history.

Finally, thanks to Mike Mashburn, Georgeann Nigh Whitener, Judge Susan Conyers, Larry Brawner, Glen Johnson, Jr., Marty Hauan, Fred Turner, Dr. Kenny Brown, Carl Reherman, John Greiner, Alex Adwan, Ed Montgomery, Hannah Atkins, Margaret Hall, Leland Gourley, Dr. Thurman Shuller, Norris and Betty Price, Connie Irby, Ruth Moore, Robert White, John Reid, Dean Gandy, Glenda Carlile, Terry Davidson, Louise Painter, Tammy Liegerot, Juanita Kidd, Michael Clingman, Rodger Harris, Shirley Cassil, Judge Steve Taylor, and James Beatty for proofreading early drafts of the manuscript and providing valuable comments.

I submit to the people of Oklahoma the saga of George and Donna Nigh.

—BOB BURKE

PROLOGUE

"*What do you want to be in life?*" the teacher asked. It was a normal question for a typical September morning in Miss Miller's eighth-grade vocations class at McAlester, Oklahoma, Junior High School.

One freckle-faced youngster might have quickly yelled "policeman!" Another lad, overcome with the futuristic power of the moment, may have whispered "doctor." Perhaps a pretty girl with curls bouncing around her smiling face said she hoped to be a teacher.

But without a doubt, from somewhere in the middle of the classroom, a 14-year-old aggressively raised his hand and beamed as he said, "I wanna be Governor!"

That confident prognostication by George Nigh would play out in Oklahoma over the next half century.

Early in life, George was destined for greatness. People of all ages and walks of life responded positively to him. He was named the best citizen of McAlester High School, outstanding student at Eastern Oklahoma College at Wilburton, and most popular student at East Central State University at Ada. Three characteristics—citizenship, academic excellence, and popularity—all served George well throughout his career.

George scored many Oklahoma firsts in his life:

1950

Youngest member of the legislature.

1958

Youngest lieutenant governor in state history and youngest in the nation.

1978

First and only statewide elected official elected governor.

1982

First governor elected to two terms and
only gubernatorial candidate to carry all 77 counties.

1983

The only person to ever serve four different terms as governor, a record that probably will never be broken.

1992

Oldest person ever hired as a university president .

The word "integrity" symbolizes George Nigh's half century of public service, as legislator, lieutenant governor, governor, and university president. He led the state during the best of times, and the worst of times, yet no one ever seriously questioned his integrity. He owed no one but the people of Oklahoma.

His administrations were never tainted by scandal because everyone, including bitter political enemies, knew George made decisions, not for personal gain, but for the overall betterment of his beloved state and its people. As Julian Rothbaum once said, "We never had to worry about anything jumping out of the closet during a campaign. With no hint of wrongdoing associated with George during his entire political career, it was always a pleasure to support him."

Many may have disagreed with George on a myriad of issues, but no one questioned his motives. This was exemplified best when George was introduced to an audience in El Reno as one who "may meet many equals but will never bow to a superior."

No one influenced the course of Oklahoma in the 20th century more than George Nigh.

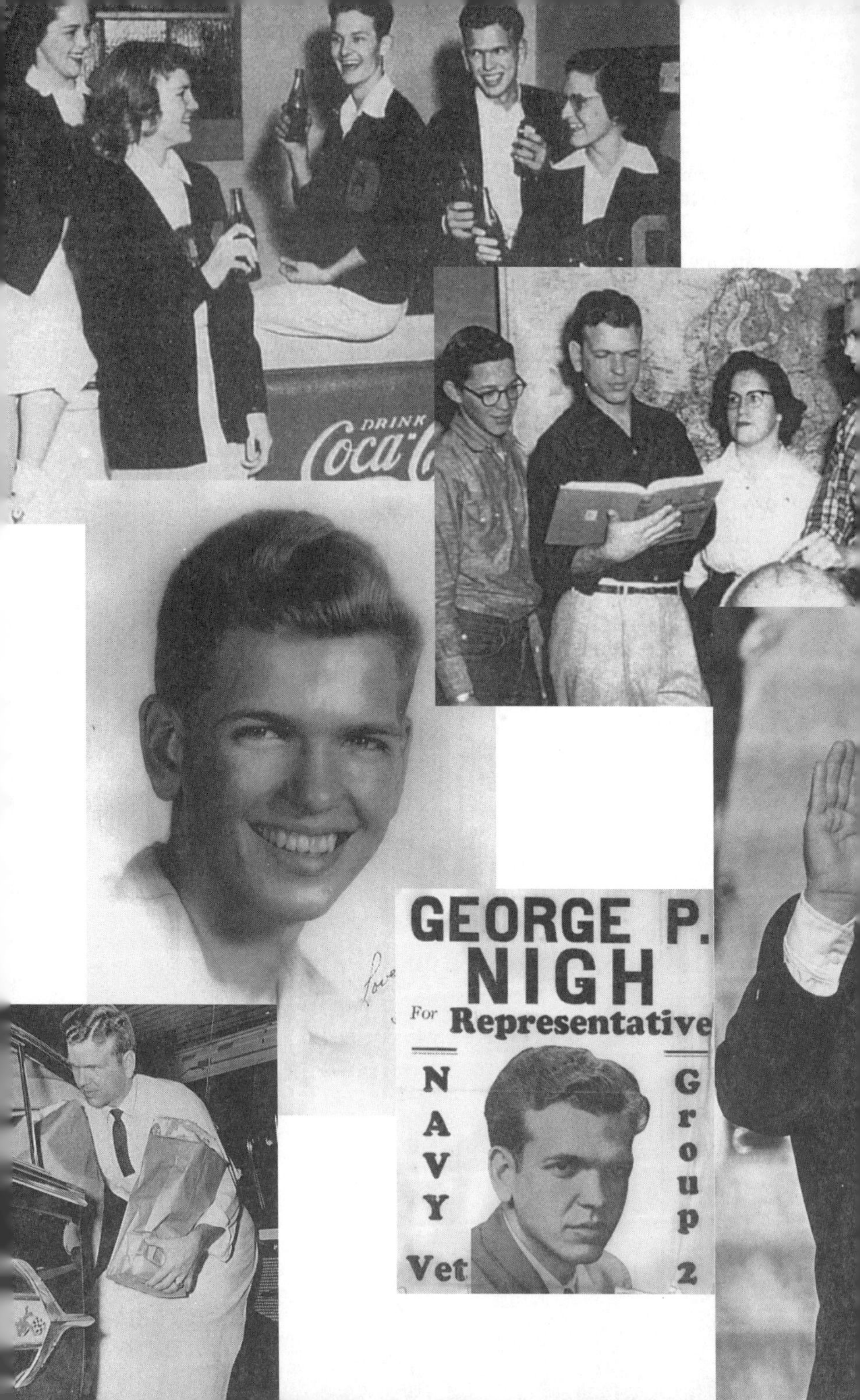
DRINK
GEORGE P.
NIGH
For Representative
NAVY
Vet
Group 2

STOPS ALONG THE WAY

CLOCKWISE FROM LEFT, FACING PAGE: Going to college; teaching history; making history; I wanna' be governor!; delivering groceries. THIS PAGE: Serving his country; youngest lieutenant governor; goal fulfilled.

Early Days in Little Dixie

George Patterson Nigh was born June 9, 1927, in McAlester, Oklahoma, in the heart of the area of the Sooner State known as "Little Dixie." Legend has it that the counties in the southeastern corner of Oklahoma were named Little Dixie because their terrain, stifling humidity, and Democratic politics were somewhat akin to those of the Old South.

McAlester began in 1869 in a spot of wilderness in southeastern Indian Territory where the Texas Road, the wagon trail from Missouri to Texas, crossed a California trail running from Fort Smith, Arkansas, to the West Coast. The town was named for prominent businessman and later Oklahoma's second lieutenant governor J. J. McAlester, who built the first tent store at the crossroads. It was the county seat of Pittsburg County, created at Oklahoma statehood from Tobucksy County in the Choctaw Nation. The new county took its name from Pittsburgh, Pennsylvania, home to many of the coal miners who came to southeast Oklahoma to work mines in the closing decades of the 19th century. The county is said to have been named when a traveler passing through Indian Territory on the Missouri, Kansas, and Texas, or Katy Railroad, commented that the area looked like a "little Pittsburgh." Somewhere along the line, the "h" from the Pennsylvania city was lost.

Little Dixie, and all of Oklahoma, was suffering from bad times in the agriculture-based American economy when George was born in the summer of 1927 to Wilber Roscoe Nigh and Irene Crockett Nigh.

The faltering economy had a direct and negative effect upon the Nigh family and its operation of the Crockett-Nigh Grocery store, one of McAlester's finest neighborhood food stores.

Irene Nigh entered the spring of 1927 with a secret wish that her fourth child might be a girl. She dreamed of relief from her three energetic boys. William Lewyn Nigh, six, had been born September 4, 1920, only nine months and three weeks after Irene married handsome Wilber Nigh on May 19, 1919. Samuel Crockett Nigh was four years old, born on September 27, 1922. Irene's youngest boy, Wilber DuBois Nigh, or Wib, was just two years old, born August 6, 1924. Irene dearly loved her boys but some days silently wondered how she was going to take care of another baby in the rambling white frame house that sat behind a big oak tree on Fifth Street in McAlester.

On the morning of June 9, Irene knew her time was near. The doctor announced to the family that the new addition to the household was another boy, and Irene had to be satisfied to have no daughter for another fifteen years, until Mary Elizabeth Nigh was born. George was named for his great uncles, George Clark and F. P. Patterson, continuing a Nigh tradition of giving children family middle names.

George's brothers always wondered about the fact that George was named after two well-to-do relatives and received a crisp dollar bill from each uncle every birthday and at Christmas. The three older Nigh boys believed that George Patterson had the luck of the Irish.

Young George Nigh began his life in a loving and hard-working household. His father labored long hours in the grocery store, often from 6:00 A.M to 10:00 P.M., and made frequent trips to his mother-in-law's farm 25 miles away near Hartshorne, Oklahoma, to pick up milk, meat, and vegetables for sale in the store.

Little is known about George's ancestral roots on the Nigh side of the family. Wilber Nigh, born in 1894, had run away from home in Missouri because of a disagreement with a haughty stepmother. Wilber settled in McAlester in 1915 and landed a job as a deliveryman at a grocery store. Within a few weeks he moved to a new job at the Crockett grocery store on East Grand Avenue. Not long after, he noticed Irene, the pretty young daughter of Lewyn and Mary Crockett, owners of the store.

Irene had been born at Vinita, Indian Territory, December 15, 1899, and was six years younger than Wilber. However, her father noticed Wilber's work ethic and good manners and approved of Wilber and Irene dating before Wilber joined the Army. In April, 1917, he left for France to fight in World War I, serving as a private in Company G, 111th Ammunition Train, 36th Division, for seven months in Europe before mustering out on March 31, 1919.[1] When Wilber returned to McAlester, his romance with Irene became serious and the couple married a few weeks later.

George Nigh's early ambition for public service may have come through the ancestral roots of his mother's family. The Crocketts, as Huguenots, fled France to England, Scotland, and Ireland, arriving in America, in Virginia, in 1715. George's great-great-great-grandfather, Anthony Crockett, a cousin of the legendary frontiersman Davy Crockett, settled in Kentucky shortly after the end of the Revolutionary War. Anthony's brother, Colonel Joseph Crockett, fought valiantly for the United States against the British and was later rewarded by President Thomas Jefferson when he was named United States Marshal of Kentucky.

George's great-grandfather, Samuel Robertson Crockett, was a schoolteacher, newspaper editor, court clerk, probate judge, and a member of the Constitutional Convention of Missouri in 1875.

Lewyn Crockett, George's grandfather, was the ninth of twelve children born to Samuel Robertson Crockett and Helen Mar Duncan Crockett between 1863 and 1887. Lewyn was born March 23, 1877, and left Missouri with several of his brothers to settle at Vinita in Indian Territory.

Lewyn married Mary Bell DuBois and moved to McAlester around the time of Oklahoma statehood in 1907 with their only child, Irene. The Crocketts established one of McAlester's first grocery stores, with Lewyn buying, selling, and bartering for meat, dairy products, and vegetables while Mary Bell kept books and served customers.

When Wilber and Irene Nigh married in 1919, Lewyn Crockett gave half his grocery business to his new son-in-law as a wedding present. The store's name was changed to Crockett-Nigh Grocery, a name that graced the neighborhood market for the next 40 years. In

Samuel Robertson Crockett was a devout Presbyterian in his hometown of Nevada, Missouri, where he owned the leading newspaper, *The Living Democrat.* He later lived in Texas and Vinita, Indian Territory, before returning to his homestead in Missouri where he died in 1913.

the early 1930s, Crockett was bedridden with cancer on his farm near Hartshorne and management of the store was left to Wilber, a "hard-working, kind man" who fell into trouble financially during the Depression because he allowed so many of his customers to buy groceries on credit. Wilber was aware that many might never pay their bills but he could not bear to see his neighbors go hungry. It was not their fault that jobs had dried up like the streams in Pittsburg County. Wilber could have been accused of running his business with his heart rather than his head, because he also extended credit to local miners even though the coal mines were shutting down.

The Great Depression had begun in 1929 when the stock market crashed and it worsened as factories shut down, stores closed, banks failed, and millions of Americans were left jobless and homeless.

Oklahoma's economy, based largely on agriculture, suffered mightily. The weather also contributed to both the severity and the length of the Depression in the state. A searing drought hit the southern plains and eventually even normally wet eastern Oklahoma around Pittsburg County became desiccated. Dust storms wracked the state. Sand blew in such quantities that travelers lost their way, chickens roosted at noon, airports closed, and trains stopped. Animals and humans alike suffered from lung disorders. The drought was accompanied by blistering heat. In Vinita the temperature exceeded 100 degrees for 35 consecutive days, and on the thirty-sixth day reached 117 degrees.[2]

Lewyn Crockett and his brothers were accomplished entertainers. They formed the Crockett Brothers Quartet which entertained at political speeches, picnics, church socials, and minstrel performances in Oklahoma, Missouri, Kansas, and Arkansas, and later toured with Oklahoma humorist Will Rogers. They once made a guest appearance on *Barn Dance* on clear-channel radio station WLW in Chicago, Illinois. The Crockett Brothers wowed audiences with their barbershop harmony in a rendition of "Break the News to Mother," a sad song popular with music lovers at the beginning of the 20th century. Left to right, Sam, Benson, Gordon, Allen, and Lewyn.

By the end of 1931, more than one-fourth of the farmers in Oklahoma were on relief and nearly 20 percent of rural landowners were in default on land loans. As if farm problems were not enough of a drag on the state's economy, the low price of coal virtually shut down production in the mines near McAlester. The coal business had been slipping for almost a decade as oil replaced coal as the fuel of choice for the country's aging railroad locomotive fleet.

When Crockett, called "Daddy Papa" by his grandson Bill, died in 1934, his wife, Mary Bell, continued as the store's bookkeeper and played a major role in the development of her grandsons, who all worked in the store in some capacity.[3]

The Crockett-Nigh Grocery was a typical 19th-century neighborhood grocery store. It was a small building with no more than two aisles. There was no need for the wide aisles later groceries would have, because the concept of commercial self-service was yet to be born. A customer typically came into the store to ask for specific items. George recalled that "The customer would ask for a can of spinach and the clerk would turn and walk from the counter to the shelf, get the can of spinach, and bring it back. Then the customer would say, 'I need a can of corn,' and the process was repeated."[4] However, most Crockett-Nigh customers never came to the store per-

Irene and Wilber Nigh. George was blessed with loving and caring parents with whom he enjoyed a great relationship. The elder Nighs were proud parents as George climbed the ladder of public service in Oklahoma.

sonally. Their groceries were delivered by one of the Nigh boys as each progressively became old enough to ride a bicycle or drive a pickup truck. A typical birthday present for a Nigh boy was a larger basket for his bicycle to allow more groceries to be delivered in a single trip.

Crockett-Nigh Grocery was across Seventh Street from the Second Ward school, also known as the George Washington Elementary School. Wilber called upon his growing sons to man the candy counter during busy times before and after school and during recess when students at the school were allowed to invade the grocery store for candy and soda pop.

Only once did George opt to work for someone other than his father. During one summer of his junior high school years he delivered prescriptions and supplies for a neighborhood drugstore by bicycle and worked at the soda fountain. It was rumored that the druggist peddled bootleg whiskey from the store so George's father telephoned the owner and reached an agreement with him that George would not be involved in the illegal activity.[5] This was the first time George observed how impossible it was to enforce most prohibition laws, a lesson he would use in dealing with liquor issues.

Irene Nigh seldom worked at the store but had her hands full making a home for her husband and four sons. She had many mouths to feed but often had to wait until late afternoon to determine her evening menu because it depended wholly upon what meat and vegetables had not sold at the store that day, the result of the lack of modern refrigeration equipment.

Irene was a gifted musician. She played piano at most of McAlester's civic clubs and, at various times, was church organist for the Presbyterian, First Christian, Baptist, and Methodist congregations of McAlester, often playing as well for memorial services at both of the town's funeral homes. Irene played the piano while her sister-in-law, Bernadine Nigh (Mrs. Sam Nigh), sang.

George's early heroes, besides his father, were mostly political leaders and Oklahoma humorist Will Rogers. George's call to public service may have come during the fireside chats of President Franklin Roosevelt who used radio addresses from the White House to calm the frayed nerves of a Depression-plagued people. It was not unusual for George to choose listening to Roosevelt over playing outside with his friends.

Everyone around George, and George himself, always knew he would end up in politics. He was called "Senator" or "Governor" by his classmates and was an extremely popular student leader at McAlester High School. During the senior class graduation assembly a make-believe fortune teller wearing a bandanna with an upside-down gold-fish bowl for a crystal ball announced that she saw "George Nigh . . . just elected President of the United States"—and she paused—"Street Cleaners Association."[6]

George, a good-looking teenager and a dancing fool, was a popular invitee to teenage parties in McAlester. Irvin E. "Buck" Conner, the son of state penitentiary warden R. B. "Dick" Conner, developed a long-standing friendship with George. Conner recalled, "Everybody liked George. He was one of those kind of guys everybody wanted to be around."[7]

Martin Hauan, press secretary to two other Oklahoma governors and a prolific commentator on Oklahoma political history, called George "a born politician."[8] There was something special about George and his ability to get along with everyone. George Brown, George's neighborhood chum and later a physician and campaign pilot, could not recall George Nigh every having an enemy in high school. George was admired by boys and girls alike and, as a cheerleader, appeared at most school functions.[9]

George's best friend for life, "literally from birth,"[10] was Paul Carris who lived a block and a half away from the Nighs. Carris and George were the same age, their parents were good friends, and Carris's mother had been Irene Nigh's nurse when her older children were born. Their parents dated each other before they were married. Carris and George often kidded that they could have been brothers.

Carris's birthday was two days after George's. From age six until Carris's death in 1986, the two friends spent time together on one of their birthdays each year, for 54 consecutive years.

George and Carris were natural entertainers. Mary Beeson Brown recalled how the two fledgling comedians entertained fellow students at the White House Cafe, owned by Paul's father. Dozens of teenagers gathered around George and Paul, who could make light of any topic about high school life.[11]

George's first flirtation with politics came at age 13 in 1940 when one of his father's customers, Tom Haile, ran for county judge in Pittsburg County. George organized a group of 40 kids who were effective attention-getters as they rode down the main streets of McAlester on crepe-paper-adorned bicycles with clacking cardboard cards clipped to their spokes with clothespins. It was the first of many successful campaigns in which George Nigh was a key player.

In the ninth grade, George learned the value of a single vote. He wanted to be home room president but so did his friend Paul Carris. Neither wanted to drop out of the race so they made a pact to nominate each other for the position. George, not believing in the old ethical commandment to never vote for yourself, did just that. In a secret ballot, he voted for himself. He reasoned, "How can you ask anyone else to vote for you if you don't vote for yourself?" Unfortunately it turned out that was the only vote he received. When Carris left the room after the election, he put his arm around George and said, "Good thing I voted for you."[12]

Only as Carris lay dying of cancer in 1986 did George tell him he knew about the ninth-grade election almost a half century before. Carris had asked everyone but George to leave the room. George laid on Carris's bed for 90 minutes. The two friends laughed and cried as they reminisced about their lives together. Finally George said, "Paul, I want you to know that back there in the ninth grade I knew you didn't vote for me because I voted for myself." Carris said, "You knew that all the time? You really are a friend."[13]

When George returned home to the governor's mansion in Oklahoma City, a telephone call awaited him. Carris had died shortly after George left his bedside.

As a high school senior, George discovered another political truth: Pick your opponent carefully. George again wanted to be home room president but knew fellow student Dick Strong, a football star and very popular with fellow students, would probably win the election. When the teacher announced that it was time to vote, George stood up and said, "Miss Whitaker, I think the most important office we could have in our home room is our voice in the Student Council. I move that we vote on that position first and I nominate Dick Strong."[14] Miss Whitaker liked the idea because she was Student Council sponsor and she allowed the change of order. Strong was elected by acclamation and was so appreciative of George that he nominated him for home room president, a race that George also won by acclamation.

It was not unusual for George to rise to the top of almost any organization of which he was a member, whether it was a student group or a state government.

George's potential was recognized by the Rotary Club when he was selected as McAlester High School Best Citizen of the Year in 1945.

George graduated from high school in May, 1945, with his dream of public service intact. His eye was still on the Oklahoma governor's mansion.

THE YOUNGER NIGHS

George, are you finally the last of the Nigh boys?

EVERY TEACHER, MCALESTER PUBLIC SCHOOLS

ALL OF IRENE'S CHILDREN were different. However, the four boys, and sister Mary Elizabeth, born November 20, 1942, inherited their mother's musical talents. Bill, who sang in a McAlester High School quartet with Ridge Bond, who later played Curly in the Broadway production of *Oklahoma!,* was the only Nigh boy to sing professionally. Bill hosted a weekly radio show on a McAlester station in the 1940s. He sang while his mother played the piano. Later, Mary sang in the high school glee club. Even though the Nigh brothers came from a long line of minstrel show performers and barbershop quartet singers, the only time they sang as a quartet was at Sam's wedding rehearsal. While Irene accompanied her boys at the organ, Wilber's eyes were misty with pride.

Bill Nigh later worked 23 years for the Missouri, Kansas, and Texas, or Katy Railroad, established an insurance business in Muskogee, Oklahoma, and served two terms in the Oklahoma House of Representatives.

Sam Nigh was a public school teacher in Cushing and at Jones Academy near Hartshorne. He was also a school administrator at Fort Knox, Kentucky, before returning to Oklahoma to take a position at the Center for Continuing Education at the University of Oklahoma.

Wib Nigh owned and managed the Union Bus Station in McAlester and a regional bus service in southeast Oklahoma.

Mary Elizabeth became an elementary public school teacher at Porter, Oklahoma, and married fellow teacher Randall Cargill. Both later taught at Fort Gibson, Oklahoma.

George, who was known as "George Pat," was the youngest of the Nigh boys. He accompanied his brothers as they played with neighborhood chums like George and Bruce Brown, James Davis, Pete Cook, Morton Klein, George Stipp, Howard Perry, Joe Basolo, Walter Howerton, Jim and Joe McConathy, and Elmer Hale, Jr. More than once, Bill, Sam, and Wilber, nicknamed "Wib," had to stop their play to pull up George's diaper that had fallen around his ankles while he chased his older brothers.

George, at six, was a favorite playmate of youngsters in the neighborhood. His brothers watched out for his safety when boyhood games became too rough for such a little tot.

George Brown remembered the sunny Little Dixie days filled with the sounds of neighborhood boys playing cowboys and Indians with rubber-band guns. Brown looked forward to the visits to Crockett-Nigh Grocery where he stuck a big fork in a wooden barrel of pickles to pull out a prize dill that he gladly wrapped a napkin around, then paid the asking price of a nickel.[1]

George was eight years old in August, 1935, when his hero Will Rogers was killed in a tragic plane crash with Oklahoma aviation pioneer Wiley Post at Point Barrow, Alaska. George remembers the morning on a Colorado Springs, Colorado, street corner when a newspaper peddler barked out the sad news of Rogers' death.

That moment was forever etched in George's mind for several reasons. It was the only time his father ever took a vacation with his family and George saw his first newspaper extra. Traffic stopped and grown men cried as they read the headlines that announced the death of George's biggest hero. It was also the first time George was aware of a tinge of pride in his native Oklahoma.

One of the favorite pastimes of the Nigh brothers and their playmates was a game called "shinny." An empty tin can was placed in the middle of the street. A reasonably even number of players lined up on either side of the white mid-stripe of the street. With long wooden sticks, harvested from nearby hardwood trees, the boys knocked the

George was a member of the Junior Police at McAlester's Second Ward School. Front row, left to right: Franklin Springer, Ross Quincy, Paul Carris, unknown, George, and Bill Eubanks. Middle row: L. G. Murphy, Alvin Latimer, James Snoddy, Dick Wheatley, Roy Clark, and James Day. Principal Jim Daniels is in the center, top row.

can toward the goal, usually marked by the end of a neighbor's driveway. If a player strayed on the other side of the mid-line, an opponent was allowed to hit him on the shin, thus the name "shinny." It was not uncommon for the neighborhood boys to play shinny until darkness fell on hot, muggy summer nights in McAlester.[2] George's hands are marked with tell-tale scars of a poor shinny player.

All four Nigh boys played in the McAlester High School band. Irene tried to give piano lessons to her boys but only George picked up on his mother's talent on the keyboard. However, George learned only three chords which enabled him to play any hymn or country and western tune ever written. On rare occasions, George demonstrates his "piano mastery," playing by ear.

Life was so busy for the Nigh family that little time was spent on discipline. Bill Nigh reflected, "Discipline was not necessary. We knew what was expected of us and simply did it. We had chores at home and at the store. Mother and Dad hardly ever had to tell us a second time what to do."[3] If a Nigh brother received a paddling at school, it was repeated at home that night by their father.

Most disputes, including which boy mowed the lawn or washed the dishes, were settled by games of dominoes or pitch at a card table in the living room. The rules were simple: no holds barred, and no mercy for any reason, including age. The loser often spent much of his day doing chores. The big-stake game, revolving around dessert time,

The children of Wilber and Irene Nigh later in life. Left to right: Bill, Sam, George, Mary, and Wib. Wilber's trademark was hard work and integrity. From their mother the Nigh children received love for community and civic involvement.

was called "eat or smell." Winners won the right to eat while losers were allowed only to smell.

The card table was an integral part of the Nigh family home furnishings. It was always set up in the living room where it stayed until the deaths of Irene Nigh in 1963 and Wilber Nigh in 1964. Afterwards, the Nigh children treasured the worn scorebooks that chronicled the thousands of family games played at the table.

Getting Ready

I've never had any quitters in my house and I'm not starting now!
Ma Richter

The Nigh family often sat around an aging RCA radio cabinet in their living room on Seventh Street, listening to news of United States involvement in World War II.

The family had grown smaller as first Bill, then Sam, and finally Wib graduated from high school and left home for the military. Even though the family was excited about George graduating from high school, their exuberance was often tempered with daily news of more American casualties. The occasional dispatch announcing that some neighbor's son had lost his life on a foreign battlefield made the seriousness of the war close and personal.

George had developed a deep love for his country and searched for an avenue of contribution to the war effort. In February of 1945, his senior year at McAlester High School, George and several of his friends, including best friend Paul Carris, joined a United States Navy program that allowed participants to complete high school before being called to active duty and basic training as a group.

In May, 1945, Germany surrendered and the battle for Europe was over. The American and British governments declared May 8 V-E (Victory in Europe) Day. However, United States troops continued the fight against the Japanese through the blood-covered islands of the South Pacific.

After high school graduation, in June, George and a dozen of his classmates were called to active duty. George received his notice while attending Presbyterian church summer camp at Dwight Mission near Gore, Oklahoma. He rushed home, packed a few civilian clothes, and left with the group of McAlester boys from the local train station. Their destination was the naval training facility at San Diego, California. While enroute to California, George and Paul Carris both celebrated their eighteenth birthdays.

While George was in boot camp, World War II came to a sudden conclusion after President Harry S. Truman, another of George's heroes who became President after the death of Roosevelt, authorized the atomic bombing of two Japanese cities, Nagasaki and Hiroshima, in early August, 1945. The defeated Japanese surrendered within days. General Douglas MacArthur accepted the formal Japanese surrender on September 2 aboard the battleship USS *Missouri* in Tokyo Bay.

Although the war was over, George's military duty continued. For the first few weeks of basic training, George never got close to a ship. He and other trainees ran the hills of the naval station, catching only a glimpse of destroyers and other naval vessels anchored far away in San Diego Bay. Naval officials asked trainees what kind of ship they wanted to be assigned to after basic training. George indicated his preference for a small ship and Paul Carris wrote down his desire to serve on a large ship. As luck would have it, when assignments came, the two friends got exactly the opposite of their requests. Carris was sent for duty in the South Pacific on a tiny landing craft while George was assigned to an aircraft carrier, the USS *Ranger,* for duty in the Atlantic.

The USS *Ranger* was an old ship, the first in the Navy actually built from the keel up as an aircraft carrier. It was the flagship for the invasion of North Africa but had been taken out of wartime service and docked at San Diego to train Navy personnel. On George's first tour, the ship left San Diego, sailed through the Panama Canal, and up the eastern coast of the United States to dry dock at Philadelphia, Pennsylvania, for repairs and repainting. While the ship was being refitted, George came home for an extended leave in McAlester at Christmas and helped his father operate the grocery store. Even mili-

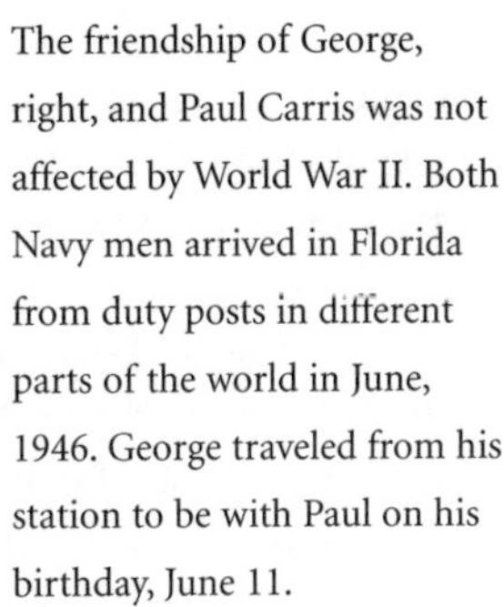

The friendship of George, right, and Paul Carris was not affected by World War II. Both Navy men arrived in Florida from duty posts in different parts of the world in June, 1946. George traveled from his station to be with Paul on his birthday, June 11.

George and Paul Carris much later in life. There never passed more than a few weeks without George and Paul talking either in person or on the telephone. When difficult personal decisions had to be made, George called Paul for advice, and vice versa.

tary service did not break the string of Christmases that George was home in McAlester to help out with year-end inventory at the family grocery store.

Back on active duty, the USS *Ranger* became home base for fighter pilot training. For a year, George, promoted to Aviation Boatswain's Mate Third Class, labored on the hangar deck of the carrier. He was a "plane handler," peeling old paint and rust off vintage airplanes and slapping a new coat of paint on the war ravaged flying machines.

George worked beneath the flight deck and valued moments he could spend out of the hole of the ship in the fresh sea air. Any observer of young George Nigh pushing airplanes onto elevators for ascension to the flight deck on the USS *Ranger* probably could not imagine that the baby-faced plane handler would someday be Commander in Chief of his home state's military forces.

George's stint in the Navy did not lessen his ambition of returning home as soon as possible and "running for something." Public service was always on his mind and he wanted to get back to southeast Oklahoma to begin his college education, to prepare him for politics. George told anyone who would listen that he wanted to be governor.

In August, 1946, George was discharged from the Navy in time to enroll for the fall semester at Eastern Oklahoma A & M, a junior college at Wilburton, Oklahoma. The school had been authorized by Oklahoma's first legislature as the Oklahoma School of Mines and Metalurgy.

George chose the school at Wilburton because it was very close to McAlester, enabling him to hitchhike home on weekends to help in the grocery store and to keep in contact with the people of Pittsburg County who George soon intended to enlist in his campaign for "something." George had no idea what office he would ultimately attempt, but he knew he was destined to serve the people of his home county.

George became a member of the College Young Democrats on the Wilburton campus, rising to the presidency of the group. At his second statewide convention of Oklahoma Young Democrats, George became the first college student ever to serve on the executive committee of the organization whose leadership was dominated by older,

Young Democrats. Later, George was elected president of the Oklahoma Young Democrats and began for the first time building statewide contacts.

With the G.I. Bill paying his tuition, George graduated in the spring of 1948 with an Associate Degree in Liberal Arts from Eastern. He worked summers at the Crockett-Nigh Grocery store and sought advice from his parents and friends on where to continue his higher education.

Assuming he needed to be a lawyer to be successful in politics, George enrolled at the University of Oklahoma in pre-law in September, 1948. His cousin, Lorena Crockett, had told him about a boarding house on Jenkins Avenue in Norman that fed varsity athletes and often provided room and board for a non-athlete who would help with chores. George interviewed with Ma Richter, the proprietor of the boarding house, and won the job. He attended classes in the mornings and helped Ma in the kitchen and dining room at lunch and in the evenings. After supper, Ma, George, and other residents gathered around an old piano in the parlor and sang songs such as the hymn "Life is Like a Mountain Railroad." It was a song that George could play by ear with those three chords taught him by his mother.

George felt like "a fish out of water" in law school.[1] He had no interest whatsoever in being a lawyer. He wanted to make laws, not to argue about them. In the third week of the semester, a professor told the students that two years hence half of the class would not be there. George thought to himself, "I'll save you a lot of time and quit now."[2] George was not following the lectures and was very emotional and unhappy with his decision to attend law school. He walked the streets of Norman at night, often ending up at the Kappa Alpha fraternity house where his best friend Paul Carris lived. Carris, a business student, tried to convince George to reconsider and stay in law school. However, George looked his friend in the eye and told him he just did not want to be a lawyer and it was too late in the school year to enroll in another field of study.

George called his mother and father and told them of his decision. His father asked, "Have you got some girl pregnant?"[3]

A long talk with Ma Richter was a turning point in George's life.

Ma lectured George for an hour about how she had never had a quitter living in her house, how she did not even want to be associated with a quitter. Ma made George promise that he would go home to McAlester to get his life straightened out and then return the next semester to OU. Ma said she would keep George's room for him.

George went back to McAlester and again worked in the grocery store, fully intending to return to Norman for the spring semester. In early January, 1949, Maurice Matheson, a cousin and former employee of Crockett-Nigh Grocery, asked George to drive his new pickup truck from McAlester to Matheson's home in Oklahoma City. George agreed and planned a stop in Ada to visit friends Bowie and Nancy Ballard. George and Nancy had graduated together from McAlester High School.

George and Jo Anne Absher of Okemah were selected most popular students on the East Central campus in 1950. Courtesy East Central Oklahoma State University.

Soon after George arrived in Ada, a massive ice storm hit the area, shutting off Ada from the rest of the world. George stayed two nights with the Ballards but thought he was imposing on their friendship. Another friend from McAlester invited George to stay in his dormitory room at East Central State College until the road to Norman thawed out. George, with no money and wondering how he was going to eat, learned that if he told college officials he was a prospective student, he would be given a coupon for room and board for two days. George signed up as a prospective student and moved into the dorm to wait out the ice storm.

Meanwhile, another fateful event occurred at Ma Richter's boarding house in Norman. While George waited out the ice storm in Ada, Ma called George's home in McAlester with news that the student occupying George's old room at Ma's had not graduated as planned and there was no room for George. Such an incredible coincidence meant only one thing to George—he was destined to attend college at East Central. There was never any regrets because George immediately fell in love with the school.

East Central began as East Central State Normal, a training school authorized by the Oklahoma legislature in 1909. For the first 11 years of its existence, East Central served as both a high school and a two-year college. Later it was converted into a four-year state college, and after several name and program changes, was renamed East Central State University.

George entered East Central with enthusiasm for his studies. After a short time on campus he was elected president of the Young Democrats, wrote articles for the student newspaper, the *Journal,* and made a legion of friends, many of whom would help George in future campaigns. On one occasion, history professor Louise Hornbeak caught George cutting class, while decorating for homecoming, and reportedly predicted, "George, you will go down in history." And he did—his grade went from A to B.[4]

George managed the campaign of Robert S. Kerr on the East Central campus in Kerr's successful bid to defeat Republican Ross Rizley to capture a seat in the United States Senate. Kerr admired George's positive outlook on the future of Oklahoma and predicted the lad from McAlester would go far.

George developed a substantial following among fellow members of the Young Democrats. Everywhere he went, he recorded on three-inch by five-inch cards the names and addresses of people he met, acquaintances he would call upon for assistance in future political campaigns.

The First Step

Remember three things, always give people your name first, so they can act like they know you, read the paper every day so that anywhere you go you'll know what people are talking about, and never pass a men's room.

Campaign advice given George
by Robert S. Kerr

I don't know what George would do if he got elected to the legislature. They don't have any jitterbug contest up there.

Willard Gotcher

The opportunity for 22-year-old George to run for political office came in early 1950 when Lonnie W. Brown of McAlester announced he would not stand for re-election to his seat in the Oklahoma House of Representatives, nor would Representative Kirksey Nix who announced he would seek the State Senate post in Pittsburg County. Brown had been elected in 1946 to one of three positions allocated to Pittsburg County in the House. Nix later served as a powerful state senator and distinguished member of the Oklahoma Court of Criminal Appeals. The third slot was held by young Gene Stipe, who had upset veteran legislator C. "Plowboy" Edwards in 1948, beginning a legendary Oklahoma political career.

All three members from Pittsburg County were Democrats. So was George who had registered as a Democrat the year before when he reached age 21. George had decided to be a Democrat early in life because he identified with Oklahoma and national Democratic leaders such as Robert S. Kerr, Carl Albert, Mike Monroney, and Presidents Franklin D. Roosevelt and Harry S. Truman.

George believed service in the legislature was a direct step toward his goal of being governor someday. However, remembering his lesson learned in high school about carefully picking opponents, he intentionally shied away from challenging incumbents. The retirement announcement of Representative Brown and the decision of Nix to run for the Oklahoma Senate gave George the opening he was looking for.

Legislative candidates in Pittsburg County did not run by district. Instead they ran at large in one of three groups. State law at that time allowed voters in only a few counties in Oklahoma the luxury of voting for all legislators in all districts in the county.

Representative Stipe announced for re-election in Group One. A popular recently-retired county home demonstration agent, Elizabeth Ward, announced for Nix's seat, Group Three. George ran for the other House seat, Group Two.

Ward was considered an unbeatable candidate, causing two other potential candidates and close friends, Willard Gotcher and Plowboy Edwards, to agree to flip a coin with the winner getting George, whom they considered the easiest to beat. Under the coin-toss agreement, the loser would face "unbeatable Ward."

Gotcher, the assistant county attorney in McAlester, and son of former County Judge W.E. Gotcher, got antsy and broke his agreement with Edwards, announcing against George. Edwards was left with no choice but to run against Ward. Ironically, the "unbeatable," Ward, lost and the "easy-mark," George, won.

The 1950 House campaign in Pittsburg County was colorful, to say the least. Stipe had been elected two years earlier as a "reform" candidate and was extremely popular with voters. Edwards continued to have a substantial following because of his colorful name and campaign tactics.

George plunged into the legislative race while yet a student at East Central State College in Ada. He did not own a car, which presented a major problem, but hitched a ride every weekend to McAlester as he began meeting with friends and local leaders to map campaign strategy. Acquaintances from the Young Democrats in Ada and George's many friends from McAlester formed the core of his group of supporters.

Not everyone was happy that George was entering politics. When he told his mother he was going to run for the legislature, she cried, and said, "It'll ruin you." However, both Irene and Wilber Nigh worked their hearts out in every campaign their son entered.[1]

George began the 1950 campaign as an underdog. His family and friends were optimistic that the positive aura that surrounded George, whether he was shaking hands with voters at a church social, or speaking from the tailgate of a pickup truck at a political speaking in outlying rural communities in Pittsburg County, would convince voters that he would represent them honorably in Oklahoma City.

One of the first visits George made in McAlester in the campaign was to an organizational meeting of a local Jaycee chapter. The Jaycees, officially the United States Junior Chamber of Commerce, was an active civic organization for the nation's young men. At his first meeting, George was elected to the local group's board of directors. Years later he would serve as Executive Director of the World Congress of Junior Chamber International.

George turned his youth into an advantage in the race against Gotcher. Students from junior high to college were excited about someone running for office who was only a few years their senior. Even though most of the students had not yet attained the voting age of 21, they turned out en masse to help in the campaign.

George's father was convinced that voters would not trust candidates or supporters who did not wear hats so George and friends such as Paul Carris, Robert Bartheld, Howard McGee, Quinton Mantooth, Fred Turner, George Lampton, Bradley Million, and Joe Gravitt either bought, or borrowed from their fathers, straw hats, short-sleeve dress shirts, and neckties and showed up at speakings, looking somewhat out of place. For all of Wilber Nigh's advice, George later found out that his father was a registered Republican and could not vote for his son in the 1950 election. That situation quickly changed.

Fred Turner was a high school senior who helped George distribute cards at speakings. Turner, whose grandfather co-founded the *McAlester News Capital* in 1918, himself became the publisher of the newspaper in later years, following in the footsteps of his father and grandfather. He remembered George's campaign strategy, "George just stood at the microphone and smiled, telling people that he loved Pittsburg County, had served his country proudly as a Navy man, and that he just wanted to do his best to represent them in the House of Representatives."[2]

George's only promise to voters was printed on his campaign card. The promise was, "Your vote for me will never be one that you will regret." Even though the promise was somewhat aggressive, and maybe unattainable, it set the tone for all of George's future public service.

Turner also recalled some of the campaign tactics of Gotcher who sincerely believed that the people of his county would not elect someone as young as George. Gotcher talked to audiences of voters more about George's youth than about the issues. Gotcher would say, "Now George is a good boy. . . and when he grows up I'm sure he'll be a good man." Voters were at first amused by the reference to George's age but apparently grew tired of the constant attacks on George's youth.

Gotcher also chided George for winning a jitterbug contest held on a flatbed trailer in front of the Aldridge Hotel on Grand Avenue in McAlester the year before. George had entered the contest with Midge Dusenberry. Gotcher said, "I don't know what George would do if he got elected to the legislature. They don't have any jitterbug contest up there." The remarks offended many young voters who were enamored with the jitterbug.[3]

At one speaking, George was unexpectedly booed by a group of sixth-graders. He was accustomed to cheers from younger members of the audience and dispatched Turner to find out why the youngsters were against him. After the speaking Turner rounded a corner behind the speaker's platform and found Gotcher handing out candy to the group that had booed George.

George's plan for his traveling band of supporters was simple. Bartheld, who later became a dentist and served as vice president of the American Dental Association, recalled, "George made certain we worked the crowd before and after his time on the stage before the microphone. We handed a card to everyone within a block of the speaking."[4]

Many of George's supporters came from Teen Town, a teenage hangout in McAlester of which George had served as its first president a few years before. The energetic campaigners knocked on doors, called voters on the telephone, accompanied George to speakings, and nailed placards announcing George's candidacy on most available trees and fence posts around the county. Teen Town members divided up the city of McAlester and became block captains in the campaign. Virtually every door within the city limits was knocked on by this group of vibrant, youthful crusaders.

Before the election George was invited to deliver the commencement address at the two-room school in the rural community of Plainview north of Arpelar and Cabiness in northern Pittsburg County. He hitchhiked from college at Ada to near McAlester. He rode the last two miles on a gravel road with parents of one of the six graduating eighth graders.

The title of his speech to the Plainview eighth-grade graduates was "From here you have a Plain View of the future." George used as an example Carl Albert who himself had graduated from a two-room school at Bugtussle in Pittsburg County and was elected to Congress.

It was the first of hundreds of commencement addresses George would deliver during each of the next 50 years. A half-century later, in May, 2000, George returned to Pittsburg County to deliver the commencement address to graduates of his hometown McAlester High School. This time the title of his speech was "You can do it from here." Once again his example was Carl Albert, a graduate of McAlester High School, who rose to Speaker of the United States House of Representatives as the highest ranking Oklahoman to ever serve in the federal government.

The long, hot days and nights of campaigning paid off. In the July 4th election, in one of Pittsburg County's largest voter turnouts in many years, George pulled a stunning upset of Gotcher, 6,772 votes to 5,009. The *McAlester News Capital* wrote, "The campaign, comparatively quiet and without marked issues, found most observers leaning toward Gotcher because of his advantage in age and experience. But the vigorous campaign by Nigh, his family and a group of energetic young friends paid off with more votes."[5]

George carried 58 of the 84 boxes in Pittsburg County, the reward for time spent at speakings, pie auctions, and church picnics at tiny communities for months of the spring and early summer. George overwhelmingly won precincts at Arpelar; Bethel Hill, where he garnered 25 of the 29 votes cast; Haileyville; Canadian; Krebs; Bower; and dozens of other rural communities with interesting Oklahoma names such as Ashland, Cabiness, and Salt Prairie.

George's father had concentrated on the Blue Valley precinct, making it his mission to talk to every single voter in the small precinct in which the Nigh farm was located. George lost only one vote in the precinct. For months after the election Wilber Nigh searched for the lone dissenter. It turned out to be his best friend who admitted voting for Gotcher because he hunted coons with him.

George lost boxes at Harpers Valley and Jackfork. In McAlester, the big prize in Pittsburg County elections, George did not lose a precinct and was only tied by Gotcher in two boxes. In McAlester's Second Ward, his home base, George scored big with voters, winning 290 to 83.

In other Pittsburg County races, Nix was elected State Senator over County Attorney Fred Whetsel, former County Judge William Jones, and newspaper publisher Hiram Impson. Edwards led the entire ticket by defeating home demonstration agent Elizabeth Ward of McAlester and G.R. Cain of Blocker. Stipe staved off a bid by Homer Geter in the other Pittsburg County House race.

In those days in Little Dixie, winning the Democratic primary was tantamount to election since Republican filings for public office were few and far between.

After the election, with a college degree on his resume, George returned to his father's grocery store and spent much of his spare time thanking the citizens of Pittsburg County for expressing their trust in his youthful enthusiasm.

George was invited by his mother's friend, Hedwig Martin, to speak to a group of civic-minded girls at a state meeting in Chickasha, Oklahoma, in the summer of 1950. Martin was state president of the American Legion Auxiliary of which Irene Nigh was an active member. The event was called Girls State. It was an opportunity for George to speak to girls from every corner of the state. He once again took their names down and recorded them in his growing card file.

In 1999, George was the guest speaker at Girls State for the 50th consecutive year. Of Girls State, George later said, "It was not only fun but a major plus for my future campaigns. Girls who had met me at Girls State became active supporters. Some became county campaign managers in future elections."[6] The girls went back to both Republican and Democrat households with a favorable impression of young George. As in all of George's campaigns, political party affiliation was seldom an issue. The girls, and their parents, simply liked George.

In the House of Representatives, George took a traditional back seat when the 23rd legislature convened in Oklahoma City in January, 1951. Oklahoma's legislators met only in odd years, and then for just a few months from January to May. Annual sessions did not come about until a 1966 constitutional amendment was approved by state voters.

The state legislature was dominated by representatives and senators from rural districts, drawn in bygone days when most of the state's population lived outside metropolitan areas. However, during the Great Depression, and at the beginning of World War II, many Oklahomans left their farms and moved to Oklahoma City and Tulsa.

The state constitution instructed future legislatures to redraw legislative districts after each federal census, to make certain that each legislator represented roughly the same number of people. But the legislature had not reapportioned itself for 40 years when George took office in 1951. Pittsburg County had a single senator, the same as far more populated Oklahoma and Tulsa counties. Oklahoma County had only twice the number of House members as Pittsburg County, despite having eight times more residents. Historians Danney Goble and W. David Baird wrote, "Although many Oklahomans regarded the legislature's long refusal to reapportion itself as a clear violation of the state constitution, their attempts to end rural domination yielded no effective results...until the federal courts intervened."[7]

Oklahomans elected Johnston Murray as governor in 1950. Murray defeated Oklahoma City attorney William O. "Bill" Coe in a bitter Democratic primary funded by a $300,000 contribution from Tulsa auto dealer William C. Doenges, and then overwhelmed Republican nominee Jo O. Ferguson of Pawnee.[8] Murray was the son of Oklahoma's former flamboyant governor William H. "Alfalfa Bill" Murray. The Murrays were the only father-son occupants of the Oklahoma governor's office.

A new era in the Oklahoma legislature began in 1951. During the war years, legislators and their constituents "kinda tolerated each other." But, after the war, colleges were bursting at the seams, new schools were needed as the population expanded and shifted from the farm to the cities, and the highway system, mostly two-lane, was inadequate as newly-prosperous citizens bought automobiles, creating traffic bottlenecks in every corner of the state. The growth forced the solons to get serious about programs and policies. It was a turning point for the Oklahoma legislature.

The new legislature, led by Speaker of the House James M. Bullard of Duncan and Senate President Pro Tempore Boyd Cowden of Chandler, faced a highly controversial issue in the opening months of the 1951 session. On the national scene, Wisconsin United States Senator Joseph McCarthy had worked the country into a frenzy over the possibility that Communists had infiltrated all levels of government. In the Sooner State, to guard against the internal damage from suspected Communists, legislation was introduced to require all state employees to take a loyalty oath. Governor Johnston Murray told the legislature, "Even though there are a minimum of Communists in Oklahoma, the oath will alert the people to the things that might creep up on them."[9]

George was certainly loyal to America and supported legislative leaders' call for a strong law requiring state employees to swear they had not been a member of a Communist organization within the past five years and would take up arms in defense of the United States. The legislature passed the bill and Governor Murray signed it into law even though he questioned its constitutionality. Opposition to the loyalty oath sprang up around the state, especially at colleges and universities. The state attorney general declared the law unconstitutional but the Oklahoma Supreme Court disagreed and upheld the law. The state tried to enforce the law by withholding salaries from employees who refused to sign the oath. However, the issue was deflated the following year when the United States Supreme Court unanimously found the law to be unconstitutional.

George supported two constitutional amendments proposed by the 1951 legislature. One, allowing women to serve on juries, received approval of state voters. The other, a proposal to allow 18-year-olds to vote, was defeated. Later, as lieutenant governor, George was state chairman of the successful effort that did lower the voting age.

George was the youngest member of the state legislature. In fact he was so young-looking a veteran House member thought he was a page and asked him for a glass of water. When George went to pick up his first legislative paycheck, he was told that members had to come in person to get their checks, not to send pages. In fact, Frank Truell, the chief sergeant of arms in the House, threatened to have George fired "if he didn't quit fraternizing with the members of the House."[10] To make certain that everyone knew that George was actually a member of the House, Representative Bill Shibley of Bristow introduced a resolution making George an honorary page.

Life Is Like a Mountain Railroad

Keep your hand upon the throttle and your eye upon the rail.

From the traditional hymn

George worked at the grocery store in McAlester when he was not attending legislative sessions in Oklahoma City. In May, 1951, he was invited to speak to graduating seniors at Hartshorne High School. George based his speech on the old hymn "Life is Like a Mountain Railroad," learned around the piano at Ma Richter's boarding house in Norman. The audience was spellbound with George's comparison of the toils of life with the problems faced by an engineer climbing a steep mountain, "an engineer that's brave, you must make the road successful from the cradle to the grave." George concluded his speech with the final words of the song he had used as his text, "As you go through life, dear brother, never falter, never fail. Keep your hand upon the throttle and your eye upon the rail."[1] The students gave him his first standing ovation.

That speech made an impression on Hartshorne High School Principal Dr. Finas Sandlin. The following year Sandlin became principal at McAlester High School, and along with School Superintendent Arch Thompson, convinced George to become a school teacher. George said he had never thought of being a teacher even though his mother and his brother Sam were teachers. But Sandlin argued that anyone who could take "Life is Like a Mountain

Railroad" and make it into a motivational speech for high school seniors should be a teacher.[2]

Having never previously considered teaching as a profession, George lacked the required six hours of practice teaching before he could receive official accreditation enabling him to teach in public schools. He returned to the campus of East Central in Ada in the summer of 1951 and completed the six hours.

George did not know what subject he wanted to teach so Superintendent Thompson sent a note to all principals that George should be called first when a substitute teacher was needed, regardless of the subject. It was an exciting and interesting time for George who taught a variety of subjects, from fourth grade music, while Elizabeth Whetsel had her appendix removed, to math in junior high and high school.

George found his niche on a day when he substituted for Oklahoma History teacher Effie Stanfield. Saying, "That's for me," George informed the superintendent he wanted to be an Oklahoma History teacher, a request that was made possible when a second Oklahoma History teacher Bob LaGrone became an elementary principal. George was a fellow teacher with faculty members in whose classrooms he had sat as a student only a few years before and taught students who had recently campaigned for him.

George was allowed to take a leave of absence in odd years in the spring semester when the legislature was in session. His annual teaching salary of $1,800 allowed him to buy his first automobile, a 1953 ivory over black Ford Fairlane. His car payment of $200 a month was more than his salary but he made up the difference with his legislative pay, $15 per day while in session and $100 a month when not in session, and money from work at the grocery store on weekends and holidays.

George was active in Democratic politics, from the precinct level to the state convention. In April, 1952, he served as chairman of the credentials committee at the Pittsburg County Democratic convention held in the district courtroom in the county courthouse. George spoke briefly to the conclave of Democrats along with Senator Nix, Representatives Stipe and Edwards, Judge Tom Haile, and County Attorney Homer W. Neece.[3]

In May, 1952, George filed for re-election to his seat in the House of Representatives. Surprisingly, he drew an opponent, *Kiowa Chronicle* publisher Manley Leonidas "M.L." Misenheimer, a peppery, old-time country newspaperman, who had served in the 14th legislature 20 years before and was a perennial candidate.

Misenheimer always filed against a popular incumbent, whether it be in a local race or for Congress, so he would be the only other candidate in that race. His theory was that surely someday one of the incumbents would die during the primary campaign, making him the Democratic nominee, tantamount to election in Little Dixie.[4]

The candidates met in early June and approved an itinerary of seven political speakings to be held the last two weeks of the month in Canadian, Kiowa, Arpelar, Krebs, Hartshorne, Quinton, and South McAlester. They agreed on a five-minute speaking limit for themselves or a representative and turned thumbs down on a proposal for formal speakings at pie suppers in the county.[5]

George, from the beginning of his political career, had run as George P. Nigh. He really did not like his middle name but thought it necessary to include the middle initial because other successful politicians in Oklahoma, such as Thomas P. Gore, Robert L. Owen, William S. Murray, Leon C. Phillips, A.S. Monroney, Robert S. Kerr, C. Plowboy Edwards, and Kirksey M. Nix, used initials. George, always trying to identify with listeners, said the "P" in his name stood for "Pittsburg County."

At one speaking, Misenheimer said the "P" in George's name stood for "pussyfootin' politician."[6] The crowd went wild and George was humiliated. When it was his turn to speak, he shot back at Misenheimer, who had run for office every two years for decades, saying, "The M.L. in Mr. Misenheimer's name means 'my Lord, he's running again.' " After the speaking Misenheimer's wife pulled George aside and castigated him for picking on her husband. Mrs. Misenheimer said, "Look, he's an old man and he doesn't stand a chance against you. Don't attack him personally."[7] George took Mrs. Misenheimer's admonition to heart and pledged to never base any campaign on personal attacks against his opponents. It was a lesson that served George well in the future.

In a statement in the *McAlester Democrat,* Misenheimer said he favored separate public schools for blacks and whites and a state university for blacks, "so they can educate their own Booker T. Washingtons and George Washington Carvers under their own college professors."[8]

Misenheimer also announced his opposition to consolidation of rural schools and toll roads "through the populous sections of the state for the tourists and transport trucks to flit to and fro through Oklahoma from the Atlantic to the Pacific and from Canada to Mexico."[9]

At speakings, George emphasized his commitment to Pittsburg County and his experience in a successful first term in the House. As usual in Nigh campaigns, he promised no jobs to anyone, agreeing only to do his best to make certain his district received its fair share in every state appropriation, a political attitude George learned from Robert S. Kerr who publicly stated that Oklahoma deserved its fair share of federal funds.

On election day, July 2, 1952, George swamped Misenheimer, polling nearly 80 percent of the votes cast. The final tally was 8,888 votes for George and only 2,307 votes for Misenheimer. Fellow Pittsburg County House members Stipe and Edwards also won landslide victories.

A New State Song

Let's do for Oklahoma what Rodgers and Hammerstein did; let's put an exclamation point there, Oklahoma!

GEORGE NIGH

PURCELL PUBLISHER JAMES C. NANCE became Speaker of the House and Raymond Gary of Madill was named President Pro Tempore of the Senate as the 24th legislature convened at the State Capitol in January, 1953. From the beginning of the session, Governor Johnston Murray's relations with leaders of the legislature were strained at best. Tension mounted when Murray proposed elimination of the legislative practice of earmarking funds for specific uses by state agencies, consolidation of some of the 77 counties, and equalization of the ad valorem property tax, all issues that are perennially controversial in Oklahoma.

George enjoyed working alongside House Speaker Nance. George watched as Nance exerted incredible power over the lower house, "His stamp was branded on almost every piece of legislation that was passed in either house. He gave a sense of purpose to the House. His goal was to raise the stature of the House to the level of the Oklahoma Senate."[1] Nance often expressed distaste of references to the House of Representatives as the "lower house" and the Senate as the "upper house."

Any keen observer of the legislative process in Oklahoma would not have expected controversy to erupt over George's introduction of a bill in 1953 to make the popular song "Oklahoma," from the Rodgers and Hammerstein Broadway musical of the same name, the official state song.

Several of the tunes from *Oklahoma!* had been among George's favorites since he listened to them on the *Lucky Strike Hit Parade* on radio on Saturday nights. He remembered the pride he felt in the summer of 1943, before his junior year in high school, when he first heard the popular songs about his home state.

Oklahoma had become a household word because of the success of the Broadway play that debuted on March 31, 1943, at the St. James Theater in New York City. The play ushered in an entire new era of musicals, played what then was a record of 2,212 performances on Broadway over a five-year period, and toured the country annually until 1954.

Although Richard Rodgers and Oscar Hammerstein, II, deserve much of the credit for the success on Broadway, the musical was based upon another play, *Green Grow the Lilacs,* written by Oklahoma native Lynn Riggs of Claremore. Rodgers and Hammerstein both lived in New York City and knew little about the West. The original words of the song were, "The corn is as high as a cow pony's eye," before Rodgers and Hammerstein discovered that corn in Oklahoma grew "as high as an elephant's eye."

The name *Oklahoma!* for the stage play had an interesting history. When selecting a new name for the play, Hammerstein's wife suggested *Oklahoma.* When told that the name needed more excitement to match the vibrancy of the play, she said, "Let's add an exclamation point and call it *Oklahoma!*"

Before 1953, the official state song was "Oklahoma (A Toast)," written in 1905 by Harriet Parker Camden. Among the words of the song were, "Oklahoma, fairest daughter of the West, Oklahoma, 'tis the land I love the best."[2]

When George's bill to replace "Oklahoma (A Toast)" as the official state song appeared on the House calendar, Representative J. W. Huff of Ada stood firmly in opposition to the move. As tears streamed down his face, he said, "I can't believe what you're doing here today. You're going to change a song written by pioneers, steeped in tradition, couched in history. You're going to change it for a song written by two New York Jews who never have even been here and they say 'taters and tomaters. You're going to change it, this song for that song?"[3]

Huff left the microphone and walked among fellow members on the House floor as he sang the words of the old song, "We have often sung her praises, but we have not told the half, so I give you Oklahoma, 'tis a toast we all can quaff."[4]

Everyone in the House chamber rose to their feet as Huff completed the final verse of the old song. After all, it was the state song. George thought his bill was "going down the toilet," but thought quickly of a way he could diminish the effect of the emotion in the chamber. He approached the only microphone at the front podium and said, "Mr. Speaker, I ask unanimous consent to lay this bill over for one legislative day."[5]

Other House members had objected to the change of the state song. Representative Robert S. Taylor of Perry objected to George's proposal. Taylor believed the Rodgers and Hammerstein song was too difficult to sing. Representative Ernest Tate of Ardmore told fellow House members that the new song had too much slang like "taters" and "termayters." Representative Richard Romang of Enid went so far to suggest that the legislature sponsor a two-year contest for a state song and offer a $500 prize.

With George laying his bill over, Huff, and other opponents of the new state song, thought they had won. However, George left the House chamber and went to work. He called Ridge Bond, a fellow McAlesterite and the only Oklahoman to star in the Broadway version of *Oklahoma!* Bond, who sang the lead role of Curly, lived in Tulsa at that time. George asked Bond to come to the State Capitol the following day, "prepared to sing."[6]

Next, George called Ira Humprhies, the House member from Chickasha, to invite the choir from the Oklahoma College for Women (OCW) to appear at the Capitol the next day, "provided they know the tunes from *Oklahoma!*" Finally, George asked Jenkins Music Company in Oklahoma City to furnish a piano.

The following day George innocently asked unanimous consent to grant privileges to the floor for a special visitor, Bond, the Broadway star, and the OCW Choir. With the House gallery packed, the college choir performed majestically. They sang "Surrey with the Fringe on Top" and "Oh, What a Beautiful Morning." As the pianist began building a dramatic introduction to "Oklahoma!", Bond, in his Curly costume, strode to the microphone and brought the house down.

After the rousing rendition of the song, the crowd, including of course the 200 friends and supporters strategically placed there by George, stood and shouted. George took the microphone from Bond and shouted above the melee, "Mr. Speaker, let's do for Oklahoma what Rodgers and Hammerstein did; let's put an exclamation point there. I move we make 'Oklahoma' the state song." . . . And they did.[7]

George told the legislature, "We should do for Oklahoma what two New York Jews have already done. . . be enthusiastic about Oklahoma! I'll take 'taters and termaters over quaff."

Thirty-five years later, in 1988, owners of the copyright on "Oklahoma" began charging the state a royalty for use of the famous song. Oklahoma paid $40,000 in royalties over a two-year period until an employee of the Oklahoma Department of Tourism found a 1953 letter written by Oscar Hammerstein, II, to a Tulsa newspaper that had inquired if the song could be used without royalty payments. Hammerstein wrote, "So tell your readers and all the people of Oklahoma that not only may they play and sing it anywhere to their heart's content, but that we want them and urge them to do so. Mr. Rodgers and I are very proud that our song has been adopted by your state. Play it and sing it loud and long and often."[8]

Persuaded by the wishes of Rodgers and Hammerstein, the daughter of Richard Rodgers and son of Oscar Hammerstein, II, accepted $1.00 from United States Senator David L. Boren in a 1990 ceremony giving the State of Oklahoma the right to use the song "Oklahoma" in perpetuity, or as newspaperman Jim Standard said, "as long as the wind comes sweeping down the plains."[9]

As a result of George's efforts to officially designate "Oklahoma" as the state song, he was invited to Hollywood for the premiere of the movie *Oklahoma!* This trip gave birth to his future successful efforts to bring Hollywood movie productions to Oklahoma.

While in California, George was invited to appear on a radio program hosted by native Oklahoman Jimmy Wakely, a popular singing cowboy in early western movies. Wakely's show was broadcast worldwide on the American Forces Radio and Television Service (AFRTS). Wakely had heard that George was the youngest member of the state legislature but mistakenly referred to him as the youngest member of the United States Senate. Not wanting to embarass the troubadour on the live show, yet worried that folks back home would think he was out in Hollywood pretending to be a United States Senator, George talked about his love for Oklahoma and gradually worked back into the conversation the fact that he was the youngest member of the Oklahoma legislature.

Later, when Wakely, his wife Inez, and other members of the family visited George and Donna's home in Oklahoma City, George played the piano while the Wakelys sang harmony to "Life is Like a Mountain Railroad."

In 1954, George's opponent for re-election was Quinton telephone company owner C.L. Elsey. George traveled his district with the message that he was the man to return to the State Capitol to represent Pittsburg County. It was an easy election for George. In the July 6, 1954, primary, George defeated Elsey 9,174 to 3,742, the most votes George ever received in his three contested legislative races.

In the same election, Representative Gene Stipe tried unsuccessfully to unseat Senator Kirksey Nix. Two years later, though, when Nix resigned to accept a position on the Oklahoma Court of Criminal Appeals, Stipe was elected to the Senate seat in a special election and continued in the same office in 2000, the longest-running service in a state legislature anywhere in the United States. Stipe was replaced in the Oklahoma House by George's friend in high school, William H. "Bill" Skeith, whose popularity was due in part to his job as the radio voice of the McAlester Rockets Class D professional baseball team.

George's popularity continued to grow. In 1956, he drew no opponent while Willard Gotcher, whom George had defeated in his first House race six years earlier, was elected to one of the other seats in Pittsburg County. Skeith was re-elected to Pittsburg County's third House seat.

Aiming Higher

If you don't know where you're going, you're liable to end up there.
Yogi Berra

EDUCATION remained George's priority as the state representative from Pittsburg County. He became vice chairman of the House Education Committee, under the tutelage of Representative E.T. Dunlap of Red Oak, and worked for increased spending and quality education initiatives in the legislature. When Dunlap left the legislature to become president of Eastern Oklahoma A & M College in Wilburton, George became chairman of the committee.

George and Dunlap developed a close professional and personal relationship for the remainder of Dunlap's life. Dunlap, as Chancellor of Higher Education, served on George's cabinet 25 years later.

Because the state penitentiary was in his home district, George was also a vocal proponent of more money to run prisons. The issue of increased funding for prisons was no more popular in the 1950s than in any other period in state history. When George supported legislation to raise the salaries of guards, other legislators screamed and hollered about programs they considered far more worthy; funding for crippled children, the mentally challenged, and public schools. George's answer was, "All of Oklahoma needs help."

George was well acquainted with the guards and administrators at the McAlester penitentiary and often walked alone across the prison yard to have lunch in the cafeteria with prison personnel. His frequent visits to the prison made him an expert on the facility, causing legislative leaders to call upon him to advise appropriations committees considering adequate funding levels.

George was a quality history teacher and a good state representative. His constituents were happy with his representation in the legislature. He was a popular teacher. He organized a boys' school spirit group, called the Wow-Wows, with more than 200 members. He was a sponsor of Hi-Y, a Christian student fellowship.

However, by 1957, the McAlester school board, whose members strongly supported George both politically and professionally, believed George should "get in or out of education or get in or out of politics." Board members would have been happy with either. Superintendent Arch Thompson called George into his office and offered him a principal's job if he chose education.

While George loved the classroom, he had no desire to be a school administratior. Also, George saw no future in continuing to hold his seat in the House of Representatives. To realize his childhood dream of being governor of Oklahoma, it was necessary to take his aspirations a step farther. He was not yet ready to run for governor and had no interest in opposing incumbent State Senator Gene Stipe. He surveyed possible statewide races that he thought he could win.

George settled on the race for lieutenant governor in 1958. However, there was possibly one small problem. George was only 30-years-old and the state constitution required that the lieutenant governor be 31-years-old. George believed he was on solid legal ground because he would be 31 by the time he took office, if, of course, he won the election.

To make certain his gut feeling about the legal filing situation was correct, George asked his friend, University of Oklahoma law student Bob Scarbrough of Altus, to set up a meeting between George and Maurice Merrill, dean of the OU School of Law. Merrill, a recognized authority in constitutional law, agreed with George that as long as he reached age 31 by inauguration day, his underage filing was irrelevant. However, Merrill anticipated someone might challenge George's filing. The dean suggested that if a challenge occurred, George should call a news conference and stand beside all the law books containing statutes he had voted on as a member of the House of Representatives for eight years. In the proposed news conference, George planned to say, "I voted on all these bills and they're trying to say I'm not qualified?"[1] There was never a protest so the brilliant strategy of Dean Merrill was not called into play. This actually was a great disappointment to the Nigh camp because close supporters believed that the obscure history teacher from McAlester needed any type of statewide publicity.

The sitting lieutenant governor was James Pinckney "Cowboy Pink" Williams, fondly referred to by many Oklahomans as just plain "Pink." He had upset longtime Lieutenant Governor James Berry of Stillwater four years before, in 1954, after he gained state and national fame from a postcard campaign aimed at making fun of United States Secretary of Agriculture Ezra Taft Benson. The postcard emphasized the plight of American cattlemen competing with cheaper foreign beef. The comical card showed a caricature of a donkey kicking up both hind legs and invited recipients to a "public ass kicking" of all cattlemen who voted for Republican presidential contender Dwight D. Eisenhower in 1952. The card was sent to judges, sheriffs, and courthouse officials all over the country.

Former Oklahoma Republican Congressman Ross Rizley had been appointed assistant postmaster general by President Eisenhower. From that position, Rizley ruled the postcard "obscene" and forbade its delivery in the federal postal system. Pink made a well-publicized trip to the nation's capital to protest Rizley's ruling, calling it a partisan political move for a defeated Republican congressman to censor a mailing by a Democrat.

It was an ideal subject for a hungry national press corps. The postcard campaign made Cowboy Pink famous, resulting in a legal name change from James Pinckney Williams to Cowboy Pink Williams.[2]

Pink owned a 1,100-acre ranch at Caddo in southern Oklahoma and appeared to many political observers to be unbeatable in 1958. However, George learned from friends in the House of Representatives and other Democrats around the state that Pink's postcard fame was wearing thin and that if anyone could get into a runoff with the incumbent, he could be beaten.

George wanted to test the validity of that theory. He and several friends, including Bruce Frazier of Sulphur, fanned out to Democratic towns such as Shawnee, Holdenville, Seminole, and Wewoka to poll prospective voters on the lieutenant governor's race. The unscientific polling, taken from brief interviews on main streets, discovered that 85 percent of the voters did not think Cowboy Pink could be beaten. However, more than 60 percent of those polled said they would personally not vote for Pink's re-election. George drew an obvious conclusion from the poll, Cowboy Pink could indeed be beaten. It was the incumbent's election to lose.[3]

Evidently, others drew the same conclusion. George was not the only person seeking to unseat Pink from his job as lieutenant governor. Thirteen men, eleven Democrats and two Republicans, filed for the position and sprinted from the starting gate for the primary election scheduled for July 1, 1958.

In addition to George and Pink, other reasonably well-known Democrats threw their hats into the ring for Oklahoma's second post. Tulsa attorney George E. Norvell, former mayor of Tulsa, was popular in northeast Oklahoma. Neville C. Kerr, sheriff of Muskogee County; Jack Johnson, McAlester; Wayne Wallace, a Norman insurance agent; Bill Wallace of Oklahoma City, a former Grady County House member; Ernest Albright; W. Otho Nichols; Leonard C. Bowen; and Andrew Fraley rounded out the overloaded Democratic primary ballot. Earl Winsel and George B. Sherritt battled for the GOP nomination.

George, the largely unknown teacher-legislator, was once again in a familiar role, a heavy underdog. However, George called upon his old and new friends around the state who organized a grassroots effort to get his name and his program before the voters.

As usual, George's campaign was based upon friendship. There were no paid workers. His friends, Paul Carris, Bob Bartheld, Bob Hinton, Floyd White, Bob Scarbrough,

Jim Hazenbeck, Dean Stringer, Ted Bonham, and hundreds of men and women George had met through his participation in such groups as the Young Democrats, Girls State, Boys State, the American Legion, and Jaycees, pitched in to help him become a familiar name in all 77 counties. A secret weapon were former classmates and students who became the nucleus of the statewide grassroots organization. Bob Bartheld described the operation as "a campaign on a shoestring."[4]

On Friday afternoons, George, right, family members, friends, and supporters boarded a bus owned by George's brother Wib, the bus agent in McAlester, and headed to a new part of the state with campaign brochures and lots of energy. At far left, on facing page, are volunteer coordinators Herman Harmon and Weldon Miller. Harmon later introduced George to Donna.

Bill Edwards, later a McAlester banker, remembered an early fund-raising banquet as being like an evangelical meeting, one supporter shouting, "I'll give $25," as another yelled, "Put me down for $30."[5]

George's brothers and sister helped in the campaign effort. Bill, working for the MKT Railroad in Texas, came home on weekends. Sam managed a one-person office in McAlester where a high school student, Leah Lee, helped George manage his campaign mail. Wib drove the campaign bus on weekends. Mary actively campaigned for her brother in the McAlester area.

No matter how much George tried to be innovative in his campaign methods, he was not attracting much attention of the Oklahoma media. For one reason, most reporters thought Cowboy Pink had the race won without much of a fight. A second reason the press shied away from George's campaign was because the political focus was on a major and bitter scramble among Midwest City builder W.P. "Bill" Atkinson, Tulsa County Attorney J. Howard Edmondson, and eight other candidates, for the Democratic nomination for governor.

A train wreck north of McAlester benefited George's sign effort. Supporters bought at a great discount damaged plywood and made hundreds of campaign signs. Former students were mobilized to build signs in the old abandoned Nigh grocery store building. The empty shelves were perfect for drying 12" x 24" signs.

Hundreds of homemade, reflective signs, simply with the word "NIGH" silk-screened onto the plywood, were placed into the backs of students' cars and pickups each week for distribution all over Oklahoma. A McAlester native, going to college, would come home on the weekends and return on Sunday with a load of signs and a map indicating where they were to be placed alongside busy highways and at well-traveled intersections. The ideal location for a reflective sign was in "the bend of the road."[6]

Early in the campaign, before the name "Nigh" became familiar, some people thought the campaign signs were advertising a new brand of soft drink or was the work of a religious fanatic.

George's supporters hosted postcard signing parties. George explained, "I would go into a community like Broken Arrow. Friends like James and Donna Newcomb would get all their friends to bring their Christmas card, family, and civic club lists. We would bring in food and for hours those people would just sit and longhand address postcards to their friends, asking them to consider me as their next lieutenant governor." The premise of the signing parties was based upon George's belief that most people did not care who was lieutenant governor but would accept a recommendation from a friend.[7]

Cowboy Pink was a nice guy but hardly visible as the lieutenant governor. George looked for chinks in Pink's armor. An unusual chink came after the lieutenant governor was authorized, for the first time, by the legislature, to purchase an official car. Pink, being a rancher, bought a new Ford pickup. The chink appeared when Pink was shown in a full-page newspaper advertisement for Ford dealers, saying, "Whether I'm at the Capitol or down on the farm, I'm at home in my new Ford pickup."[8] George capitalized on Pink's advertisement and contacted, both by mail and in person, dealers for other brands of automobiles. George promised the dealers he would never appear in an advertisement for their competitors.

Pittsburg County had the fourth largest Democratic voter registration in the state, behind Oklahoma, Tulsa, and Muskogee counties. That fact alone gave George confidence that he had a good chance to force Cowboy Pink into a runoff. He recognized that Pink, as the incumbent, would probably win the primary in Oklahoma County; that Norvell, endorsed by the *Tulsa World*, would win Tulsa County; and that Sheriff Kerr would be the frontrunner in his home of Muskogee County. George assumed he would do as well in Pittsburg County. He predicted whomever could come reasonably close to Pink in the other 73 counties could sneak into a runoff.

Jaycees around the state played a major role in the campaign. In nearly half the counties, a Jaycee whom George had known through the organization, served as the campaign manager. Among them were Floyd White in Hugo; Bowie Ballard in Ada; Kermit Ingham and Joe Johnson in Stillwater; Francis Hollingsworth of El Reno; Frank Coates of Tonkawa; John McAnaw of Bartlesville; and Bert Mackie of Enid.

Jaycees were young business leaders who were mostly registered Democrats but tended to be conservative in their politics. George's

George taps a stake into the ground to anchor his temporary headquarters on the State Capitol Lawn in June, 1958. The publicity stunt worked. This photograph appeared on the front page of *The Daily Oklahoman.* Courtesy *The Daily Oklahoman.*

ideas on fiscal responsibility and accountability in government warmed Jaycees' hearts and motivated them to work hard in George's campaign. George often would deliver a batch of mail to Jaycee couples who could type well enough to answer inquiries from prospective voters and campaigners.

Another group of Nigh supporters was girls who had attended Girls State. Entire familes were dragged to Nigh rallies by daughters and granddaughters who had met George over the previous eight years at Girls State.

In mid-June George hatched up an idea to attract the needed press coverage to his campaign. He and a contingent of 21 former students headed out from McAlester in two cars and a bus, driven by Wib Nigh.

Their mission was to spend the night on the lawn of the State Capitol in pup tents and bedrolls. Television cameras and newsmen were on hand as the entourage arrived at the Capitol at dusk.

The plan worked, causing one newsman to remark, "This is the first real gimmick to come out of any campaign this year."[9] To George it was not just a gimmick, but an inexpensive way to garner much-needed publicity for his campaign.

The *McAlester News Capital* reported on the event in the next day's edition, "Wrapped in blankets, somewhat moist from a heavy dew, George's student campaigners were up wandering around at 5 A.M. Some stayed on the grass while others crawled into the traveling bus or inside the Capitol. George stuck to the pup tent labeled 'temporary headquarters.' This implied he would be ensconced a bit farther to the southeast come election day." [10]

Asked by a reporter why he was camping on the Capitol lawn, George said, "If Pink can camp in the Capitol corridors, then I guess it's all right for me to camp on the Capitol lawn."[11] Several of George's friends, including State Representative Bill Bradley of Waurika, and Oklahoma County school superintendent Carlton Poling, came by the Capitol to encourage him.

After handing out campaign brochures in Oklahoma City's shopping districts all day, and spending a second night attracting the attention of the press and automobile travelers along Northeast 23rd Street, George and his supporters traveled to Edmond, Guthrie, Stillwater, Cushing, Drumright, Sapulpa, Sand Springs, and Tulsa for quick campaign stops. As soon as the bus and cars in the caravan arrived in a town, campaigners saturated the area with literature while George shook hands in the business district.

In the following two days the Nigh campaign troupe made stops in Claremore, Miami, Vinita, Pryor, Muskogee, Okmulgee, Henryetta, Checotah, and Eufaula before returning to McAlester.

George's campaign budget did not allow for the renting of motel rooms for his campaigners. Instead they camped out in tents and slept in the bus and cars. One night, while the youthful campaign team slept in sleeping bags on the bottom of an empty swimming pool at Boulder Park in Tulsa, a driving rainstorm filled the pool with water and drove the campers to the safety of nearby public bathrooms. In Stillwater, youngsters campaigned door to door during a tornado alert, until George heeded the warnings of would-be voters and pulled the campaigners to the safety of the campaign bus.

With the newsworthy campaign swing to many of the state's major population centers, George had the publicity he needed to vault him into a runoff with Cowboy Pink Williams. People began telling George that they would vote for a teacher who could get his students working as hard as they did on the campaign blitz.[13]

George burned the candle at both ends during the final week of the campaign. He spoke to Young Democrats in Bartlesville, was the principal speaker of a banquet in Clinton, and made campaign stops in Altus and Lawton.

At a state Jaycee convention in Lawton, one of the more famous George Nigh stories was born. Several women, in varying stages of pregnancy, wore campaign tee-shirts that read "Nigh is the Guy." Thus was born one of Oklahoma's most colorful campaign slogans.

His hometown newspaper, the *McAlester News Capital,* called for last minute help in a front page story, writing, "George Nigh needs more than your vote. His crew is getting ready for a last minute statewide appeal, and George will need about 200 volunteers Saturday. The workers will be provided transportation to spread out over the state handing out cards and soliciting votes. Any age, single or married. Oh, yes, if you have a car bring it along but it isn't absolutely necessary. If you want to work just call Garden 3-0215 or drop by the Nigh headquarters at the Aldridge Hotel tomorrow." [14]

By the time Saturday morning arrived more than 300 volunteers had signed up to take George's message to every corner of the state. The volunteers were told by George to stress to the people that the lieutenant governor is just a heart beat from the governor's office and was a position to be taken seriously instead of in a joking manner.

When the primary election ballots were counted, George fulfilled his strategy and made the runoff with a strong showing in second place, ahead of Mayor Norvell and Sheriff Kerr, and the remainder of the field. George polled 80,727 votes, but was still 90,000 votes behind

Cowboy Pink Williams' total of 176,171 votes. Williams received only 40 percent of the primary vote, meaning that 60 percent of the voters voted against the incumbent.

George was not disheartened but instead was pleased with his position as runner-up in the primary. He and his campaign manager and best friend, Paul Carris, strongly believed the old political axiom that incumbents get all their votes in the primary and that votes going to losing candidates usually ended up in the column of the runner-up in the runoff. At least that is what George counted on as he stepped up his campaign for the July 22 runoff.

The *McAlester News Capital* editorialized on behalf of George, citing a selfish reason for his election as lieutenant governor, "Nomination of George would give Pittsburg County the third largest legislative delegation in the state. George would sit as the head of the senate as its president. In that same senate will be Gene Stipe while across the way in the House side will be three representatives from Pittsburg County. Our county, thus would rank third to Oklahoma and Tulsa counties... For the future of Pittsburg County, we owe George Nigh our wholehearted support."[16]

George's friend, Joe Johnson, former state president of the Jaycees, came home from Texas after the primary, ready to work full-time in the runoff campaign. Johnson, not believing that George could make the runoff, arrived at George's hotel room at the Biltmore Hotel in Oklahoma City at 3:00 A.M. the morning after the election. Johnson knocked on the door. When a sleepy George inquired, "Who is it?," Johnson answered, "It is a friend who has come to give you three weeks of his life."[17]

A Heartbeat Away

I want to be the insurance policy you never have to cash.

George Nigh

On July 13, George, Joe Johnson, and Paul Carris organized Oklahoma's first statewide political rally for a lieutenant governor candidate. About 450 supporters crowded into the Biltmore Hotel ballroom in downtown Oklahoma City. Two defeated primary candidates, Bill Wallace and Otho Nichols, spoke in favor of George. Two other former candidates, Wayne Wallace and Ernest Albright, sent letters of endorsement to the rally.

Carris opened the meeting and then turned the microphone over to George who told the cheering crowd that his victory in making the runoff was a clear signal from Oklahoma voters that it was time for a change. As newspaper reporters scrawled in their notebooks and television cameras whirred in the background, George slammed home the point that the lieutenant governor was just a heartbeat away from the governor's mansion. George said, "We must stress that we are sincere in our efforts to return this office to its proper position. And the awakened majority of Oklahomans want to replace horseplay with horse sense." [1]

George also told his supporters that he was interested in the youth of Oklahoma, had served as chairman of a legislative council committee studying juvenile problems and corrective legislation, and promised to create a permanent committee to work with the state's youth. Finally George said he wanted to make the lieutenant governor's office "a job instead of a position."[2]

It seemed inconsistent to him that the second highest office in the state, and only a heartbeat away from the top position, was a part-time job with no responsibilities or authority.

George was hungry for speaking engagements, anywhere, anytime. He was elated when he was asked to be the principal speaker to a group of about 40 voters gathering for a meeting in Blanchard, a small town southwest of Oklahoma City. He soon recognized that the reason he was the main draw in Blanchard was a giant rally that expected a crowd of 5,000 people in Shawnee the same night. George made two phone calls, one to the people at Blanchard asking to be first on the program. The second call was to the organizers of the Shawnee rally, asking to be last on their program.

George delivered a stem-winding speech to the tiny group in Blanchard and sped toward Shawnee, making it in time for the last half of the elongated program that featured J. Howard Edmondson, Bill Atkinson, and dozens of other candidates. George asked the master of ceremonies to not mention the fact that he was the last speaker, for fear that the crowd might leave. However, the emcee forgot George's request and announced to the fan-waving crowd on the hot summer night that George was the final candidate and would speak for seven minutes.

Fearing that a typical crowd would start making a mad dash to the parking lot to beat the crowd, George ran to the podium yelling at the top of his voice, "Wait a minute! The next seven minutes might be the most important seven minutes of your life." George was excited because no one left. In fact, no one moved as George, snapping his fingers continuously, talked about the importance of the lieutenant governor. He said, "The snap of a finger, the tick of a clock, a heartbeat. It's just the beat of a heart that makes this job so important. It's just the beat of a heart that makes the lieutenant governor the most important office in the state." The entire crowd sat motionless for seven minutes.

A tear of humility and pride ran down George's cheek as he was humbled by the crowd's attention. He thought to himself, "George, you've done it. You have reached the pinnacle. The greatest speech you ever made has held captive 5,000 people." The master of ceremonies retook the podium and said, "Thank you very much Mr. Nigh. Now we will draw for the $500 cash."[3]

A late push for financial help from supporters around the state assisted George in placing a few television spots on stations in Oklahoma City and Tulsa. Martin Hauan, who had been press secretary to Governors Murray and Gary, put together ads with the help of David Hudson and Larry Frazier in Frazier's recording studio.[4]

Even though the campaign was operating on a limited budget, George was able to fly to many rallies and meetings with the assistance of Dr. George Brown of McAlester and other friends who owned airplanes. Brown ferried George to stops in Ada, Pauls Valley, Chickasha, and Ardmore, all in one day. Campaigning by airplane allowed George to cover three times as much territory as he could by car. Brown remembered, "When we landed at a town, George always looked out the window to see who was waiting. If he recognized anyone in the crowd, he was the first out the door to greet them. But if he did not recognize anyone, Paul Carris was the first out, to shake hands and find out their names, a job that would later become Donna Nigh's in future campaigns."[5]

Dr. Brown advised George to cat nap between campaign stops to stay fresh throughout a grueling day of campaigning. Dr. Brown believed most mistakes and mis-speakings were made by political candidates when they were tired.

George received help in the runoff from unlikely sources, the camps of both Democratic gubernatorial hopefuls, Edmondson and Atkinson. Edmondson's campaign advisers did not want to run in the general election in tandem with an elderly candidate such as Cowboy Pink.

The Edmondson line to their supporters was, "Vote for two fine young men."[6] Atkinson's campaign managers, in an attempt to capture a part of the youth movement, took a different approach by saying, "Mature and experienced Atkinson and young Nigh will be a balanced team."[7] Martin Hauan wrote, "George got the best of both worlds, each camp in the governor's race favoring him."[8]

"Nigh is the guy," a slang fixture in many later campaigns, was the center of an editorial in the *McAlester News Capital* on the day before the runoff election. The newspaper said, "Nigh is able, willing and well qualified to fill the lieutenant governor's office. He is honest, fair and progressive and will devote himself to giving the people of Oklahoma the best that is in him. . . He is attempting to return dignity and experience to an office that once was considered a joking matter. He has conducted a clean, above-the-board campaign and is deserving of a big majority of the votes."[9]

As the results of the runoff election voting began to filter into the Nigh headquarters in Oklahoma City on the evening of July 22, it became apparent that the school teacher from McAlester had pulled off an incredible upset of Cowboy Pink Williams. George beat Cowboy Pink by more than 110,000 votes, 302,050 to 190,530. In just three short weeks there had been a 200,000 vote swing.

United Press International reported that it was a bad day for Cowboy Pink. Not only did he lose to George in the election but he was given a traffic summons by an Oklahoma City police officer for making an improper turn.

The youth movement was alive and well in the Democratic governor's race in which Edmondson overwhelmingly defeated the older Atkinson.[10]

Back home in McAlester, supporters were so happy that they put together a lengthy telegram of congratulations that was delivered to the Nigh watch party at the Biltmore Hotel. George was touched deeply by the show of support from his neighbors.

A grand celebration was planned in McAlester for a few days after the election. Mayor Fritz Neil proclaimed the day "George P. Nigh Day." The daily newspaper called George a good example for the youth of McAlester, "proof that a young person can succeed in almost any field of endeavor, if he is determined, sincere and interested."[11]

Dr. Brown flew George from Oklahoma City to McAlester where he was met by his family, Mayor Neil, and a host of friends and supporters. George quite naturally began working the crowd until Mayor Neil told him to save his effort because the real celebration was downtown.

The McAlester High School marching band, containing a large number of his former students, led a parade for George down McAlester's streets, the same streets where George had organized his first political bicycle parade and won his first jitterbug contest. George rode in an open convertible, escorted by highway patrolmen and city police officers.

More than 500 well-wishers crowded into the ballroom of the Aldridge Hotel to hear George thank the people of Pittsburg County for their help. He said, "As I traveled throughout the state on my campaign, people everywhere told me they were going to vote for me because they heard the whole city of McAlester was behind me. Wherever I have gone, I found a McAlester person had been there before me, asking a vote for George Nigh."[12]

With a bold, black headline of "OUR GUY IS BACK," the *McAlester News Capital* reported on the celebration in the next day's newspaper. The big welcome was described as, "With all the fanfare possible for the return of a favorite son... Nigh stepped to the ground with the wide smile that has been his trademark since first seeking office more than eight years ago... Many people still remember Nigh as the local grocery boy who drove the Nigh grocery truck. Or as the high school boy that could really 'cut a rug' with the latest jitterbug steps. But, Nigh has come a long way since those days. He has proved beyond a doubt that hard work, sincerity, friendliness and integrity can accomplish almost anything—no matter what the odds are."[13]

The Daily Oklahoman called the nomination of Edmondson and Nigh a result of people "in a mood to banish every familiar face from Oklahoma's sometimes smelly political vineyards."[14] The newspaper wrote of George's victory over Cowboy Pink Williams, in an editorial entitled "Oklahoma's New Broom," saying, "Incumbent Lt.-Gov. Cowboy Pink Williams got the political comeuppance that his notorious postcards once advocated for President Eisenhower's supporters. He bowed to George Nigh of McAlester, a neophyte in statewide politics."[15]

Neophyte or not, George was the Democratic nominee for the state's second highest elective office. After resting a few days at home

In 1958, for the first time in Oklahoma history, candidates for governor and lieutenant governor ran as a team. J. Howard Edmondson was 33-years-old, not quite two years older than George. They appeared together on billboards, in radio and television advertisements, and in this campaign brochure.

with his parents in McAlester, George sat down with Paul Carris, Joe Johnson, and a few other close friends to plan for the general election campaign against GOP nominee George B. Sherritt of Tishomingo.

The next step of George's plan to become lieutenant governor took a most unusual turn. Sherritt, the mayor of Tishomingo, not only did not campaign for himself, but introduced George at a rally on Tishomingo's Main Street, and even contributed financially to George. The Republican nominee told George the only reason he entered the race was to make certain that someone was running against Cowboy Pink Williams. It is hard to imagine in a political climate that one party's nominee would openly support his opponent.

The headlines the morning after the November 4 general election was "Democrat Win Paced by Nigh," the story of George's overwhelming victory over Sherritt. George won by more than a quarter million votes, 384,431 to 100,068 for Sherritt, and 15,674 for independent candidate Paul W. Updegraff. On election day, even before the polls had closed, came a letter from Sherritt, saying he wanted to be the first to congratulate George and that he himself had voted for him.

The Democratic landslide swept Edmondson into the governor's mansion with the greatest majority ever given a candidate in the governor's race in Oklahoma. George carried every county in the state while Edmondson carried all but one, Major County. During their service together, George often kidded Edmondson that he, George, was the governor of "all of Oklahoma."[16]

By the time inauguration day arrived in January, 1959, George was constitutionally old enough to serve as lieutenant governor. At age 31, George Nigh finally had a full-time job.

Second in Command

The official lieutenant governor's handshake is to, the first thing in the morning, shake hands with the governor with the index finger extended to check the pulse. If it's OK, go back to bed because you don't have anything to do.

George Nigh

The powers and duties of the lieutenant governor in Oklahoma have been less than clearly defined since the first day of statehood.

The office of lieutenant governor was created by Article 6, Section 15 of the state constitution. Only a "male citizen,"at least 31 years of age, and who had resided in Oklahoma for the previous ten years, could be elected lieutenant governor, the same qualifications as governor.

Females were excluded from the top jobs in state government even though Kate Barnard was elected Oklahoma's first Commissioner of Charities and Corrections in 1907.

Women were not allowed to run for governor, lieutenant governor, and other major statewide offices until voters overwhelmingly approved SQ 302 in 1942, 35 years after statehood. It would be another 52 years until a woman, State Represenative Mary Fallin, a native of Tecumseh, was elected lieutenant governor of Oklahoma in 1994. Interestingly enough, Fallin was the first Republican lieutenant governor in history, having defeated another woman, Democrat Nance

Diamond of Shawnee, the granddaughter of James C. Nance of Purcell, the only man in Oklahoma history to head both houses of the legislature.

Lieutenant governor was one of 12 independent statewide elective positions created as part of an "executive department" by the constitution. The bulky executive department resulted in a "weak governor" form of state government. The lieutenant governor, and all other heads of constitutionally created agencies, have never been answerable to the governor, the chief executive officer of the state. Instead the elected officials are beholding only to the voters who exalted them to office.

The position was part of the executive branch of government, yet constitutional convention chairman William H. "Alfalfa Bill" Murray believed, "the Lt. Governor's function is wholly legislative." Except to fill in for the governor when he is vacant from the state, is disabled, has resigned or is impeached, the only duty assigned by Sections 15 and 16 of Article 6 is:

> *He shall be president of the Senate, but shall have only a casting vote therein, and also in joint vote of both houses.*

The "legislative" facet of the lieutenant governor's job was emphasized when Oklahoma voters approved, 94,686 to 71,742, a constitutional amendment in November, 1914, to reduce the state legislature to one house of 80 members and give the other legislative house's powers to the lieutenant governor. The amendment failed because it did not receive a majority of the votes cast in the election that day.

The hearty souls who crafted the Oklahoma constitution realized the importance of having a qualified person waiting in the wings in case something happened to the governor. Chairman Murray loudly preached that, other than to preside over the Senate, the "emergency governor" purpose was the only valid purpose of the lieutenant governor's job.

Article 6, Section 16 of the Oklahoma Constitution reads:

> *In case of impeachment of the Governor, or of his death, failure to qualify, resignation, removal from the State, or inability to discharge the powers and duties of the office, with its compensation, shall devolve upon the Lieutenant Governor for the residue of the term or until the disability shall be removed.*

Not long after the birth of the State of Oklahoma, appeals courts were asked to interpret the legal rights of the lieutenant governor. In *Ex parte Hawkins,* in 1913, the Criminal Court of Appeals held that during the absence of the governor from the confines of Oklahoma, the "Lieutenant Governor has all powers of the Governor." In a sweeping opinion, the Court recognized its limitations, "Courts have no right to substitute their discretion for the discretion of the acting Governor, or to nullify any of his official acts."

The *Hawkins* decision contained many tidbits of reasoning: "The Governor may go to other states, and travel in foreign countries, with all of the military pomp and glory of the Commander in Chief of the Oklahoma militia, as he pleases, without forfeiting his office, and may carry his title with him; but his powers as Governor become dormant the very moment he crosses the state line, and they revive again as soon as he returns and is within the borders of the state."

The *Hawkins* case and other cases arose in 1913 when Lieutenant Governor J.J. McAlester granted pardons to convicted criminals while Governor Lee Cruce was out of state. Defendant Hawkins' pardon was ruled invalid because the governor was actually on a train inside the borders of Oklahoma at the moment the lieutenant governor granted the pardon. But in other cases in which the governor was clearly out of state, pardons given by the lieutenant governor were recognized as a constitutionally accepted act by the chief executive officer of the state.

The Oklahoma Supreme Court was later called upon to determine if there was a difference in the lieutenant governor as an "acting governor" or as a "permanent governor." The constitution provided that the lieutenant governor officially assumed the office of governor when a governor was impeached. Impeachment was simply the act of the state senate officially accusing the governor of misconduct.

In 1923 when Governor James C. Walton was impeached, Lieutenant Governor Martin E. Trapp took over the governor's office and began exercising duties of the office. Walton successfully obtained from a district judge an injunction prohibiting Trapp from doing his duty as governor. But the Supreme Court, in *State ex rel Trapp v. Chambers, District Judge,* vacated the injunction and said all "duties and emoluments of the office of Governor automatically devolve [defined by the Court as rolling down, tumbling down, or descending] upon the Lieutenant Governor" at the moment a governor is impeached, even though the governor may later be found not guilty of the accusations. In that case, the governor would assume his duties, as if he had simply been out of state for awhile.

In a later case, *Fitzpatrick v. McAlister,* the Supreme Court said Trapp, when he succeeded Walton and completed his term, could not have succeeded himself as governor, even though he had never been elected governor. When a lieutenant governor succeeds to the office of governor, the high court wrote, "He is the 'Governor' for the simple reason that he governs. Therefore he is the official Governor... Section 4 (of the Constitution) speaks for itself: 'The Governor... shall not be eligible immediately to succeed himself.' " Oklahoma voters have since amended the constitution and now a governor is allowed to serve two consecutive terms, even though the length of a "term" has not been legally defined. George later became the first governor to succeed himself.

However, with so little constitutional guidance, Oklahoma's lieutenant governors have been left to their imagination to define their role in state government. Some have been figureheads who spent their days filling out certificates for supporters. Others have quietly stood in the shadow of the governor, truly waiting in the wings should something happen to the chief executive. George Nigh would neither stand in the wings waiting nor be satisfied spending his day filling out certificates. He wanted to make a difference in his beloved state. Frankly, he had to create a job out of the position of lieutenant governor.

The status quo of the lieutenant governor's office in Oklahoma in January, 1959, was brilliantly described by Martin Hauan, "It was an office of small prestige and no duties. It was rare to find the office open. A typed card pasted on the door told the phone number of the man just a heartbeat away from becoming the state's chief executive, in case you wanted to get 'hold of him,' which nobody did."[1]

The status quo was about to change!

George is congratulated on his election as lieutenant governor by his mother, Irene Nigh. Mrs. Nigh was extremely fond of her son and even though skeptical of the propriety of a career in politics, she supported her son's decisions to run for public office. Courtesy *The Daily Oklahoman.*

A gracious Cowboy Pink Williams, left, hands the gavel, symbol of the lieutenant governor's constitutional post of president of the state senate, to George in January, 1959. Courtesy *The Daily Oklahoman.*

George, right, as the nation's youngest lieutenant governor, and J. Howard Edmondson, the nation's youngest governor, were featured in this full-page photograph in *Life* Magazine in November, 1958, in an article featuring the newcomers to American politics, including New York Mayor John Lindsay, Arizona United States Senator Barry Goldwater, Minnesota United States Senator Eugene McCarthy, and New York Governor Nelson Rockefeller. Courtesy *Life* Magazine.

George genuinely wanted to serve the people of Oklahoma. His humorous and easy manner made him a much sought-after speaker at civic clubs, mens and womens groups, and commencement exercises. Commencement addresses were important to get to know as many Oklahomans as possible, George remembered, "You go into a town and talk to a Lions, Kiwanis, or Rotary Club, you get to meet just that one group. But at a commencement, you have a cross section of the community, rich, poor, all races, influential, common folk. You really get to know Oklahoma by making commencements."[2] An added benefit was that the people who made up commencement audiences got to know George.

Beginning in 1950, George made a practice in his entire political career to set aside the month of May to accept all commencement invitations that would fit his calendar. In 1999 he delivered the commencement address for the graduation class of the University of Oklahoma School of Law, his 50th consecutive year of giving at least one commencement speech. Several years he gave as many as 20. In the year 2000, George returned to his roots and spoke to students from McAlester High School where he had graduated and later taught.

One thing George had going for him as lieutenant governor was a close friendship with the new governor, Edmondson, who publicly stated he wanted to give George more responsibility than any previous lieutenant governor.

George took seriously his job as presiding officer of the state senate. He shocked many members of the upper chamber when he appeared at the beginning of the 1959 session to preside. At first, some senators believed George was out of line for wanting to be involved in the senate's daily activities. However, George soon soothed ruffled feathers by assuring senators that he was only interested in fulfilling his constitutional responsibility.

For the first five months in office George worked diligently to gain the confidence of the senate. He became an expert parliamentarian and learned senate rules backward and forward. His goal was "to give each senator the feeling that he had a fair shake in any debate or on any issue with him, as an unbiased and fair presiding officer." George was such a gentleman in the way he approached his new position in the senate that his relationship with senators grew positive with each passing week. Ultimately, George presided over the senate far more than any lieutenant governor in Oklahoma, before or after.

Unfortunately, presiding over the senate occupied George's time only five months of every two years, leaving George 19 months to do something else. He believed that the lieutenant governor's office should be the state's public relations office. He developed a "Pride in Oklahoma" campaign, pushing tourism and convention business. He put the promotion of Oklahoma first on his list of things to do in his new job.[3]

George, a single lieutenant governor, and eight others rented an old sorority house, called "The Shed," near the University of Oklahoma campus in Norman. Left to right, Jim Hazenbeck, John Steincamp, Bob Scarbrough, and George. The Shed produced the nucleus of George's future campaign teams. Members of the "Shed mafia" were some of George's closest advisors. Several residents of the house later served as members of George's gubernatorial administration. David Hudson of Sulphur was George's legal advisor, Bob Scarbrough of Altus was general counsel for the Oklahoma Turnpike Authority, and Paul Reed of Sulphur was Commissioner of Public Safety. During football season, George and his roommates paid for their entire yearly rent by parking fans' cars in the yard of The Shed.

Each year George accepted hundreds of invitations to speak, cut ribbons, and serve as master of ceremonies of events from Broken Bow to Guymon and Commerce to Hollis. He made friends with most of the rural newspaper publishers and radio and television station managers in the state. His frequent travels won him much front-page space in small town weekly and daily newspapers. George, always the promoter, traveled over 74,000 miles in his first year in office, telling Oklahomans that before they could sell their state to new residents and people in other states, they first had to sell it to themselves.[4]

George found his new office in the north wing of the fifth floor of the State Capitol almost bare of furniture or official trappings. Not having much to do, George developed the lieutenant governor's handshake. He explained, "It is where you extend the index finger to get the governor's pulse each morning while you are shaking his hand. If the pulse is strong, you don't have a thing to do that day and can go back to bed."[5]

Prohibition was the main issue before the legislature as it convened in January, 1959. Oklahoma had been dry since statehood. Newspapers reported that drinks flowed freely on the eve of statehood, November 16, 1907, with "men drinking from streams of liquor in the streets," as saloon keepers emptied whiskey, gin, and beer into the gutters. Their actions were necessarily hasty to comply with the midnight deadline for the new state's law against the sale of intoxicating liquors.[6]

Oklahoma humorist Will Rogers had long poked fun at Oklahoma prohibition, writing, "Oklahomans will always vote for prohibition as long as they can stagger to the polls," and "Look at these towns and people after prohibition has hit them. Everybody looks like they had just had a puncture and no extra tire."[7]

Prohibition made hypocrites of many people. Moonshine whiskey was a big business in many areas of the state. Law enforcement officers turned their heads and ignored the stills that turned corn mash into "shine" along sparkling creeks and streams. Bootleggers prospered in cities, towns, and rural areas, even advertising their prices and home delivery, while clergymen and other drys preached about the dangers of "Demon Rum" to their congregations.

Finally, by 1959, much of Oklahoma's population lived in metropolitan areas and began to recognize the financial advantages of liquor sales, especially the notion that legal liquor would generate huge sums of new state tax revenue.

When Edmondson took office, he appointed Joseph "Joe" Cannon, a 34-year-old, crew-cut district attorney from Muskogee County, as Commissioner of Public Safety, and ordered him to enforce the winked-at statutes that prohibited the sale of liquor. Edmondson had promised voters in 1958 to bring the question to a vote of the people within 90 days of taking office. Edmondson's point was clear, "You have a clear choice. One or the other. You can't have it both ways. Either vote for legal liquor or there will be no liquor at all."[8]

Cannon rode herd on state troopers, deputy sheriffs, and city police officers in a three-month campaign to enforce the prohibition laws. Elite country clubs were closed, fraternal organizations were raided, roadblocks and midnight raids shut down bootlegger operations. "Crew Cut Joe" told people that if he caught them with one jar of moonshine in their car he would arrest them and sell the car. Cannon, later a district judge in Oklahoma County, recalled, "It scared hell out of them."[9]

As Cannon destroyed stills and closed speakeasies, and shut down drinking at country clubs and fraternal halls that had long violated the law, dry supporters organized rallies at many of the state's churches. Public debate erupted with a fury saved only for a handful of hot topics. Dry leader Sam Scantlan told members of the First Baptist Church in Lawton, "If we don't sober up, we're going to lose our nation."[10]

Champagne was proposed to be served at the Oklahoma Club at a private reception honoring George. Knowing that George would not want to set a bad example, friends substituted beer in the champagne glasses. The 3.2 beer was not prohibited by the liquor laws. A *Life* Magazine photographer caught for posterity George at the end of the table being toasted with beer. The story about Oklahoma prohibition problems in *Life* gave birth to the practice, called a "Cannon ball bomb," of serving beer in champagne glasses.

The "wets," supporters of liquor sales, and the "drys," groups that opposed legalized liquor sales, debated the issue for 52 years before the legislature, empowered by Governor Edmondson's call for a public vote, authorized a special election in April, 1959. Voters had six times previously defeated attempts to legalize liquor sales.

George, as lieutenant governor, presided over the State Senate during seven hours of emotional debate over prohibition. He never left his chair at the head of the Senate chamber. After a long closing speech about the evils of intoxicating liquor, Senator Ray Fine of Gore, an opponent of repeal, turned to George and said, "God, I need a drink."

United Oklahomans for Repeal successfully convinced voters that repealing prohibition would end the notorious double standard and hypocrisy and create a single-minded respect for the law. On April 7, 1959, voters approved the repeal of prohibition by an 80,000-vote margin.

George was speaking to a press convention at Lake Murray Resort in southern Oklahoma in September, 1959, when he literally fell into a big story. While taking a water skiing lesson, George was thrown into the water, his ski striking a hapless fish. When the stunned fish floated to the top, George grabbed it by the gills and waited for the ski boat to come around and pick him up. He wrapped the fish in a towel and took it back to the lodge to show a disbelieving group of reporters. He finally convinced news reporters of the authenticity of the story and posed with the fish for this photograph. In proof of its newsworthiness, the event was chosen as the number two "sports oddity" photograph of 1959 by the Jackson Brewing Company, the makers of Jax Beer. Number one was a baseball pitcher who threw a no-hitter and lost the game. Courtesy *The Daily Oklahoman.*

An honorary colonel's certificate is presented to George by Bob Stewart, left, Bartlesville, Boys State Governor, in June, 1960. Others are, left to right, Delbert Frieze, Skiatook, state treasurer, and Jim Crownover, Norman, secretary of state. George made friends, and future supporters, of participants of Boys State. Courtesy *The Daily Oklahoman.*

In his journeys to every corner of the state, George recognized Oklahoma's tremendous potential for attracting tourists. State government had traditionally spent very little money on advertising the beauty of state parks and lodges to residents of other states. Governor Edmondson approved of George's plan to make the lieutenant governor the chief cheerleader of Oklahoma's tourism effort. George, with the backing of the Planning and Resources Board, which oversaw the operation of the state's parks, lodges, and recreation areas, launched a vigorous public relations campaign to tell the world about Oklahoma, its people, and its natural beauty.

While Governor Edmondson was attending the Washington, D.C., inauguration of President John F. Kennedy, George signed into law the first bill passed by the 28th legislature in January, 1961. The law corrected an error in Oklahoma's unemployment compensation statutes. It was rushed through the legislature to prevent a $13 million increase in federal payroll taxes. With George are, left to right, Morris Leonhard and Laymond Crump of the Oklahoma Employment Security Commission, and Representative Jim Bullard, author of the bill. Courtesy *The Daily Oklahoman.*

George presides over the state senate in 1963. On the wall behind him is a photograph of President John F. Kennedy. Courtesy *The Daily Oklahoman.*

George met with officials of the Oklahoma League of Women Voters at the State Capitol in February, 1961. Left to right, Mrs. Ernest Palo, Oklahoma City; June Morgan, Norman; and Mrs. P. P. Manion, Jr., Tulsa. Courtesy *The Daily Oklahoman.*

The tourism promotion effort gained George many new personal and political friends. Local chamber of commerce and business leaders flocked to George with ideas of how to promote their areas. They finally had a leader with statewide clout who could mobilize them. George's fifth floor office in the State Capitol was always accessible to citizens. Anyone who wanted to talk to the lieutenant governor simply had to show up at the door. It was yet another first.

In 1959, the legislature had not yet seen fit to provide security for the lieutenant governor. George drove himself, in his state car, to appearances around Oklahoma.

Falling Short of the Mark

Frankly, in retrospect, I probably would not have voted for myself.

George Nigh

There was one time in George's life that he did not listen to his great instinct. George did not really want to run for governor of Oklahoma in 1962, but he did. His first term as lieutenant governor was judged extremely successful by most observers and George could have waltzed to re-election. However, two forces pushed him toward the governor's race. He still lived with the dream of becoming governor of his home state and longtime friends convinced him this might be the golden opportunity.

The gubernatorial campaign of 1962 began as yet another uphill climb for George. Other candidates were ahead of George even from the starting gun. An early poll conducted by the *Young Democrat,* the monthly publication of the Young Democrat Club, showed former Governor Raymond Gary of Madill on top; followed by Midwest City builder W.P. "Bill" Atkinson, who had lost to Edmondson in the bitter 1958 runoff; Court of Criminal Appeals Judge Kirksey Nix of McAlester; Oklahoma City attorney and former state senator George Miskovsky; House Speaker J.D. McCarty of Oklahoma City; Mayor Earl Sneed of Norman; and George.[1]

As George met with supporters in the fall of 1961 to strategize and raise money for the campaign, other possible contenders surfaced, including State Senator Fred Harris of Lawton; Sulphur banker Glen R. Key; Broken Bow telephone company owner Jewel B. Callaham;

Senate President Pro Tempore Everett Collins; University of Oklahoma football coach Bud Wilkinson; Oklahoma Education Association executive secretary Ferman Phillips; and Preston Moore, a prominent Oklahoma City attorney who had served as both the state and national commander of the American Legion. [2]

George thought long and hard about whether or not to run for re-election or run for governor. Odds were good that he could be re-elected perhaps without serious opposition, but history was not on his side in moving up from lieutenant governor to governor. Only two lieutenant governors, Martin E. Trapp and William J. Holloway, had ascended from the number two spot to the governor's office but only because both of the governors under which they served were impeached and removed from office.

Another negative for George's chances of a successful run for governor was the unpopular end of the Edmondson administration. Edmondson had taken office as one of the state's most popular governors ever, but ended his term as one of its most unpopular.

George and Edmondson had run as a team, part of the "youth movement." There was a possibility, maybe even a probability, that Oklahoma voters' zeal for youthful and fresh faces in the State Capitol was soured.

Edmondson's term was controversial and politically unsettling. A gubernatorial historian, observed, "His determined efforts to make needed changes in Oklahoma's governmental patterns and practices led him to challenge its political establishment and aim at reform in the state legislature, the Democratic Party, and business operations of state government. As a result, the days of rural domination of Oklahoma politics, the Democratic Party, and Oklahoma government were numbered."[3]

Edmondson lost control of both the legislature and the Democratic Party. His popularity plummeted as battles raged over prohibition, county government, central purchasing, and placing employees under a merit system. One of Edmondson's secretaries told George that the governor had received thousands of Christmas cards and gifts his first three years in office but, during the last Christmas season, only a few dozen cards arrived at the mansion.[4]

The turning point in George's decision to run for governor came during a meeting of his advisors and friends in Norman on December 2, 1961, the night before the annual Oklahoma-Oklahoma State football game. Late into the evening, several friends met at The Shed and laid out the road map to victory, discussed issues, and convinced George, admittedly against his better judgment, that the time was right for him to make the leap to the governor's mansion. George later reflected on the campaign, "I don't think I would have voted for myself." [5]

George's decision to run for governor in 1962 opened the gates for politicians who believed they could replace him as lieutenant governor. Fifteen Democrats and two Republicans ran, including such big names as Corporation Commissioner Wilburn Cartwright of McAlester; State Representative and former Oklahoma Semi-Centennial Chairman Lou S. Allard of Drumright; future state legislator L.H. Bengtson, Jr., of Oklahoma City; and Leo Winters of Hooker, who was serving as the secretary of the Oklahoma Senate and the State Election Board.

Some candidates entered the race for lieutenant governor hoping to attract voters with their famous names. Donald Nye of Midwest City hoped voters would think he was the incumbent. It was an interesting runoff in the lieutenant governor's office between Cartwright, a perennial office holder and household name, and Winters who had support in every precinct because of longstanding contact with county election officials. Winters won the runoff by more than 100,000 votes.

George's campaign strategy was basic and sound. Attorney and political historian Stephen Jones wrote, "George and the others all felt that Raymond Gary would lead in the primary, but that he was ripe for defeat in the runoff with the prospect of facing only one opponent, who would have the backing of urban voters. Therefore, the strategy of George was the same as Atkinson, Harris, and Moore—get into the runoff by attacking Gary and by proving you are the man to tackle him."[6] Therefore, it would be the same scenario of George's previous successful race for lieutenant governor, try only to be number two in the primary and knock off number one in the runoff.

One poll showed George faring better than any of the other contenders in a one-on-one race with Gary. Nigh forces believed that because George hailed from Little Dixie, he would probably garner a large vote in Pittsburg and surrounding counties, cutting into Gary's strength in the Third Congressional District. Another reason George was finally convinced he could win the race was the fact that he and Gary were the only mentioned candidates who had actually won a statewide election.

During the primary filing period, 12 Democrats threw their hats into the ring, including seven candidates who were considered serious contenders, Miskovsky, Harris, Gary, Moore, State Treasurer William A. Burkhart of Pawhuska, Atkinson, and George. The other candidates were Paul J. Summers, a Carnegie merchant; Max B. Martin, a Prague rancher; Tulsa attorney Thomas Dee Frasier; Oklahoma City public relations consultant Harry R. Moss; and Ben Elmo Newcomer, a Norman grocer.

George opened a statewide and Oklahoma County campaign headquarters in a vacant furniture store building in downtown Oklahoma City. Crystal Mounts, the telephone receptionist for the House of Representatives during legislative sessions, was the campaign office receptionist. She was aided by two other paid secretaries and statewide campaign manager Joe Johnson, who volunteered his time to coordinate dozens of unpaid workers, making and distributing yard signs, and manning telephone banks for "Nigh Watch" telethons, where supporters were each asked to call four other voters the night before the election. John Ingram, longtime Jaycee friend, was the Oklahoma County campaign manager.

"I make no promises to anyone," George firmly pledged as he opened his campaign for governor. He stressed the importance of new industry and the value of tourism as a major economic factor in the state.

With limited campaign funds, George bought large newspaper advertisements during the final three weeks of the campaign. With a slogan of "For a u-NIGH-ted Oklahoma," the advertisement quoted a United Press International poll that showed George gaining momentum from one side of the state to the other, subtly hinting that

At right is Floyd "Red" Rice who, as a band leader, became a fixture at George's rallies and inaugurations during the next 20 years. The campaign kickoff was held at Oklahoma City's Wedgewood Amusement Park in 1962.

Oklahomans would lose their vote if they voted for one of the other candidates who did not have a chance of overtaking Gary.[7]

A full-page advertisement in *The Daily Oklahoman* ballyhooed George's pledge for no sales tax increase, no "back-breaking" bond issues, $10.5 million in additional school funding, a $600 million road program, and $1 million more for mental health facilities. The advertisement contained a detailed $280 million budget George promised to propose to the legislature if the voters elected him governor.

George depended upon young people to staff his campaign effort. Pittsburg County campaign treasurer Irvin E. "Buck" Conner, remembered, "Young people liked George and were attracted to his campaign. Even high school kids believed in George and tried to convince their parents to vote for him."[8]

Two new state office buildings, the Will Rogers and Sequoyah buildings, were dedicated in 1962. Attending dedication ceremonies were, left to right, John Kilpatrick, Oklahoma City civic leader; George; Governor J. Howard Edmondson; and Edmondson administrative assistant H. I. Hinds of Tahlequah. The shiny Cadillac in the background was Governor Edmondson's limousine, courtesy of a private fundraising effort headed by Kilpatrick. Courtesy *The Daily Oklahoman.*

By the end of April, 1962, most experts agreed there were only five Democratic candidates from the field of twelve who had any reasonable chance of winning the primary. They were former Governor Gary, described by most political writers of the day as the man to beat; George; Fred Harris; Preston Moore; and Bill Atkinson. Meanwhile, Republican wheat farmer, former legislator, and GOP state chairman Henry Bellmon of Red Rock was the frontrunner for the Republican nomination over political unknown Leslie C. Skoien.

Gary believed he would carry rural Oklahoma by a large margin and gain a respectable vote in Oklahoma and Tulsa counties, enough to emerge from the primary with a majority, thus avoiding a runoff.

Harris had been planning the campaign for two years but had not served long enough in the Oklahoma Senate to be counted among the Old Guard. He based his presentation to the state's voters on his fresh face and a new image for the State Capitol.[9]

Moore, a close personal friend of Oklahoma's senior United States Senator Robert S. Kerr, raised a reasonable campaign budget, enabling him to become a formidable candidate. Members of the American Legion formed the nucleus of Moore's supporters in most counties.

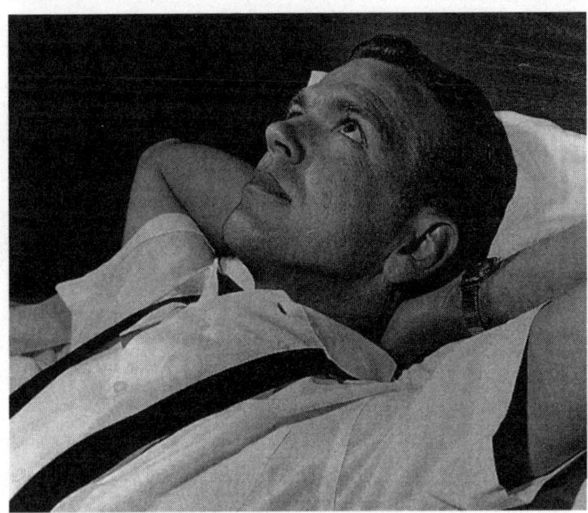

The newspaper cutline said George was "contemplating his future" in this May, 1962, photograph. Courtesy *The Daily Oklahoman.*

Atkinson, still smarting from his second place finish in 1958, was determined to change his public image "from the kindly religious gentleman who permitted thousands of children to ride free on his Shetland ponies to the elder statesman of the Democratic Party and the man who had made his personal fortune in the best traditions of Oklahoma and was now prepared to devote his senior years to furthering the best interests of Oklahoma."[10]

Two weeks before the primary, a major poll showed George running second to Gary in both urban and rural areas of the state. The numbers came as a shock to Atkinson, Miskovsky, and Moore who had constantly attacked Gary during the primary campaign. With the new poll results in hand, Atkinson and Moore turned their attention to George, showing they had to first beat George before having a chance to face Gary in a runoff. Atkinson and Moore questioned George's youth, his tie to the Edmondson administration, and asked voters, "Do you want another four years of what has happened to us in the Edmondson years?"

On the Sunday before the primary, veteran political writer Otis Sullivant wrote in *The Daily Oklahoman*, "Nigh continues to show strength statewide. Three or four weeks ago, it appeared that Nigh, given a boost by aid from the Edmondson administration, might go on and lead in the first primary. However, the ground swell of support didn't continue to give him the lead, if the polls and soundings are correct."[11]

The boost from the Edmondson administration referred to by Sullivant was assistance given the Nigh campaign by Leland Gourley, Edmondson's former chief of staff and director of the State Insurance Fund, who used his knowledge of newspaper advertising, as editor of the *Henryetta Daily Freelance,* to convince George to spend the bulk of his campaign kitty on print advertising.

The *Tulsa World,* after endorsing Atkinson, possibly to temper the vicious attacks on Atkinson's moral fiber and honesty by the state's largest newspaper, *The Daily Oklahoman*, commented that George was making inroads in Tulsa County, "Nigh forces are counting heavily upon Tulsa County and an organization is at work for him. Quinton Mantooth, accountant and former McAlester classmate of George, heads the campaign, with assistance from Elmer Wilson of Okmulgee, sent by Nigh state headquarters to coordinate the county effort."[12]

On election day, as expected, Gary made a strong showing with voters, finishing far ahead of the pack in first place but far below the vote needed to win without a dreaded runoff. In a close race for second place, Atkinson nosed out Moore by less than 6,000 votes. George was only 800 votes behind Moore. Fred Harris was fifth, 8,000 votes behind George. George carried only one county in the state, a slim victory over Gary in his home county of Pittsburg. In the final analysis, attacks on George during the closing weeks of the campaign successfully kept him out of a runoff, which he missed by less than 7,000 votes.

George's loss and Governor Edmondson's later resignation left unanswered the constitutional question of what would have happened had George won the election and tried to succeed himself after serving the final nine days of Edmondson's term.

In the runoff election that shocked veteran political analysts, Gary, who had a large lead in the primary, lost to Atkinson by a scant 449 votes, out of nearly a half million votes cast. A one vote change in less than a fourth of the state's precincts would have changed the outcome of the election.

Gary was bitter because George traveled the state in support of Atkinson in the runoff. Gary's biographers wrote, "He felt particularly betrayed in this instance, for it was Gary who once had used his influence to get the young lieutenant governor out of jail in Mexico. The incident had been innocent enough, but it figured large in Gary's thinking because of his belief in personal loyalty. . . He thought that if he could take time in the middle of the night to help a friend avoid serious public embarrassment, that friend should repay the favor. Nigh apparently had forgotten his debt to him, Gary felt."[13]

The Mexican incident Gary remembered occurred in 1960 as George and five of his students from McAlester High School were in old Mexico on a camping trip. George left Mexico earlier than planned because of a call from Governor Gary who needed George back in Oklahoma City to help the governor elect his choice as Speaker of the House. While en route, George hit a chughole filled with water near Victoria, Mexico. When the car rolled over, one of the students, Jimmie Martin, suffered a concussion and was hospitalized.

George was incarcerated in a Mexican prison, a customary practice of Mexican authorities in automobile accident situations that involved personal injury. However, after two days, George, accompanied by a guard, was allowed to visit Martin in the Victoria hospital. Doctors were concerned that Martin would contract dysentery if he ate Mexican food served by the hospital. George informed the doctor that the trunk of his wrecked car contained large amounts of canned and packaged food that George and the students had brought with them from Crockett-Nigh grocery in McAlester.

George, left, and Preston Moore, right, threw their support behind W. P. "Bill" Atkinson, center, in the bitter Democratic gubernatorial runoff in 1962. Gary dubbed Atkinson, Moore, and George as "the three-headed monster," accusing George of lying about him in the runoff.

Police officers assisted George in transferring the food from the pried-open trunk of the crumpled car in a nearby junkyard. George was moved from the prison and placed under hospital arrest with a guard posted outside his room 24 hours a day. After all other patients in the hospital had been served their normal Mexican food, George prepared Martin's meals in the hospital kitchen. Dr. C.E. Lively, Martin's family doctor in McAlester, conferred by telephone with the doctors at the Victoria hospital, and was assured that Martin was receiving adequate medical care.

George was handicapped by his inability to speak Spanish. Another patient in the hospital, the daughter of an American railroad worker and a Mexican native, spoke both English and Spanish fluently, and became George's interpreter. The woman, hospitalized for injuries sustained during a suicide attempt, was good news for George. Her interpretation allowed George to communicate with doctors and police authorities.

George's interpreter played a vital role in winning his release from house arrest. The woman's best friend was the sister of the governor of the Mexican state in which Victoria was located. After a call from Governor Gary's office, confirming that George was who he said he was, the Mexican governor ordered charges against George dropped and provided his personal automobile to take George and Martin to an airport for the flight back to the United States.

Feeling that maybe her life was worth something after all, George's interpreter turned to him before he left Mexico and said, "Thank you for saving my life."[14]

Gary's hard feelings toward George did not soften for almost two decades. In 1988, George was invited to speak at a dinner honoring Gary at Southeastern Oklahoma State University in Durant. George informed planners of the event that he would not come unless Governor Gary approved. However, organizers of the dinner were aware of the Gary–Nigh rift and had already received Gary's approval.

Gary was ill and unable to attend the banquet honoring him. But he heard from his family how George lauded his accomplishments, especially the improvement of Oklahoma's rural highway system and Gary's critical leadership during integration of the state's public schools after the *Brown v. Board of Education of Topeka, Kansas* United States Supreme Court case rocked the nation's segregated schools in 1954. Following the banquet, George received a letter from Gary thanking him for his remarks. Gary told George, "In reflection, you have been a good governor of Oklahoma."[15]

As a result of the quarrel among Democrats in 1962, a Republican bandwagon rolled across the state. Then the unthinkable happened. Republican Henry Bellmon was elected Oklahoma's first GOP governor in history in the November general election.

With his term about to end, George began planning for a life out of politics. It was something new for him. Since before he had graduated from college a dozen years before, his total attention had been focused on public service.

A Dream Fulfilled

Get your cotton pickin' feet off my desk, Howard, I've got work to do.
George Nigh

Oklahoma Democrats were still reeling from the Bellmon defeat of Atkinson in the November, 1962 general election when the state's most powerful Democrat, Robert S. Kerr, died on January 1, 1963, just two weeks before the end of the Edmondson administration. Kerr's death left a large vacuum among Democratic leaders and had a stunning impact upon the state's colorful political history.

The state constitution at that time provided the governor would appoint a United States Senator should a vacancy occur. Governor Edmondson was attending a University of Oklahoma football game at the Orange Bowl in Miami, Florida, leaving George as "acting governor." George had ruffled feathers because Edmondson had not reserved him a spot on the national guard airplane going to the Orange Bowl. Before the trip, George told the governor, "I've been very loyal to you, right by your side the whole four years in office. That airplane holds several dozen people. I can't believe there's not room for me."[1]

Nevertheless George stayed home from the Orange Bowl game and traveled to McAlester to spend New Years Eve with his parents. While upstairs in his old bedroom, George received a call from Ed Montgomery, a newspaper reporter for *The Daily Oklahoman*, with news of Kerr's death. Speaking officially for the state, George made appropriate comments about the terrific loss that Oklahoma would suffer because of Kerr's demise.

Moments after the phone call from Montgomery ended, the Nigh phone rang again. It was a state senator who was startled to hear George's voice. The senator said, "Oh, I thought you were at the Orange Bowl." When George replied, "No," the senator replied, "OK, I was just checking how you were doing," and hung up.

If George had been out of Oklahoma, the duty of appointing a new United States Senator would have fallen to Senator Everett Collins of Sapulpa, the president pro tempore of the state senate, and then to House Speaker J.D. McCarty.[2]

A few minutes later, the phone rang again. This time it was John Criswell, Edmondson's press secretary, who said, "Hey George, old buddy, how are you doing?" George said, "John, cut the shit, I heard the news." Criswell paused a moment and then told George that Governor Edmondson wanted to talk to him and would call shortly. Edmondson at that moment was visiting with President John F. Kennedy who was also attending the Oklahoma-Alabama game at the Orange Bowl.

Remembering that George was upset over his exclusion from the national guard airplane trip to Miami, Criswell was concerned that George would immediately appoint a new United States Senator. Criswell informed George the entire Oklahoma delegation at the Orange Bowl was being rounded up for a quick trip home. Criswell said, "We need to get home because you're going to be under a lot of pressure to appoint somebody before we get back."

George told Criswell, "Let me tell you a story. You tell it to Howard. I've been your lieutenant governor for four years. I've not yet done anything to embarrass you. And I won't now. That's not my role. Appointing a new senator should be done by the real governor. I won't violate that principle. On the other hand, if I were going to, you couldn't get back here quick enough, so what difference does it make?" [3]

"I won't be under any pressure I can't handle," George assured Criswell. George avoided any further phone calls until he could return to Oklahoma City.

The flight for Edmondson and his guests from Florida to Oklahoma was anything but relaxed. Veteran State Capitol newspaper reporter Ray Parr later said, "One of the engines conked out and the pilots wanted to turn back and land at Montgomery, Alabama. But Edmondson wasn't about to stop, until he crossed the state line, and we flew to Oklahoma on three engines."[4]

The day following Kerr's death, bold headlines in state newspapers blared the sad news and speculated that either Governor Edmondson or his brother, Congressman Ed Edmondson of Muskogee, were front-runners to succeed Kerr. Behind the scenes Robert S. Kerr, Jr., the son of the late senator, was mentioned as a possible successor. Under Oklahoma law, whomever the governor appointed would serve two years until the next general election.

Otis Sullivant, reporter for *The Daily Oklahoman*, and whose inside information was usually accurate, wrote, "Edmondson can arrange for George Nigh to appoint him senator and resign before his term expires on January 14. Or the governor can appoint his brother, or someone else, to serve the two years and contest for the senate seat in the 1964 primary."[5]

George was kept in the dark about high-level talks at the governor's mansion concerning the course of action Edmondson would take. Edmondson did not call George for three days, a development that did not bother George as he tried to downplay the appointment of a new senator until the state had paid appropriate homage to Kerr, his longtime friend and hero.

The governor at first did not want the appointment, even though newspapers speculated he would be the logical choice because he was a close friend of the Kennedy clan, including the President, and would have instant influence for Oklahoma, certainly a plus to fill the large power loss created by the death of Kerr. Newspaper stories indicated Governor Edmondson preferred that his brother take the job. However, Ed Edmondson wanted the appointment only if the Kerr family, and top Kerr allies such as House Speaker J.D. McCarty, Burl Hays, Ardell Hines, and Rex Hawks, would assure him of the Kerr machine support when re-election time rolled around in just two short years.

At a meeting with Robert S. Kerr, Jr., and his brother, Breene, Ed Edmondson asked if the family wished the appointment for Grayce Kerr, Senator Kerr's widow. "Under no circumstances," was the reply.[6]

Another name mentioned for the job was Oklahoma Secretary of State William "Bill" Christian. Tom Finney, a powerful state senator from Idabel and Jack Cornelius, Secretary of the State Board of Agriculture, believed the governor should appoint some faithful friend, such as Christian, or Ed Edmondson, to be a caretaker of the seat in the Senate. Finney and Cornelius surmised that Christian could hold the office while Edmondson spent two years mending political fences, absolutely necessary if he had any chance to be elected two years hence.[7]

Howard Edmondson later told Martin Hauan that Vice President Lyndon Johnson had talked to President Kennedy to try to get him to use his influence with Edmondson to appoint Robert S. Kerr, Jr. Kerr seemed interested, telling Edmondson, "All I know is I want to work on my father's program, help carry it out. I just don't know. We'll talk about it later."[8]

Later never came because Edmondson offered the Senate post to his brother the following day. Ed declined, because of the lack of promises that the Kerr family would support him later. With his brother out of the picture, it became increasingly evident that the governor was seriously considering resigning and asking George to appoint him as Oklahoma's next United States Senator.

On Friday, the morning of Kerr's funeral, Governor Edmondson sent for George to come to his second floor Capitol office. After a short, "How are you doing, George,?" George cut the governor off, and said, "Howard, before you tell me anything, before you tell me I'm a great guy or we're great friends, I want to tell you something. If you want to resign and want to be United States Senator, I'll appoint you, based upon three conditions." Edmondson replied, "It depends on what the three conditions are." Imagine his surprise when he heard what they were.[9]

The first two conditions were that Edmondson must promise to never appoint George to any federal job or position nor show special favoritism to members of George's family when it came to federal

As lieutenant governor, George leads the procession bearing the body of Robert S. Kerr from the State Capitol, where Kerr had laid in state in the rotunda. Kerr had been George's hero since his college days. He looked up to Kerr who he thought had been great for Oklahoma and its future.

help. George was concerned that Oklahomans would consider any such action a payoff for the appointment. The third condition was that Edmondson would not oppose George in any future race for governor.[10]

With the assurance that George would appoint him as United States Senator if he wanted the job, Edmondson continued high-level discussions with friends, aides, and supporters. To allow Oklahoma to pay tribute to Kerr, it was decided to delay until the following Monday the decision of whom would be appointed.

President Kennedy attended Kerr's funeral service in Oklahoma City later that day. George accompanied Governor Edmondson to Tinker Air Force Base to meet the President who had arrived on *Air*

Force One. Edmondson asked George to remain in the hangar while he boarded the airplane to speak with the President. When Edmondson returned, he told George the President did not want to see him, "He has come to pay honor to Bob Kerr, not to give the impression of influencing the appointment of a United States Senator." [11]

On the steps of the First Baptist Church in downtown Oklahoma City following the memorial service, Kennedy was asked by Governor Edmondson if he should appoint Robert S. Kerr, Jr. to the Senate seat. Kennedy shrewdly asked the governor, "Would he appoint your son if your positions were reversed?" Edmondson snorted, "Hell, no!" The President chuckled and said, "Then that answers your question, doesn't it?"[12]

After a meeting with three of Kerr's most trusted friends, McCarty, Hawks, and H.I. Hinds, it was decision time. Martin Hauan chronicled the moment, "Edmondson knew there were drawbacks to taking the job himself. A new campaign would start immediately. He could sense that Kerr-McGee's wealth and power, plus Senator Kerr's close political friends, might be fighting him. And he had enough political scars to cause serious adhesion pains in a new race without this added force against him. But a decision had to be made. Right then. Howard Edmondson made it. Bob Kerr, Jr. and...Ed were reluctant dragons. So Gov. Edmondson, with just a few days in office, grabbed it for himself."[13]

Edmondson called Breene Kerr and informed him of the decision, promising to help the Kerr family in any way he could and openly asking for continued Kerr family support, support that never came.

By phone, Edmondson confirmed his decision with George to resign and have George, as governor, appoint Edmondson to the Senate post. The official transfer of power was scheduled for Monday.

However, a second phone call from Edmondson to George on Saturday morning changed the schedule. Edmondson had learned that he really needed to be appointed before Monday to gain all important seniority on newly elected senators who would be soon sworn in in Washington, D.C.

George was reluctant, wanting a full-blown, open news conference and ceremony on Monday so that the historic event could be accomplished in full view of the public. Instead he was persuaded to come to the governor's mansion on Sunday afternoon for the transfer. George understood the importance of Edmondson gaining seniority on the incoming freshman senators because of the loss of power Oklahoma would suffer at the national level with Kerr's death. George also recognized that Edmondson's close personal friendship with the President would give Oklahoma a direct line to the White House, possibly filling some of the vacuum.

On Sunday morning George talked by phone with President Kennedy for a few minutes, assuring the President that he wanted Kerr's programs carried on with all possible speed. Kennedy pointed out to George that he was indebted to Edmondson because the governor had stood alone for him against an angry Oklahoma delegation at the 1960 Democratic National Convention that was pushing the nomination of Lyndon B. Johnson. Kennedy said he really should not be involved in the decision because it was George's decision. However, the President told George he would certainly appreciate the appointment of his good friend, Governor Edmondson. Nigh told the President that in the end, he, as governor, would appoint Edmondson because "it was best for Oklahoma."[14]

Secretary of State William "Bill" Christian, a native of Broken Bow; Commissioner of Public Safety Joe Cannon of Muskogee; gubernatorial press secretary John Criswell of Stigler; and Oklahoma Highway Patrol Captain Bill Fisher of Tulsa were present in the upstairs office of the governor's mansion as Edmondson handed George his resignation. Always a master at infusing humor into a critical moment, George looked at Edmondson and said, "Howard, get your cotton pickin' feet off my desk, I've got work to do."[15] It was 4:44 P.M.

Immediately after resigning, Edmondson handed George another piece of paper, a typed statement, that, among other things, said, "I hereby appoint J. Howard Edmondson a senator from said state to represent said state in the senate of the United States." George looked at Edmondson and said, "What's this?" Edmondson's countenance fell a few stories in the following eternity of seconds until George smiled and signed the appointment.

At that moment George Nigh accomplished the dream he had carried since age 12, although not under circumstances even a gifted screenwriter could envision. At the age of 36, George Nigh was Governor of Oklahoma.

Christian, accompanied by Captain Fisher, took the originals of the two documents to the Secretary of State's office in the State Capitol. Although normally closed on Sunday, Christian officially filed the documents. He made certified copies and delivered them back to Edmondson and George.

Possibly the most intriguing passage of power in Oklahoma history had taken but 20 minutes.

Nine Days of Nigh

If I had had the ten-day virus, I would have missed the whole damn thing.

George Nigh

"Relaxed and smiling, George Nigh arrived Sunday at the place he aimed for last May and missed—the governor's office." Reporter Katherine Hatch used those words to open her front-page story on Monday morning, January 7, under a headline, "BIG Job is Nigh's If Only for Week."

George had laid awake the night before, planning his next few days as chief executive. He certainly expected no major issues to arise and had such a short time to work on a state of the state message required by the state constitution to be delivered on Tuesday to the opening session of the legislature. What would he talk about? What would the people expect of a governor who was to serve only nine days? He decided to make the theme of the speech a tribute to Senator Kerr.

George talked on the telephone constantly with friends and family, inviting them to Oklahoma City to stay in the mansion or to become members of his staff. Martin Hauan called the time, "nine turbulent days filled with cots and happiness... stately rooms filled with cots and roll-aways. The mansion's long, winding 3-stories banister... a thrilling roller coaster for dozens of squealing kids."[1]

Feeling that he might never have the opportunity to live at the mansion again, George recalled a campaign promise to his younger relatives that they could have a slumber party at the mansion.

George Patterson Nigh was sworn in as Governor of Oklahoma by Supreme Court Justice Earl Welch on January 6, 1963. George realized the dream he had borne since the eighth grade. Courtesy *The Daily Oklahoman.*

Hundreds of George's family members, friends, and supporters crowded into the Blue Room of the State Capitol as George was formally sworn in as governor for nine days in 1963. The swearing-in capped the most exciting political maneuvering in state history. Courtesy *The Daily Oklahoman.*

Still a bachelor, George invited his nieces and nephews, uncles, aunts, cousins, and some of their friends, for a sleepover at the mansion. George closed his lieutenant governor's office and moved his secretary, Glenda Temple, of Chandler, to the governor's office. He appointed Paul Carris as chief of staff, Joe Johnson as legal counsel, Fred Turner as press secretary, and other friends and supporters as aides to the governor. Carris, Johnson, and Turner were known as the "McAlester Mafia."

The Biltmore Hotel provided cots and roll-away beds for friends and relatives to sleep on at the mansion. As was the custom, the outgoing governor had removed all his personal furnishings from the mansion. All that basically remained were the dining room and living room furniture so even George, the governor, had to sleep on a roll-away bed.

After the Edmondsons moved out George had his small staff move into the mansion. They ate three meals a day at the mansion. The first affair was to be a state dinner, complete with candles, china, and historic silverware on the big dining room table. However, the one remaining cook had gone home for the day. After everyone was seated, the candles lighted, and the lights turned low, the kitchen door opened and pizza from a nearby Northwest 23rd Street pizza parlor was delivered.

George talked to the Capitol press corps Sunday afternoon less than two hours after becoming governor. In a light-hearted, informal news conference, George said he would like to raise teachers' salaries in his nine days, but knew that was just a dream. He announced he had turned down a job with a public relations firm and had no plans after he left office. George said, "I would love to teach school, but I have to be realistic about it and with my campaign debts, I just couldn't afford taking a job as a school teacher."[2] He said he wanted the nine days to be on-the-job training since he fully intended to run for governor again someday.

George was formally sworn in as the 17th governor of Oklahoma by Supreme Court Justice Earl Welch at 10 a.m. on Monday morning. The brief ceremony was witnessed by an overflow crowd of family, friends, and government officials in the Blue Room of the Capitol, just feet away from the cavernous office occupied by Oklahoma's chief executive. Nigh and United States Senator Edmondson received a rousing ovation from the throng. In a brief statement after he took the oath of office, George called on the people of Oklahoma to double their efforts to carry the state forward. Reflecting on the death of Senator Kerr, George said, "It is with regret that I even have the opportunity to serve you as governor." [3]

Justice Welch, who later was removed from office in a scandal involving the Oklahoma Supreme Court, had administered the oath of office to both Kerr, 20 years before, and Edmondson. He pointed out to George that both of the others became United States Senators and George would have to become president to top them. [4]

George remembered that he had made a bet in the 1962 campaign that he would be the next governor. After he lost in the primary, George paid off the $100 wager. However, the day he took office, George called the person and demanded his $200, the repayment and the original bet. The reply was, "But you weren't elected governor." George reminded him that the bet technically was who would be the next governor. Because George was the next governor after Edmondson, the bet was paid off.

On Tuesday members of the state legislature convened in joint session in the House Chamber on the fourth floor of the Capitol to hear the customary state of the state message from the governor. Before George addressed the legislature, the Senate had a brief constitutional crisis because, for the first time in history, there was no lieutenant governor to call the Senate into session, and Senator Roy Boecher of Kingfisher had yet to be formally elected by fellow members as the President Pro Tempore.

George began his speech on a humorous note, pointing out his record on highway construction. That very morning the state highway commission, at George's request, had approved $10.4 million for road construction, more than a million dollars for each day George would be in office. George declared himself, "the road-buildingest governor in history."[5] The Oklahoma General Contractors Association gave George that title seriously 25 years later in recognition of a remarkable statewide highway construction and improvement program.

Royalty for one night were George's nieces and nephews who were present for a gubernatorial sleepover during George's nine days as governor. Courtesy *The Daily Oklahoman.*

George moved his secretary, Glenda Temple, from the lieutenant governor's office into the governor's office. Courtesy *The Daily Oklahoman.*

George spent much of the brief speech honoring the life of Senator Kerr, saying, "From the rank and file of John Q. Public came our champion, the one who would tell our story louder, longer, and more lovingly than all the others."[6] George reviewed the accomplishments of his own 12 years in state government, his attempts as a circuit rider to instill state pride, in hope that pride would help improve the economic condition of Oklahoma.

After the state of the state message, everyone assumed that George's final six days as governor would be calm. How wrong they were! On Wednesday, the Oklahoma Planning and Resources Board, the governing body of the state's parks and lodges system, voted to delay approval of a lease that would allow construction of two new state lodges on Lake Eufaula, Arrowhead, on an arm of the lake in

George invited his family to a "state" dinner at the governor's mansion. Left to right, back row, Sam Nigh, Vickey Nigh, Linda Nigh, Lewann Nigh, Bill Nigh, Marlene Nigh, and Wib Nigh. The children are Sharon Cain, Leah Cain, and Cindy Cain. Left to right, seated, George, Mary Nigh, Irene Nigh, Wilber Nigh. Courtesy *The Daily Oklahoman.*

northern Pittsburg County, George's home county, and Fountainhead Lodge, on the northern portion of Lake Eufaula in neighboring McIntosh County. The delay would have pushed the signing of the agreement beyond the federal deadline and jeopardized the federal funds.

The lodges were to be built at a cost of $9.5 million. The federal government had agreed to underwrite the loan if the state would agree to an annual lease payment of $552,000. George, under pressure from folks back home who saw the lodges as a boon to the local economy, and fearing that a delay would cause the federal government to withdraw its offer to fund the project, demanded that the Planning and Resources Board approve the lease.

The recent death of Senator Kerr, and the loss of his unusual prominence in the United States Senate, played a role in George's decision to strongly back the lodges project. George spoke with federal officials who would not guarantee Oklahoma would receive the allocated federal funds if there was a delay beyond a Friday deadline. Because the influence of Kerr was gone, other United States Senators from all across the country were clamoring for the money, if Oklahoma turned it down.

The Planning and Resources Board balked, partly because some of its members thought the state would have difficulty paying the annual lease, and partly because the Oklahoma Senate, which had become a bitter anti-Edmondson body, had passed a resolution the day before suggesting that the board delay any action until the issue could be further studied by the legislature. Leland Gourley of Henryetta, chairman of the Oklahoma Lake Redevelopment Authority, and strong proponent of the program to build the lodges, accused Governor-Elect Henry Bellmon of Billings of asking the Planning and Resources Board to put off any decision until after he took office.

The federal government had promised to back the lodge project because of high unemployment in Pittsburg, McIntosh, and Okmulgee counties. State and federal officials before Kerr's death were so convinced that the project would go forward that ground had been broken in much-publicized events even before the state legally signed off on the deal.

United States Senators Edmondson and Monroney fully supported the plan, as did Congressmen Carl Albert and Ed Edmondson. Kerr and Albert were two of the most powerful legislators in Washington, D.C., and were able to push through congressional authorization for the funding of the two lodges. Originally, there were plans for only one lodge. But, when Albert and Edmondson disagreed over in whose district the lodge would be built, two lodges were authorized, Fountainhead in Edmondson's Second Congressional District, and Arrowhead, in the Third District represented by Albert, who had risen to the lofty position of House Majority Leader.

Members of the Planning and Resources Board complained that they had not had time to read the contract so George called a public meeting in the underground auditorium between the Will Rogers and Sequoyah state office buildings at which members of the administration alternated in reading aloud the lengthy contract. Hundreds of supporters from eastern Oklahoma attended the reading which was broadcast live on television.

Board member Jack Griffith of Stillwater told George that even after the contract was read, he and most other members of the board would still vote to delay approval of the agreement. When the motion was made and seconded to delay approval, George, as governor was recognized. He reminded the board members, "You serve at the pleasure of the governor. Your service is no longer this governor's pleasure, so I hereby remove you from office." With most of the board gone, there was no quorum and the meeting adjourned at 10:30 P.M.

George and his staff went to the mansion and searched for an answer. Within hours George appointed eight new members to the board, members he knew would vote for the lease. All, including *McAlester News Capital* publisher Richard R. "Dick" Hefton, had sat through the lengthy reading of the legal documents during the day-long public meeting. They were called at home in the middle of the night and told to return immediately to Oklahoma City and to come to the mansion.[7]

Fearing that the opponents of the new state lodges might ask for a court injunction to prevent the sale of the bonds, George closeted new members of the Planning and Resources Board at the governor's mansion the rest of the night before their meeting so they could not be served with court papers. Highway patrolmen sealed off the mansion, coming and going was allowed only with the personal permission of the governor.

Five of the new members came from Pittsburg County, two from Okmulgee County, and one from McIntosh County. The new Board met at 7:00 a.m. the following morning and unanimously approved the lease. The meeting was open to the public, and the press, at the urging of George's press secretary, Fred Turner, who thought any attempt to vote in secret, in executive session, would be frowned upon by the public and could possibly be a violation of the open meetings law.[8]

The federal government was the only bidder for the $9.5 million in bonds for the project. *The Sunday Oklahoman* columnist Ray Parr wrote, "I would certainly like to commend Governor Nigh on one thing. I guess he appointed about the smartest bunch of fellows to his new planning board I ever heard of. It took 'em only about five minutes to digest that 56-page lodge contract and 120-page trust indenture and come up with the conclusion it was a great thing for Oklahoma."[9]

After the bonds were sold, some members of the Senate were irate. One historian observed, "Comparing Nigh's governorship to Adolph Hitler's dictatorship of Nazi Germany and describing Gourley as a worse thief than the Old West's Jesse James, many of the senators felt the lodge deal would haunt Oklahoma's economy for years to come."[10]

George explained to both supporters and opponents of the quick lease deal that his efforts were directed at firmly holding the federal government to its commitment to underwrite the bonds, and no more. He adamantly denied that the lodge lease had anything to do with his appointment of Edmondson to the United States Senate. Attorney General Charles Nesbitt later ruled that George's firing of the Planning and Resources Board was void and the lease was invalid. George told the press that if he was only going to be governor for nine days he would rather be remembered as the man who saved the state a $9 million project than be remembered as the man who lost a $9 million deal. George's action had done what he said it would do, save

George signs the Lake Eufaula lodges lease agreement on January 10, 1963. Standing is W. E. "Bill" Allford, McAlester, a new member of the Planning and Resources Board. At right is Leland Gourley, principal architect of the lease deal with the federal government. Courtesy *The Daily Oklahoman.*

the federal money for Oklahoma. Governor Henry Bellmon renegotiated the final agreement, not only saving the Arrowhead and Fountainhead lodge projects, but in the process securing even more federal funds for state lodges and parks.

In his final days as governor George was busy on several fronts. Criminals Appeals Court Judge John A. Brett decided to retire because he did not want incoming Governor Bellmon to appoint his successor. George appointed his close friend, Stillwater attorney Joe Johnson, to the post to replace Brett.

George paroled five prisoners, including a Muskogee County man, J.C. Fast, Jr., who had killed a Muskogee banker a quarter century before. The Pardon and Parole Board had previously recommended clemency for Fast but Edmondson, while still governor, would not grant a parole because he was a personal friend of the families of both the killer and the victim.

Earlier legislative action placing most state employees under the merit system had exempt the State Insurance Fund whose employees remained unclassified. George placed 63 employees of the Fund under the state merit system, a move to protect workers whose jobs were threatened by incoming Governor Bellmon. The attorney general later ruled that George's action was legal.

Earlier in the week, George announced a gala event to close out his nine-day administration, an open house at the governor's mansion, on Sunday from 1:00 to 5:00 P.M., complete with cookies and punch. He appointed 12 Oklahoma City women to an arrangements committee. Wynetka Armor was chairman with Dolly Hoskins, Glenda Phillips, Mrs. David Bridges, Mrs. John Ingram, Mrs. Louis Darrell, Crystal Mounts, Mrs. John Perry, Mrs. Cruce Trice, Billie Fagerquist, Mrs. John Conner, and Mrs. Ben Brown as committee members. Another 50 women were named to a reception and tour committee.[11]

Thousands showed up for the governor's mansion open house before the gates opened. George saw people huddled in the cold on both sides of Northeast 23rd Street and gave the order to open the gates early. The mansion was so clogged with visitors that the fire marshal halted the serving of refreshments. Cars were parked for blocks around. It was estimated that more than 22,000 people attended.

George's close advisers told him that the size of the crowd at the Sunday open house at the mansion would be a referendum on his drive to push through approval of the Lake Eufaula lodges and perhaps a referendum on his political future. If only a handful of people showed up, they reasoned, George's actions would be deemed a failure. Conversely, if a large crowd attended the event, it would be a sure sign of approval of George's leadership.

Sunrise brought bad news. The morning dawned with teeth-chattering cold gripping the state from Boise City to Broken Bow. It was three degrees below zero at 8:00 A.M. as George's volunteer committees began arriving at the mansion with punch bowls and cookies. George feared the bone-chilling temperatures would severely limit the crowd and send a crushing signal as to his future.

George had invited everyone, and it seemed as if everyone came. Planners had expected only a few hundred people, but literally thousands swarmed over the mansion grounds, "looking at books, studying the kitchen, climbing the spiral staircase" and finally meeting their host, the governor.

The official guest book was signed by 10,000 people. The signing started out at the front door, but as the crowd grew, the book was split three ways. There was a logjam at the few bathrooms in the mansion. People waited up to half an hour outside bathroom doors. Mrs. Howard Everest, one of the official greeters, estimated that 20,000 to 22,000 people visited the mansion.

George worked the crowd, shook hands with everyone, and kissed more than a few babies. Doing what came naturally, he stayed at the door until the last Oklahoman left the open house, hours after the scheduled closing time. George loosened his tie and sat down with friends on the historic staircase inside the mansion's front entrance. He was pleased with his fellow citizens' response to his invitation to the open house. All agreed that it sent a signal that indeed George was still a major player in Oklahoma politics. It was a fitting end to the first term of Governor George P. Nigh.

Donna

Donna is the best thing that ever happened to me.

George Nigh

I had a job, I had a house, I had a car, I wasn't a hundred thousand dollars in debt. Where was the good deal about me marrying the "state's most eligible bachelor?"

Donna Nigh

On Monday, January 14, 1963, Henry Bellmon was sworn in as Oklahoma's first Republican governor, and George was out of government and out of a job. He formed a public relations firm, George Nigh, Incorporated, and opened offices in downtown Oklahoma City, intending to use his recognition and experience in tourism as a drawing card to work with organizations to plan conventions and events in Oklahoma.

Newspapers called George the most eligible bachelor in the state. He had never found the girl he wanted to spend the rest of his life with. That is, until a former student and campaigner from the 1958 bus tours, Herman Harmon, a reservations agent for American Airlines, introduced George to a brown-haired Trans World Airlines (TWA) ticket agent. Donna Mashburn worked at the TWA desk at the Skirvin Hotel. Harmon arranged a get-acquainted "Coke date" for Donna and George at the Skirvin Tower Coffee Shop across the street.

The Daily Oklahoman talked about George's bachelor status, noting that the girl who caught up with him would have a lot of traveling to do. George logged 74,000 miles in his first year as lieutenant governor. The newspaper hinted that George had been seen in the company of a former Miss America. Courtesy *The Daily Oklahoman.*

Donna, a 30-year-old single parent with a ten-year-old son, Berry Michael "Mike" Mashburn, born October 8, 1952, during a previous marriage. Donna had graduated from Oklahoma City's Capitol Hill High School and attended Central State College, now the University of Central Oklahoma, in Edmond.

Donna's parents were Raphael and Gertha Mae Dunham Skinner. After working at Wilson & Company for years, Donna's father, like George's dad, opened a neighborhood grocery store. The Skinner grocery was on South Walker Avenue near Capitol Hill High School. He later managed the Skinner's Coffee Shop in the Oklahoma Natural Gas Building in downtown Oklahoma City.

Even though the public thought of George as a highly eligible bachelor, Donna wanted to know what the big deal was. The truth was that George had no job, no house, no car, was a defeated candidate, and up to his ears in campaign debt. However, his relationship with Donna blossomed from the very beginning. George said it was love at first sight, but Donna was not sure. She was not accustomed to appearing in public with a face that everyone knew.[1]

On their first official date, George took Donna, in her car of course, to an evening of dining and dancing at a restaurant at the Habana Inn in northwest Oklahoma City. George financed the evening with a due bill the restaurant owed George's campaign printer, Roy Thomas. When George told Thomas, owner of Royal Printing, that he had a date with Donna, Thomas gave George the due bill. Donna later asked, "Why are we going here?" George simply replied that the restaurant had always been one of his favorites.

George has never forgotten that first date with Donna. In the summer of 1999 he leaned back in his chair, folded his arms across his chest, and reflected on the date 36 years before, "I never shall forget the first evening we went out, the dress she wore, and how beautiful she looked. From that very moment I knew this was the woman I wanted to marry and spend my life with."[2]

Most of their dates were to the nearby University Hospital where George's mother was hospitalized. Irene Nigh had lost a kidney and was receiving dialysis daily at the hospital.

Wedding bells were near when George and Donna purchased a marriage license at the Oklahoma County Courthouse. Courtesy *The Daily Oklahoman.*

Donna and Mike Mashburn, 1963. Donna took awhile to answer George's proposal for marriage. She was making it well as a single mom. She owned a small house, a good car, and had a decent job.

Both Irene and Wilber Nigh loved Donna from the first time they met her. Wilber immediately cemented a wonderful, loving relationship with Donna's son Mike, whose first question was could he call him "Grandaddy Nigh."

George and Donna's relationship grew serious. One night during a visit with George's mother Irene asked George to leave the hospital room. With George standing in the hallway, she gave Donna her diamond ring. Everyone cried that night.

It was difficult to find a romantic moment during the courtship because George had no money for elaborate dates and Mike reversed roles and was chaperone. However, in September, George planned a special way to ask Donna to marry him. Their song was "I Left my Heart in San Francisco," by Tony Bennett. George had noticed that Donna had an album with "San Francisco" on it. That evening George quickly pulled the record from the album cover and placed it on the turntable on Donna's stereo. He turned the lights down low and lit a candle. His plan was to ask Donna the magic question while Bennett sang.

Unfortunately, the mood was not quite what he had hoped for. George had picked up a Judy Garland record about San Francisco.

Instead of the melodic sounds of Tony Bennett, George was shocked to hear the raspy rendition of Judy Garland belting out, "San Francisco, open your golden gate!" But George popped the question to Donna anyway.

Donna could not give George an immediate answer. She had a lot to think about. She had proven she could take care of herself and Mike. She had a good job, a home, and an automobile. She knew she loved George but wanted to make certain she was ready for marriage. After a week, maybe the longest in George's life, Donna said yes, and the partnership began.

George and Donna sprang the news of their upcoming marriage to 10-year-old Mike while attending the prison rodeo in McAlester. Over breakfast, Mike was told for the first time that his mother was marrying George. Mike was shocked. He had been the man of the house for most of his life. He was less than enthusiastic about George playing such a major role in his mother's life. Hours later, the marriage plans were announced to a Nigh family gathering.

In September, wedding plans were publicly announced. Mary Jo Nelson wrote in the *Oklahoma City Times,* "Oklahoma's ranking bachelor finally has succumbed to the lure of matrimony."[3] The wedding was planned for October 19, 1963.

Ten days before the ceremony, George took his mother, her health deteriorating, home from University Hospital to McAlester, stopping long enough at a dress shop to buy a dress to wear to the wedding. Instead it became her burial dress as she died two days later.

Her doctor, George Brown, told George that Irene had "willed her death," that she knew she was in her last days and did not want her death to postpone George and Donna's wedding. She had been excited about George abandoning his bachelorhood and about his future life with Donna. The wedding plans continued at Wilber Nigh's request, with feelings of both joy and sadness enveloping the following week. George and Donna were married at the Capitol Hill Baptist Church in Oklahoma City, Donna's home church.

Donna wore a beige lace dress, accompanied by her sister, Ann Davis, of Dallas, Texas. Paul Carris, George's friend since boyhood, stood as best man. The vocalist was Florence Ambrose, a McAlester

The newlyweds at Capitol Hill Baptist Church in Oklahoma City, October 19, 1963. Clergymen for the ceremony were Capitol Hill Baptist pastor Dr. Hugh Bumpas and Dr. Lawrence W. Johnson, pastor of George's church, First Presbyterian Church of McAlester.

George and Donna with their parents. Left to right, Raphael Skinner, Gertha Skinner, Donna, George, Wilber Nigh. Everyone knew that Irene Nigh surely was watching the wedding from heaven.

native, then living in Ada. Florence was one of Irene Nigh's best friends and had sung at her funeral just a week before. After the 8 P.M. wedding, a reception was held at the nearby Hillcrest Golf and Country Club in Oklahoma City.

After a November honeymoon in Israel and Europe, George and Donna settled down in Donna's house near Southwest 68th Street and Villa Avenue in south Oklahoma City.

George resumed his planning of an international convention, or congress, of the Jaycees scheduled for Oklahoma City the following year. George had contracted with the Oklahoma City Jaycee chapter to coordinate the convention. It was a long and laborious task. First, George and the Jaycee team had to convince American Jaycees that Oklahoma City should be the bid city from the United States. Competition was stiff among delegations from New York City; Los Angeles, California; and Miami, Florida, but Oklahoma City won out over the others as the official United States bid sight.

At a world meeting of Jaycee leaders, George led the successful convention bid in head-to-head competition with Rio de Janeiro, Brazil and Montreal, Canada. George was proud of his nickname as "Oklahoma's cheerleader." He strongly believed that young men of the world, members of Jaycee chapters in 70 countries, could see in Oklahoma City the real meaning of what living in the heartland of America was all about.

In October, 1964, Jaycees came from points around the globe, in their native dress, to the Jaycee Congress headquarters at the Skirvin Hotel in Oklahoma City. George invited the famous Washington, D.C., party-giver Perle Mesta to return to the hotel built by her father, William Balser "Bill" Skirvin, to host a gala event for visiting Jaycees.

George traveled to Mesta's office in Washington, D.C., to extend the formal invitation. Mesta was known on the social scene as the "Hostess with the Mostes." As a former United States Ambassador to Luxembourg, appointed by President Harry S. Truman, this Oklahoman was the first female ambassador in American history.

She was thrilled with the idea of returning to the hotel where so many of her formative years were spent and said of course she would be the official hostess. She told George that her normal fee for hosting a party was $5,000. George was terribly disappointed because there was no money available in the Jaycee convention budget to pay the $5,000 fee and he did not know how he could withdraw the invitation. George asked, "Mrs. Mesta, can't you cut the fee for this hometown event?" Mesta told George that, as a matter of principle, she never never cut her fee. However, with a twinkle in her eye, she said she would be pleased to host the party free, but made it clear that she was not cutting her fee. George could hardly contain his enthusiasm as he telephoned Jaycee officials back in Oklahoma with news of Mesta's agreement to come for the convention.

Oklahoma Congressman Carl Albert, left, arranged an appointment with President Lyndon B. Johnson, right, in the Oval Office of the White House, where George invited him to speak to the International Jaycee Congress in Oklahoma City. Johnson was already booked but sent Secretary of State Dean Rusk. Courtesy The White House.

George launched a fund raising drive to support the Oklahoma City Jaycees' effort to land the International Jaycee Congress. Here George hands his dollar to Joe A. Cunningham, tag committee chairman. Courtesy *The Daily Oklahoman.*

Perle Mesta, the nation's most famous hostess, and daughter of the builder of Oklahoma City's Skirvin Hotel, poses with George and Donna at the 1964 International Jaycee Congress in Oklahoma City.

Mesta's party at the Skirvin Hotel to welcome the thousands of Jaycees was one of the gala events in Oklahoma party history. Mesta stood at the head of the reception line as delegates entered the large ballroom for the event. Oklahoma politicians and socialites were as thick as children gathered around a broken fire hydrant on summer's hottest day.

The exchange of international ideas was the highlight of the world gathering. Delegates spoke in their native tongues, as other members sat with headphones to hear interpretation in one of the four Jaycee official languages, English, Spanish, German, and French. Many future world leaders shared ideas on how to make a community a more productive and forceful place to live. United States Secretary of State Dean Rusk was the featured speaker for the Jaycee Congress. President Lyndon B. Johnson had been invited by Jaycees to appear. However, a conflict in the President's schedule sent Secretary Rusk, one of the better known men in the American government, to Oklahoma City.

In the period when George was not lieutenant governor, he was in the private sector, promoting and managing conventions in Oklahoma for business and civic groups. However, most of his income came from fees from out-of-state speeches. Because of his first exposure as a speaker at Jaycee events across the country, George became a motivational speaker on the national scene, traveling to almost every state in the nation and several international conventions. At one time he was under contract as a national speaker for General Motors. GM offered to sign him to a handsome multi-year contract if, and a big if, he would agree not to run for public office. GM pointed out that General Electric had cancelled a contract with Ronald Reagan because of political views being expressed. They were concerned about George being viewed as a political speaker, rather than a motivational speaker.

The choice could have been a tough one, a choice between a guaranteed family "lucrative gut cinch," or the uncertainty of returning to the political arena. George wanted to keep his options open so he declined the GM offer.

Fortunately, no out of Oklahoma speeches were scheduled for the first week of January, 1965. On January 14, Donna gave birth to Georgeann Nigh, a seven-pound, thirteen ounce bundle of joy for the Nigh household. Mike was 12-years-old when Georgeann was born and was very proud of his new little sister. He became a reliable big brother, helping to raise the new member of the Nigh household.

In 1965 George began mulling over his future. In their first two years of marriage, George and Donna had developed a unique and close relationship. When George considered running for public office again, he told Donna, who simply said, "It's your decision. Whatever you do, I will support you 100 percent." George's sharing of his innermost thoughts with Donna, and her instant expression of unequivocal support for all his decisions, were demonstrative of their relationship throughout George's political career.[5]

After he left his nine-day term as governor in early 1963, George genuinely had doubted he would ever run for public office again.

However, he was still in the spotlight because of his successful coordination of the Jaycee Congress and as chairman of statewide fund raising campaigns for worthwhile causes such as the Oklahoma Association for Retarded Children, Inc. George's friends and former campaign supporters frequently urged him to run for governor or lieutenant governor.

In early October, 1965, the *Oklahoma Journal* reported that George was "definitely interested" in running for his old job as lieutenant governor. George told a United Press International reporter that he was checking with his past associates around the state and was optimistic about his entry into the race. The newspaper story speculated that the incumbent, Lieutenant Governor Leo Winters, would run for re-election. Winters said he welcomed George into the race.[6]

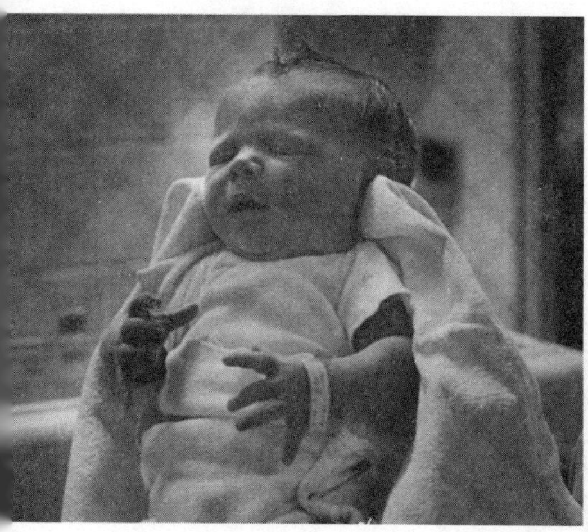

Georgeann Nigh was born January 7, 1965. Mother, father, and big brother Mike were very proud.

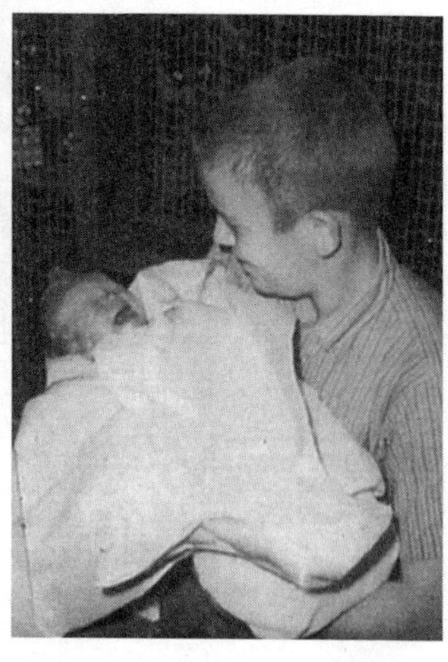

Mike Mashburn bonded with his new sister, Georgeann, immediately on her 1965 birth. He became her chief babysitter and surrogate parent, refusing to allow other babysitters to come to the Nigh home. Mike, lovingly, said she was "his."

After talking to family and friends, George decided that he would definitely run for lieutenant governor again as a starting point on a comeback trail. Surprisingly, Winters announced he would not stand for re-election but instead ran for and was elected state treasurer.

A month later, an error-filled Associated Press dispatch from Phoenix, Arizona, announced that George would run for governor of Oklahoma. George was in Phoenix speaking to a meeting of the Arizona National Livestock Show.

Back home in Oklahoma, the Associated Press report made bulletin material for radio and television and set off a flood of telephone calls to George and Donna's home and the Capitol pressroom. Donna, reached at home by an Oklahoma City reporter, said she doubted the story, musing, "He wouldn't announce anything in Phoenix. I think he must have been misunderstood."[7]

A reporter said he overheard George talking about running for something but later admitted George might have been talking about a race for lieutenant governor.

George relished the publicity surrounding the erroneous news report. He quipped, "Just say the report of my candidacy has been grossly exaggerated," a paraphrase from language used by the late American humorist Mark Twain, in replying to the false report of his death.

With Donna at his side, and pledging once again to be a "working lieutenant governor," George officially announced his candidacy on December 7, 1965, at a press conference in the state senate lounge. George told reporters that the lieutenant governor should be given additional responsibilities. He promised to be available for industrial trips and to work with individual communities who sought new and expanding industries. Asked if he could work with a Republican governor, George replied, "I think I could work with anyone."[8]

With the incumbent, Winters, out of the race, George faced little organized opposition in the May 3, 1966, Democratic primary. His opponents were "Fence-Cutter" Roger Willis, famous for a run-in with the Oklahoma Planning and Resources Board over a fence at Fort Cobb Lake; Bob A. Trent, a former legislator and farmer from Caney, Oklahoma; and Woodrow Weaver, an Oklahoma City engineer.

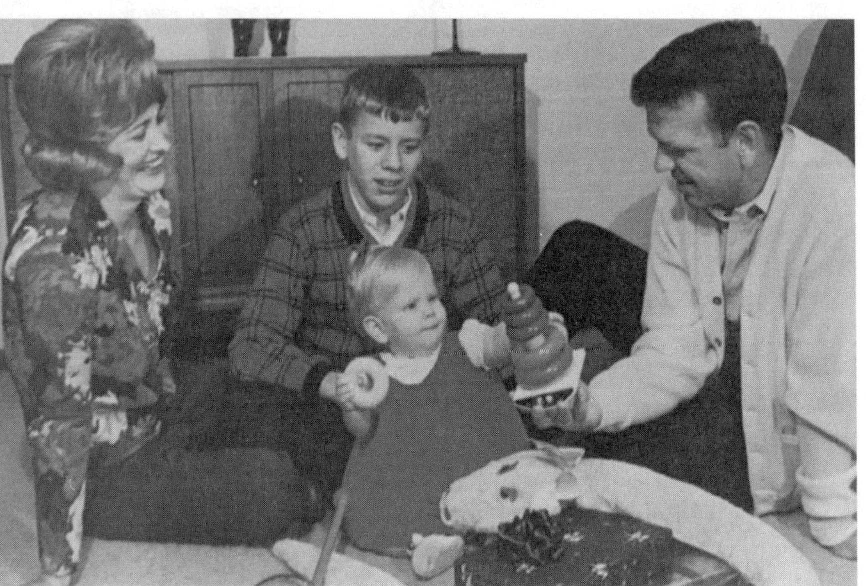

George's 1966 campaign brochure promoted his enthusiasm about Oklahoma and its future. It also showed Oklahoma his new family.

George had little difficulty in swamping his primary opponents, winning nearly 80 percent of the vote. His political comeback had begun. George tallied 303,518 votes, a quarter million more than his nearest challenger, Trent.

In the Democratic primary for governor, Raymond Gary and Preston Moore led a 13-man field into the May 24 runoff where Gary, the former governor, was upset by Moore.

George's opponent in the general election was Republican J. Robert Wootten, a Yukon banker, who beat Ernest O. Martin, a veteran employee of Skelly Oil Company in Tulsa, in the GOP primary.

Believing that he would win the November election by a landslide, George devoted most of his attention to Moore's campaign for governor against Tulsa State Senator Dewey F. Bartlett, an oil man who had survived a runoff challenge from John N. "Happy" Camp of Waukomis.

George moved his headquarters into the Moore headquarters on North Lincoln Boulevard in Oklahoma City and began directing Moore's calendar of appearances. Moore had many contacts among veterans organizations because of his past service as state and national commander of the American Legion. However, Moore was void of support in many communities where no American Legion post existed. George used his card file of supporters, Jaycees, families of Girls Staters, and Young Democrats, to set up campaign events for Moore all over the state.

The Daily Oklahoman endorsed George's opponent, Wootten, editorializing, "Wootten should be elected so that Republican Dewey Bartlett, this newspaper's choice for governor, would have a member of his own party as his assistant in the event of his election."[9]

Wootten criticized George's nine-day term as governor, the handling of the Lake Eufaula state lodges lease; the appointment of Joe Johnson to the Court of Criminal Appeals, an appointment made without consulting the Oklahoma Bar Association; and George's appointment of J. Howard Edmondson to the United States Senate, a decision reversed by voters when they refused to re-elect Edmondson in 1964.

George's inattention to his own race almost cost him the election. On November 8, nearly 700,000 Oklahomans went to the polls. A Republican mid-presidential year landslide cast Bartlett into the governor's mansion by more than 80,000 votes over Moore.[10]

George defeated Wootten by only 24,000 votes, 328,580 to 306,053. George learned a valuable lesson—worry about your own race first and never have a watch party with other candidates. On the night Moore lost to Bartlett, the Moore-Nigh watch party at the Sheraton-Oklahoma Hotel in downtown Oklahoma City was a mishmash of mixed emotions. Nigh supporters were forced to restrain their shouts of victory amidst the disappointed supporters of Moore.

Other remarkable outcomes of the general election were the defeat of House Speaker J.D. McCarty in his south Oklahoma City district and the election of Leo Winters as state treasurer. Political reporter Otis Sullivant considered both George and Winters as future possibilities to wrest control of the governor's office from the Republicans, writing, "Winters can succeed himself as treasurer and would have to cut loose from the office now prized because of demand of banks for state deposits. Nigh will have to do his homework and outgrow the 1958 picture of being just 'a nice guy' "[10] Other observers publicly stated that George being a nice guy was a political disadvantage for the future.

Oklahoma City television personality Ida Blackburn, or Ida B, took partial credit for George's victory. Since he lived near the television studio, George was a convenient fill-in guest on the *Ida B Show,* when scheduled guests failed to appear for the live telecast. George was thankful for the free air time for two reasons. It gave him exposure and taught him to be comfortable in front of television cameras where there was no live audience. Mrs. Blackburn's son, Dr. Bob Blackburn, later became the executive director of the Oklahoma Historical Society.

Return to Public Service

No matter how we choose to view ourselves in the abstract, in the world of work and politics Americans live in a constant state of debate and contention.

Ralph Ellison

Even before he took office again as lieutenant governor, George encountered problems with the Bartlett administration. Troubles began when the Bartlett inaugural planning committee allotted George just two seats on the giant inaugural platform on the south steps of the Capitol. George called an inaugural committee official and asked for a third chair for his step-son Mike. George was informed that there were no additional seats available. George then asked if the Bartlett children were going to be on the platform and the answer was, "Yes, they are the first family."

George inquired why the family of the lieutenant governor could not be included. He was told again that there was no room. The inaugural committee official said, "Are you suggesting I kick someone off the inaugural platform?" George replied, "No, I am not asking you to remove someone. I'm just asking you to simply add another chair."[1]

George stated that unless one more chair could be added to the platform for Mike, he, George would sit in the far rear of audience and would slowly and methodically come forward when it was his turn to be sworn in. George knew the press would inquire why he was not on the stage. Bartlett committee officials quickly added another chair.

George's persistence was because he thought his relationship with Mike was fragile, although normal, under the circumstances of a 12-year-old having a new father figure in the household. George worked diligently to show Mike how much he cared for him and believed leaving him out of the inaugural activities would do permanent harm to their relations.[2]

As inauguration day approached, George had little contact with the Bartlett inaugural committee who had never asked for a list of George's family members and supporters to invite to the inaugural ball. The lieutenant governor's supporters were anxious to celebrate also.

Finally, two weeks before the big day, with the help of his closest allies, George initiated plans for his own inaugural celebration at the Sheraton-Oklahoma Hotel. Ted Bonham of Oklahoma City and Paul Carris of McAlester were co-chairmen of the $25-per-couple affair to honor the state's new lieutenant governor.

When Governor-Elect Bartlett heard of the plans for a separate inaugural party, he sent for George to come to his temporary quarters in outgoing Governor Bellmon's office on the second floor of the Capitol. Bartlett chastised George for planning the separate, competitive ball. George pointed out that it was not in conflict because he and his supporters were not invited to the ball Bartlett was having. As a result, Oklahoma had two separate inaugural balls.

The pre-inaugural friction between George and Bartlett carried over into the administration. An *Oklahoma Journal* headline, "NIGH HITS OUT AT BARTLETT," greeted readers on the morning of March 18. The story quoted George as saying that he wanted to work but Bartlett would not let him.

Another example of the hard feelings between George and Bartlett was a flap over George's declaration of "DeMolay Week," honoring the student organization sponsored by Masons. George himself was a former DeMolay Master Counselor and had advanced through the ranks of his local Masonic Lodge in McAlester to the level of a 32nd degree Mason. Even while yet a bachelor, George had been selected as a "DeMolay Dad" by the McAlestser DeMolay chapter.

Bartlett refused to sign the declaration so George, as acting governor, signed the document when Bartlett was out of state. Even though George had agreed to limit his actions while acting as governor, he defended this particular move as a simple recognition of a worthy organization.[3] He believed he could not turn his back on an organization which he had headed.

During the campaign Bartlett had promised voters that he would appoint the lieutenant governor as chairman of the Industrial Development and Park Commission, to give the lieutenant governor an active and official role in promoting the state. However, Bartlett shocked George by calling him to his office and informing him that he was appointing his general election opponent, J. Robert Wootten, to the post.

George was enraged by the appointment but offered a compromise solution. He told Bartlett that he would not object to Bartlett appointing someone else besides him to the commission chairmanship, and he would not object to Wootten being appointed to any other state position. But to appoint his former challenger to that specific position he had earmarked for the lieutenant governor was too much to take calmly. Bartlett told George that he would not change his position. Thus began a major legislative partisan fight.

The Democrat controlled legislature came to George's aid and passed legislation making the lieutenant governor the voting chairman of the Industrial Development and Park Commission, as had been promised in the campaign by the gubernatorial nominees of both major parties, and raised the lieutenant governor's salary from $9,000 to $15,000 annually. George used his privilege as a former member of the House of Representatives, to actively campaign on the floor of the House and Senate for passage of the bill.

In an effort to soothe the feelings of Democratic legislators, Wootten resigned as chairman of the commission. But still Bartlett vetoed the bill. The legislature promptly overrode the gubernatorial veto and the legislation became effective 90 days later.

One day before the new law took effect, Bartlett appointed Sam Noble of Ardmore as chairman of the commission. Under the old law,

Smiling from ear to ear over their catch of four silverking tarpon are Mike, left, and George, in July, 1967. George sandwiched the deep sea outing in the Gulf of Mexico off the coast near Cameron, Louisiana, between speaking engagements. The largest of the fish weighed 160 pounds. Courtesy *The Daily Oklahoman.*

the governor had the authority to name the chairman, but under the new legislation, still being considered by the Supreme Court, the lieutenant governor automatically became chairman. A month later, Noble quit the job and Bartlett appointed George chairman, a move rejected by George because he believed he did not need to be appointed as he was already chairman by virtue of the new law.

When George tried to attend meetings of the commission to serve as chairman, the members of the commission, all appointed by Bartlett, voted to refuse George's participation as chairman. Every month George attended the meeting, only to be rebuffed by commissioners.

George filed a lawsuit in district court in Oklahoma County seeking to uphold the law designating him chairman of the commission and allowing the pay raise. The following day, Attorney General G. T. Blankenship ruled that George was entitled to serve as voting chairman of the commission but that the pay raise was unconstitutional.

Eventually, the Oklahoma Supreme Court ruled that the pay raise was appropriate and legal because the lieutenant governor had been given additional duties not previously designated.

In October, 1967, George began his official job as chairman of the Industrial Development and Park Commission. His role was as overseer of the seven state lodges, the massive state park system, the search for new industry, and the limited advertising campaign employed to advertise the benefits of living in and vacationing in Oklahoma. George called for closer cooperation between the state agency and the governor's office and asked each commission member to be fully and equally involved in making decisions regarding Oklahoma's industrial and tourism promotion policy.[4]

As chairman of the commission that oversaw the agency, George asked for specific daily duties to push the goals of the department forward. Agency executive director Robert H. Breeden, a former Republican state senator from Pawnee, and Governor Bartlett challenged the move as an attempt by George to take over the leadership of the agency. George defended his action, saying, that as chairman, he needed to know what the department was doing, and he could not have any working knowledge of the state's industrial development and tourism promotion activities by only attending a three-hour monthly meeting.

Most of the members of the Industrial Development and Park Commission argued that George had overstepped the limits of his chairmanship. Clarence Wright of Yukon, who agreed with George's expanded role, was fired from the commission by Bartlett. The legislature again stepped into the battle on George's side and proposed legislation making the lieutenant governor executive director of the department. The bill died in committee, at George's request.[5]

During the Bartlett administration Oklahoma reached new heights in attracting new industries. New or expanded industries added an investment of more than $700 million in 67 of the state's 77 counties. The Ozarks Regional Commission spent $4.8 million on developing industry in high unemployment counties in eastern Oklahoma.[6]

George and Donna attended the 1968 Democratic National Convention in Chicago, Illinois, as a delegate from Oklahoma. The convention made headlines not only for nominating Vice President Hubert Humphrey as the Democratic presidential candidate, but also for clashes between demonstrators and police on the streets of downtown Chicago.

When the American Civil Liberties Union (ACLU) asked George and other members of the delegation to sign a letter criticizing actions of the Chicago police, George fired off a reply, saying, "Your letter stated that some delegates faced obstacles to free expression in Chicago. I was among those, but let me make it clear that my obstacles to free expression were not the police, but rather thousands of non-delegates who tried to restrict my freedom of expression." "As a delegate," he continued, "who was spat upon as I simply walked from my bus to the hotel; as a delegate who was nauseated by the stink bombs thrown into the lobby of my hotel; as a delegate who was repulsed by the vulgarity of the demonstrators, may I say clearly that I think you are representing the wrong group."[7]

The rift between George and Bartlett simmered until one day George asked for a meeting with the governor. George and Bartlett both agreed that publicity surrounding their difficulties was not good for the state. George suggested that they concentrate more on what pulled them together and less on what pulled them apart. Both agreed

George met with Democratic presidential nominee Hubert Humphrey during a 1968 campaign visit to Oklahoma City. Courtesy Oklahoma Tourism and Recreation Department.

George and Donna spent much of 1968 inspecting state facilities, including parks and recreation areas.

that they looked like two spoiled kids who each wanted to have their own way and pledged to work together for the good of Oklahoma.

Bartlett immediately showed good faith by sending George, accompanied by Donna, to inspect all state facilities, from hospitals and institutions to colleges and universities. Protests over the Vietnam War had resulted in campus unrest. George talked with protest leaders on several campuses. After his extensive tour, George gave a full report to Bartlett on the status of state facilities.[8]

Another benefit of George's reconciliation with Bartlett was an assignment to check out the vocational education system in South Carolina. Bartlett believed, and was proved correct, that a well-trained work force was critical to attracting new industry to Oklahoma. South Carolina Governor Robert McNair invited a 40-member Oklahoma delegation, headed by George, to visit vocation technical schools in South Carolina that were described as a model for vocational training by many nationally recognized experts.

George and Bartlett became non-partisan partners in many areas and George came to admire and respect Governor Bartlett.

George spent a great deal of his personal time in the summer of 1968 campaigning for older brother Bill, a member of the Oklahoma House of Representatives, who was running as a Democrat for a seat on the state corporation commission. When questioned about his support for his brother, George said he thought it would be unnatural if brothers did not help one another. He told a reporter, "Don't you think someone's brother ought to help him? If he didn't, something would be wrong, wouldn't it? I bet if Charlic Nesbitt [Bill Nigh's major opponent in the primary] has a brother, he's helping him too."[9] In fact Nesbitt did not have a brother.

Bill hired Dave Dank, a former aide of Democratic publicist Martin Hauan, to manage the closing weeks of his campaign. Bill made the runoff with Nesbitt, a successful Oklahoma City attorney, over formidable famous name candidates Joe Bailey Cobb of Tishomingo, John M. Rogers and A.F. Shaw of Oklahoma City, and Andy Payne, famous for winning a cross-country bunion derby race

Framed by the charred remains of a window in the burned NAACP Freedom Center in Oklahoma City, George spoke at ground breaking ceremonies for a new center in February, 1969. Sitting far left is Hannah D. Atkins. Courtesy *The Daily Oklahoman.*

in the 1920s. However, Bill lost to Nesbitt by 22,000 votes in a bitterly contested runoff on September 17, 1968.

By 1967, Oklahoma had regained population that had left during the dust bowl of the 1930s. George, as the chief promoter of the state, told audiences that all Oklahomans must become "walking, talking, breathing" salesmen for the state to attract industry and tourism and offer opportunities to young people. At a fund raiser to help George and the Democratic Party pay off 1966 campaign debts, George pledged to do everything in his power to be a stepping stone toward building Oklahoma and not be a stumbling block.[10]

After eating crow over comments made about Boise City, Oklahoma, George smoked a peace pipe with Panhandle leaders and apologized. The move made George many friends in the Panhandle. Earlier in the day, residents of Texhoma gave George a four-feet-long replica of a hypodermic needle which was intended to cure "hoof and mouth disease." In Guymon, the local mayor handed George a crate of live crows. In Hooker, the mayor said, "Governor, you sure have got a lot of publicity for Boise City by saying something bad about them. Can you say something bad about Hooker?" Because Governor Bartlett was using the state airplane that day, George was flown to the Panhandle by Jude Northcutt and Jody Taylor, owners of Jude & Jody Furniture of Oklahoma City. Courtesy Oklahoma Tourism and Recreation Department.

At every opportunity, in every speech and interview, George stressed the need for Oklahomans to be proud of their heritage and tell others of the state's advantages. He continued to spend several weeks each year outside the borders of the Sooner State, telling the nation about Oklahoma.

Not every George Nigh speech ended in acclamation. In 1969, speaking to the Hereford Breeders Association in Amarillo, Texas, George referred to Boise City, Oklahoma, as "where we send highway patrolmen who get out of line."[11]

Residents of all three counties in the Oklahoma Panhandle were upset. The *Boise City News* charged that George's comment was intended to ruin the area's chance of luring a large feed lot and feed processing plant.[12]

George and actress Beverly Garland, star of the movie *Where the Red Fern Grows,* filmed at Tahlequah, Oklahoma. The movie co-starred Jack Ging, a native of Muskogee.

News organizations around the world, including the American Forces Radio and Television Service, carried the story. George apologized for the comment and launched an intensive effort to soothe the ruffled feathers of people in the Panhandle. When Governor Bartlett was next out of state, George, as acting governor, declared a "Panhandle Empire Appreciation Day," and traveled to towns in the three counties to make his apology. Television crews from all Oklahoma City and Tulsa stations and surrounding states met George at every stop. George gave such tender attention to the Panhandle that residents forgave him, although he was given six live crows, symbolic

George and Donna raise the Oklahoma flag over a Hollywood, California, hotel owned by Oklahoma singing cowboy Gene Autry, on a 1969 trip to Hollywood to convince moviemakers to consider Oklahoma as a shooting location. Courtesy Oklahoma Tourism and Recreation Department.

George, left, welcomes to Oklahoma Dan Rowan and Dick Martin, hosts of the popular television show *Rowan and Martin's Laugh In*.

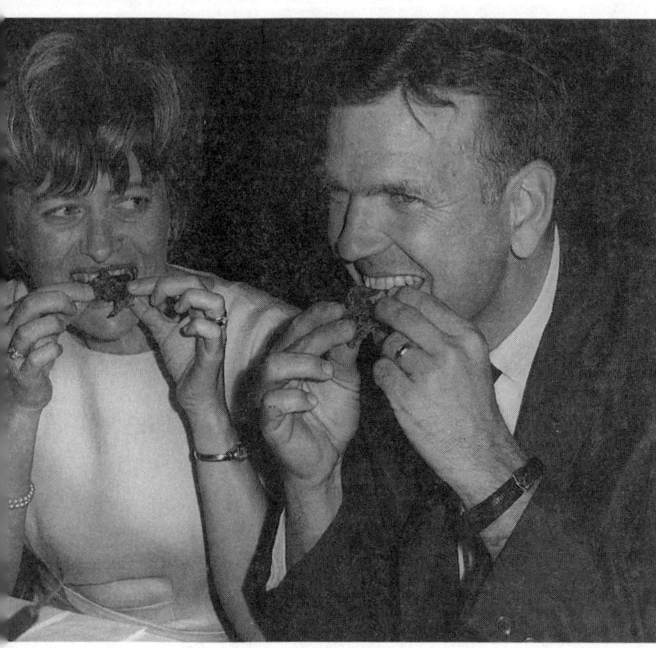

Part of the job of a lieutenant governor was to appear at the hundreds of local celebrations held each year in Oklahoma. In 1968, George and Donna tried fried rattlesnake at the world-famous rattlesnake hunt at Okeene. Courtesy International Association of Rattlesnake Hunters.

During a 1969 joint session of the legislature, George, left, talks with Senate President Pro Tempore Finis Smith of Tulsa and House Speaker Rex Privett of Pawnee.

of his "eating crow." George also smoked a peace pipe during the event with a local newspaper publisher.[13]

George began calling on California movie-makers to ask them why they did not film in Oklahoma. Their answer was simple, no one had told them about Oklahoma. George enlisted the aid of 120 volunteer Oklahomans who flew to Hollywood to spread the word. The invasion and propaganda effort worked. *J. W. Coop,* a movie starring Cliff Robertson; *Welcome Home Soldier Boy,* produced for Twentieth Century Fox; Universal Studio's *Two Lane Blacktop;* and *The Only Way Home,* produced by Washita Films, were filmed primarily in Oklahoma.

Armed with information of the positive economic impact of tourism in Oklahoma, George renewed his efforts to convince citizens of surrounding states to spend their weekends and vacations in Oklahoma. On the way home from a tourism meeting, the idea of splitting Oklahoma into tourism "countries" was born. George and Donna unfolded an Oklahoma road map and the two of them divided the state into six regional "countries": Red Carpet Country, Great Plains Country, Frontier Country, Green Country, Lake Country, and Kiamichi Country. The promotional program, called "Oklahoma—State of Many Countries," was patterned after a most successful private promotional effort by civic and government leaders in northeastern Oklahoma called Green Country.

This concept attracted national attention and several states adopted similar efforts and placed their lieutenant governor in charge, referring to the idea as "The Oklahoma Plan."

Also under George's leadership, the state lodges were renovated and tourist centers were built along Oklahoma's major highways and interstates to provide information to travelers about nearby special state places and events.[14] As Oklahoma moved into the top ten states in the nation in attracting tourism, *The Daily Oklahoman* commented that George had "certainly changed the previously inconsequential and unassuming role"[15] of the Oklahoma lieutenant governor's office. By 1970, visitors were spending hundreds of millions of dollars each year at Oklahoma tourist attractions and special events.

Teaming with a New Governor

The trouble with a politician's life: somebody is always interrupting it with an election.

Will Rogers

George decided early in 1970 that he would follow his principle of not running against an incumbent governor, a principle that served him well. Governor Bartlett announced he would attempt to become the first governor to succeed himself since voters had amended the constitution to allow such a feat. George told a news conference in January, 1970, that he would be a candidate for re-election.

George had unanimous support from Oklahoma's Democratic congressional delegation. For one reason, George and fellow Democrats agreed on major issues. A second reason for the delegation's support was George's secret weapon. He privately and publicly told members of the Oklahoma delegation that he was not interested in running for an office that would move him to Washington, D.C., a pledge that George kept throughout his political career.[1]

In the Democratic primary, George rolled over his lone opponent, Jack K. Gillespie of Oklahoma City, 299,152 to 63,880. Former Tulsa County County Attorney David Hall won the Democratic nomination for governor in a tough runoff with Oklahoma City attorney Bryce Baggett.

Oklahoma City attorney and State Representative Ralph G. Thompson was the Republican nominee for lieutenant governor.

George and Donna campaigned by airplane across Oklahoma in 1970. Donna often remarked that she got off the airplane first, to "check for land mines." During the campaign they guarded their roles as active parents and taught the senior high Sunday School class at Council Road Baptist Church.

By 1970, George's name was well-known enough in Oklahoma for campaign billboards to just say "NIGH." It was Marty Hauan's idea to print the posters in reverse black and white, a big saving over expensive color posters.

Thompson was an excellent campaigner, the son of well-known Republican Lee Thompson, and grandson of former University of Oklahoma President Dr. William Bennett Bizzell. Incumbent Governor Bartlett and Thompson ran as a team, taking a page from George's playbook, emphasizing the need for the governor and lieutenant governor to be from the same party, to work together as the president and vice president of the nation did. George and Bartlett were living proof of the difficulties of being teamed with a governor of a different party and political philosophy.

As usual, the state's largest newspapers split their editorial influence. The *Tulsa World* endorsed Hall and George. *The Daily Oklahoman*, on the other hand, urged continuation of the eight years of Republican rule in the governor's office, and picked up on the team concept being ballyhooed by the Bartlett-Thompson camps. The editorial in *The Sunday Oklahoman* two days before the election was powerful:

> Oklahoma has been fortunate that feuds between governors and lieutenant governors of different parties have not developed on a more regular basis. However, the decision of Governor Bartlett and State Representative Ralph Thompson, nominee for lieutenant governor, to campaign as a team offers Oklahoma voters a chance to establish in practice what many feel will eventually be the law of the state. Thompson is a man of considerable legislative experience and has worked closely with the governor in developing his programs. The team idea is a good one...
>
> Bartlett deserves the assistance, in the legislature and in his absence on official state business, of a lieutenant governor, dedicated to the same goals he is working toward as chief executive. Ralph Thompson should be elected to serve with Governor Bartlett for the next four years.[2]

George agreed with the idea that the constitution should be changed so contenders for governor and lieutenant governor could run as a team, from the same political party. However, he told voters they could do the same and elect two Democrats. And that's what the voters did.

George went on daytime television to stretch his campaign advertising budget. He scheduled four 30-minute shows, called *George and Donna Nigh Coffees*, between 9:30 A.M. and 11:00 A.M. on television stations in Ada, Lawton, Tulsa, and Oklahoma City. George mailed appeals to 7,500 supporters, requesting them to ask 10 neighbors to a neighborhood coffee to watch the television shows, reminiscent of George's early campaigns in which coffees were held to address postcards to potential voters.

In one of the most unusual display of support in Oklahoma political history, more than 200 newspaper editors in the state announced their support for George's re-election bid. Larry Hammer, editor and publisher of the *Fairview Republican,* was chairman of the group of editors. Members of the executive committee were James C. Nance, Purcell; Jim Pate, Madill; Ben Langdon, Mangum; Fred Turner, McAlester; Bob Peterson, Durant; August Stoll, Garber; Jack Christy, Waukomis; and Larry Wade, Elk City.

On November 3, 1970, in a major upset that shattered all predictions, Hall defeated Bartlett to become the state's 19th governor, ending eight years of Republican rule. Hall, the 40-year-old silver-haired underdog, rode a tide of rural support to the surprise victory. After a recount, Hall's margin of victory was slightly more than 2,000 votes of nearly 700,000 votes cast.

On the other hand, the prediction that George would garner more votes than Hall proved correct. George defeated Thompson, 382,249 to 270,535. They remained close friends even after battling for the lieutenant governor's job. Thompson later was appointed United States District Judge for the Western District of Oklahoma by President Ronald Reagan.

In a post-victory celebration visit with reporters at the Lincoln Plaza Hotel in Oklahoma City, George attributed his impressive win to his travels trying to sell Oklahoma. George was 43 years old, actually older than Governor-Elect Hall, certainly a new position for George, who had always been younger than everyone else.

George saw his re-election as the people's approval of his efforts. George promised, "I'll give them four more years of going anywhere to promote Oklahoma. Oklahoma's good to me and I'll try to be good to it."[3] George immediately launched a new promotional program called "Think Oklahoma."

George's relationship with Governor-Elect Hall was excellent. There was absolute cooperation between the Hall and Nigh campaign staffs to plan both the transition into office and inaugural activities. Hall told George he wanted him to be an active lieutenant governor, a vital part of his administration.[4]

George and Donna are all smiles after hearing early returns at the Nigh watch party in November, 1970, at the Lincoln Plaza Hotel in Oklahoma City.

George stepped up Oklahoma's efforts to attract movie-makers to Oklahoma. He used friendships with Oklahoma actors such as James Garner and producer Gray Frederickson to set up movie seeking trips to Hollywood. George was even dubbed as "Hollywood George" by *The Daily Oklahoman.*

A major plank in Governor Hall's successful campaign had been the promise of a stepped-up effort to attract industrial development and tourism in Oklahoma. George, who had preached that sermon for 20 years, offered his complete cooperation to Hall. In April, 1971, George chaired a series of community forums in ten cities in Oklahoma to give citizens an opportunity to assist in planning the state tourism program.

George told a meeting of local business leaders in Shawnee that promotion was the key. He said, "You can build a better mousetrap, but you have to advertise it. We must continue to make Oklahoma a place to go to, not through."[5]

George, right, at the groundbreaking of a new production plant for Highland Supply Corporation at Hobart, Oklahoma, in 1970. Left to right, Erwin Weder, president of Highland, an Illinois company; Illinois Congressman Philip Crane; and George. The Weders were introduced to George by friends John and Nellie Perry of Hobart who managed George's campaigns in Kiowa County.

The tourism community forums, instituted by Governor Hall, were held in Shawnee, Guymon, Fairview, Talihina, Lawton, Clinton, and at states lodges at Western Hills State Park, Fountainhead, and Lake Texhoma. Three-hour morning and afternoon sessions were moderated by George, with participation by local and state experts on attracting out-of-staters to Oklahoma destinations.

On June 4, 1971, George was addressing a downtown Oklahoma City luncheon honoring Congressman Wilbur Mills of Arkansas with Governor Hall in attendance. While George was in the middle of his speech at a restaurant in the Skirvin Tower, Oklahoma Highway Patrol troopers began circling the room. George, as lieutenant governor, was not provided security so he assumed the troopers were there to protect the governor. He cut short his speech and was surprised as Hall and Congressman Mills left the restaurant and the troopers encircled him. George was informed that a threat had been made on his life. An anonymous male caller had phoned the lieutenant governor's office with a chilling message: "Nigh will be killed at 3:00 P.M."

It was not the first nor last time that George's life was threatened. As was his normal procedure, he had no public comment about the threat.[6]

On June 20, George was the guest on the state's most listened-to interview show, *Headliners,* broadcast on KTOK Radio in Oklahoma City and 47 stations of the Oklahoma News Network. George told interviewers Tracy Rowlett and Doug Fox that Oklahoma must do more to compete with states like Texas for the tourism dollar. George said, "Man has more money and more time to his leisure, and more wheels to make him mobile, so he wants to get out and spend that time and that money." "The tourist and recreation business," he continued, "is the fastest growing industry in the world. You can't pick up any periodical or look at any television show that is not talking about places to go or things to do. Oklahoma can expect some increase just by being here but we will not get our fair share until we spend adequate money to compete on a level with our neighbor to the south."[7]

In the fall of 1971, George's secretary, Glenna Hunt, resigned. Betty Price, who regularly filled in for Glenna, suggested to her friend Margaret Hall that she apply for the position. Margaret, who had worked as a secretary for the House of Representatives and a private law firm, had no desire to leave her present job but agreed with Price that she should at least take advantage of the opportunity to interview with the lieutenant governor.

George quizzed Margaret on dozens of unrelated topics during the interview. She left George's office thinking he was a nice man but surely she would not be hired. A day later, George's administrative assistant, Carl Clark, called Margaret and offered her the job. Thinking she "would do it just for awhile," Margaret accepted. She left George's office 16 years later, only when George retired from politics.

Margaret prepared the budget, paid bills, kept up with George's schedule, and maintained records regarding his speaking tours. From the very beginning Margaret was aware of George's great love for Oklahoma. She recalled, "There's not a part of Oklahoma that he did not know something about. I saw him as an incredibly eager and talented person who wanted to make this state look good."[9]

As the 1972 session of the Oklahoma legislature convened, Governor Hall, at George's request, proposed a constitutional amendment that would require the governor and lieutenant governor to run as a team. The proposal provided that, after party primaries, the nominees for the two top spots in state government appear on the same ballot, eliminating the possibility of electing a governor from one party and a lieutenant governor from another, as has happened twice in state history.The bill also provided for the replacement of the lieutenant governor if he should leave office before the end of his term.

The proposed constitutional amendment never made it through the legislature. The main reason was that the lieutenant governor, who constitutionally was the president of the Senate, would become a running mate with the governor, to some, a clear invasion of the separation of powers between the legislative and executive branches. George offered a solution, suggesting that the amendment require the governor and lieutenant governor to run as a team but remove the lieutenant governor as president of the Senate. No agreement was reached and the proposal was never submitted to a vote of the people.

As part of George's efforts to enlarge the role of the lieutenant governor, he suggested, and Hall agreed, to ask the legislature to divide the responsibilities of the Oklahoma Industrial Development and Park Department into two separate state agencies, one to promote industrial development and the other to guide the state's park and lodge system and promote tourism.

George aggressivly lobbied for passage of the bill. As chairman of the Industrial Development and Park Commission, he had traveled to many states seeking industry. However, he had always believed that prospective new industry presidents and chief executive officers really wanted to talk to the governor, not the lieutenant governor, about coming to Oklahoma. The leaders of companies needed commitments from the top official who could pledge support for roads, tax-breaks, and other advantages businesses searched for before making a final decision about the location of a new plant or business.[10]

The 1972 legislature agreed and abolished the Industrial Development and Park Department and its governing commission. To replace the old agency, the legislature created the Oklahoma Tourism and Recreation Department, with the lieutenant governor as its permanent chairman. The Oklahoma Department of Industrial Development was made a part of the governor's office. Commissions were created for both agencies with members appointed by the governor and confirmed by the Senate.

The new tourism and recreation agency was responsible for 21 state parks, 17 recreational areas, several museums, Fountainhead, Arrowhead, Western Hills, Roman Nose, Lake Murray, and Texhoma lodges, and a new lodge being built at Quartz Mountain State Park in southwest Oklahoma.

I Love Oklahoma

Oklahoma is more than just another state. It is a lens in which the long rays of time are focused into the brightest light. In its magnifying clarity, dim facets of the American character stand more clearly revealed. For in Oklahoma all the experiences that went into the making of the nation have been speeded up. Here all the American traits have been intensified. The one who can interpret Oklahoma can grasp the meaning of America in the modern world.

Angie Debo

Statistics from the early 1970s showed more and more people traveling through Oklahoma, largely because three major interstate highways, I-35, I-44, and I-40, crisscrossed the state. However, George was concerned that most people passing through were not stopping. He believed if motorists only knew the pearls of Oklahoma, they would stop and spend time, and money.

In April, 1972, George dedicated five new tourist centers, all in one day. He began the ribbon-cutting at 9:00 a.m. at the newly completed Blackwell center on I-35 in far northern Oklahoma. Ninety minutes later, he was in Miami, to dedicate the tourist center serving drivers along the Will Rogers Turnpike.

The third leg of the all-day jaunt carried George to Sallisaw, where limited services had been provided at a tourist center on I-40 since the year before. At 2:30 P.M. George was in Colbert to officially open the center on U.S. 69-75 highways. From there George flew to Thacker-

ville to survey the facilities of the tourist center on I-35. George was accompanied on his 1,000-mile journey by state tourism public information officer Harry Wilson.

The new tourism information centers moved Oklahoma up a step in its battle with neighboring states such as Arkansas and Texas who already operated such centers. Oklahoma added two more centers, in Erick and Lawton, within the next two years.

George continuously looked for other ways to get the word out about Oklahoma. *Oklahoma Today,* the official magazine of the Oklahoma Department of Tourism and Recreation Department, edited by Bill Burchardt, was one of the best state publications in the nation, considered second only to *Arizona Highways* in professional content and appearance. One Oklahoma newspaper editor, Milt Phillips of the *Seminole Producer,* lauded George for his promotional efforts and urged the lieutenant governor to encourage the staff of *Oklahoma Today.* Phillips wrote, "George Nigh will have an enormously popular tool with which to work in developing Oklahoma tourism with the *Oklahoma Today* Magazine."[1]

George was hobbled following a round of tennis in 1972. He pulled a muscle and ligament and ruptured a blood vessel in his foot. Courtesy *The Daily Oklahoman.*

George presides over a joint session of the Oklahoma legislature in 1973, flanked by Governor David Hall, left, and House Speaker William "Bill" Willis of Tahlequah. Courtesy *The Daily Oklahoman.*

The month of May, 1972, like most Mays in the many years of George's service, was devoted primarily to commencement addresses. George told 304 graduating seniors at Edmond Memorial High School, "The world is really yours. Tomorrow is yours, the future is yours. I can remember speaking at many senior commencements but the one I remember best was at Weatherford High School."

George continued, "That night as I went to the podium a full harvest moon was in the sky. I looked at the moon and realized that astronaut Tom Stafford, a native of the town where I was speaking, was headed home and was somewhere between us and that moon. That night I told those seniors that they, too, could do anything they put their mind to."[2]

As an example to all state agencies, Oklahoma hosted the annual meeting of the nation's lieutenant governors in 1972. George had lobbied his fellow lieutenant governors for years for the opportunity to show off Oklahoma.

Oklahoma Indian maiden, Princess Wa-le-lah (Jody McCrary) of Warner, presided over the opening presentation of the 1972 National Lieutenant Governor's Conference at Fountainhead Lodge on Lake Eufaula. The princess crowned George as Chief Afanchkuse Eapayah, meaning great leader. Courtesy *The Daily Oklahoman.*

Upon arriving at Fountainhead Lodge on Lake Eufaula for the August 9-13 event, each lieutenant governor was presented an Indian chief's headdress and an Indian name signifying something important about his home state.

The lieutenant governors were treated to some of the world's tastiest Italian food in nearby Krebs, known far and wide for its superb Italian cuisine. Bill Pritchard of Pete's Place, Dom Giacomo of the Isle of Capri restaurant, and the owners of Minnie's restaurant prepared the palate-tempting surprises for the visiting dignitaries.

To promote a different image, George planned an Oklahoma beach party. The Oklahoma Houseboat Association, under the leadership of Slim Blalock of Oklahoma City, provided boats for a cruise around Lake Eufaula. The flotilla, each houseboat bearing the banner of its guest state, beached on a scenic cove for a luau-style party.[3]

The national meeting of lieutenant governors also featured an air show, with parachute jumpers, and a barbecue, followed by a performance of the Trail of Tears drama at Tahlequah.

Following the national lieutenant governors conference, George agreed to become state campaign director for Congressman Ed Edmondson's bid for the United States Senate seat after Fred Harris' decision not to run for re-election. Harris had defeated Edmondson's brother, Howard, six years before. Ed Edmondson defeated 10 opponents in the Democratic primary but faced stiff opposition from former Governor Dewey Bartlett in the general election.

George assumed control of campaign operations in the Edmondson state headquarters while Donna coordinated special missions of Edmondson volunteers. Edmondson's son, James, concentrated on field work in the state's 77 counties.

Republican State Chairman Clarence Warner denounced Nigh's involvement in the Edmondson campaign, calling on George to forfeit "his state salary, his state-owned car, and his large expense account." George assured voters that his efforts for Edmondson would in no way detract from his pledge of being a full-time lieutenant governor. George told reporters, "It is every man's right to volunteer his extra time for a cause in which he believes."[5]

Warner also demanded that George's chief aide, Carl Clark, be removed from the state payroll and that Edmondson campaign staffers be barred from George's state office. George laughed at the Republican Party challenge to a Democrat office holder supporting another Democrat and simply pointed out all the incumbent Republicans who supported other Republicans. It turned out to be a non-issue. George took great care to keep separate his official duties as lieutenant governor and his efforts for Edmondson who lost the November election to Bartlett.

George's personal knowledge of the layout of the state penitentiary in McAlester proved valuable to Governor Hall in July, 1973, when 20 prison officials were taken hostage during a riot. More than 1,000 national guardsmen, state troopers, and local police officers surrounded the prison compound and waited for word from the governor's office.

Governor Hall, who made an emergency flight back to Oklahoma from Denver, Colorado, set up a command post in his State Capitol office. George was present to interpret maps of the penitentiary. When inmates phoned their grievances to the governor, George was able to pinpoint their location inside the penitentiary walls. After hours of negotiation, the hostages were released. However, the riot was the worst in state history. Three inmates were killed by other inmates, 20 people were injured, and fires caused $20 million in damage.

George dutifully went about his business promoting tourism. In 1973 the tourism industry contributed $500 million to the state economy, a $50 million annual increase over two years before.[6] Speaking to a Yukon Rotary Club, George pointed out that getting ten people per night to stay in Yukon was equivalent to a $100,000 annual payroll to the community.[7] George also announced that $1 million had been spent shooting two movies, *Oklahoma Crude* and *Dillinger,* on location in Oklahoma.

When a newspaper editor accused George of wasting taxpayers money by flying a state airplane from Oklahoma City to an appearance in nearby Guthrie, George set the record straight. He would have never taken a plane for such a short trip, he wrote, but was forced to use the quickness of flight to make four state appearances that day. He had an Oklahoma Aeronautics Commission luncheon in El Reno at noon, a 2:00 P.M. speech at a Guthrie radio station, a late afternoon dedication of the new Ethan Allen manufacturing plant in Atoka, and a banquet that evening back in Oklahoma City.[8]

In June, 1973, rumors were rampant that George might retire from politics. Indeed, George and Donna had talked many times about retiring from the public spotlight. George admitted to a Tulsa reporter that he had told some of his closest supporters that he would not run again, saying, "If the election were tomorrow, I would not run." [9]

The election was still a year away and George kept open his options. Some Democrats urged him to oppose Oklahoma Sixth District Congressman John N. "Happy" Camp. That prospect was attractive to top Democrats because George traditionally polled more votes than any other Democrat in any race. George would have been able to run in the Sixth District because legislators had previously intentionally included his residence in the district. What the legislature did not realize was that Camp was one of George's closest friends and George would have not run against the incumbent congressman under any circumstance. Later, Camp, a Republican, supported George in his bid for the governor's office.

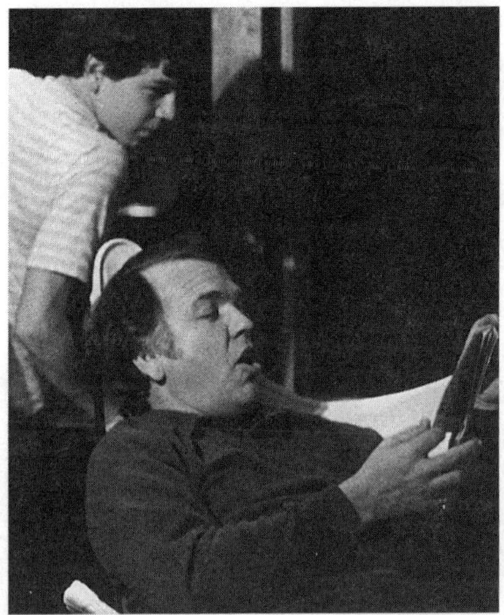

George singing Christmas carols with John Randall Price, at the home of close friends Norris and Betty Price. When the youngster was critically injured in a motorcycle accident in 1975, George and Donna spent countless hours at Midwest City Hospital. Often George spent the entire night beside Randy who tragically died shortly before his 18th birthday in November, 1975.

George was 46 years old, a veteran of 20 years in public office and countless days and months of tiring campaigns. However, by the time other candidates were sorting out their options, George decided, with Donna's full support, to run for lieutenant governor again.

In February, 1974, an *Oklahoma Journal* editorial, with a headline of "Stay in There, George," urged George to "wash out of his mind" any thought of quitting or "withholding his services from the state he has served so well."[10]

As a national energy crisis gripped America in 1974, George went on the attack to preserve Oklahoma's vital tourism industry. Citing figures that showed tourism generated $500 million annually in the Sooner State, George lobbied federal energy officials to develop conservation measures and a national energy policy that recognized the needs of the tourism industry. George said, "Oklahoma is not going to sit idly by and allow a $500 million industry to be destroyed."[11]

By 1974, annual tourism expenditures in the United States topped $70 billion, exceeded in retail expenditures only by grocery store sales. The tourism industry employed 3.5 million workers, almost five percent of the nation's civilian work force.[12]

Georgeann accompanied George once on an official visit to the Great Salt Plains in Red Carpet Country. George promised Georgeann that she could hide Easter eggs sometime that afternoon. During the trip, Georgeann announced, "Daddy, I want you to hide the eggs right here." George hesitated because his car was in a caravan of officials. However, Georgeann reminded her father, "You promised." George, being a good daddy, stopped the official caravan and hid easter eggs for his daughter.

George found an ally in the fight to save the tourism industry in Duke R. Ligon, an Oklahoman who had been appointed assistant administrator of the Federal Energy Office. Ligon agreed with George that travel connected with tourism was a minor factor in gasoline consumption in the United States. In 1972, transportation from tourism had accounted for only about 12 percent of the total national demand for petroleum fuel.[13]

Honorariums for out-of-state speaking engagements supplemented George's annual state salary of $18,000. George called his after-dinner speaking his "hobby" and "an additional tool used to sell Oklahoma."[14]

George never took money for a speech regarding policy matters or his role as lieutenant governor. He also declined invitations which would keep him away from his official government duties. George became so well-known as a convention speaker that he was listed in a book of select lecturers and entertainers by a prominent national booking agency. Others on the list included political columnist Jack Anderson; psychologist Joyce Brothers; seeress Jeane Dixon; television celebrity Art Linkletter; and radio commentator and fellow Oklahoman, Paul Harvey.[15]

In April, 1974, George announced an Oklahoma tourism mission to Germany and the Netherlands. State school children responded with letters, recommending ways George could promote the state's assets. Students in Betty Hefner's third grade class at Central Elementary School in Tulsa sent letters to George. One third grader wrote, "Dear Mr. Nigh... When you go to Germany tell the people to come to Oklahoma to see our lakes and wheet [sic] and cattle and our schools and pones [sic]... Yours truly, Kim Smith." Another letter said, "Tell them to come see our state flower is a misseltone [sic]. They really ought to see the lands and the oil wells and the Redbud trees and Dogwood tours [sic]." Another child wrote, "Tell them we got fly-tail sizzor [sic] catchers and tell them we're friendly."[16] Despite the misspellings, the students' enthusiastic support was evident for George's trip to Europe, a trade mission sponsored by *Pulse* Magazine.

THE 1974 CAMPAIGN

I'm not trying to break Jim Berry's record for longevity as lieutenant governor. It's just my feeling that the incumbent lieutenant governor should not run against the incumbent governor, regardless of party.

GEORGE NIGH

FOLLOWING IN HIS TIME-HONORED POLICY that as lieutenant governor, he would never run against an incumbent governor of either party running for re-election, George would have no part in the scramble for the Oklahoma governor's mansion in 1974. To keep down any speculation and send the right message to potential opponents, he announced early his intention to run for re-election as lieutenant governor.

Governor Hall, facing major hurdles in his bid to be renominated and re-elected, nevertheless was optimistic about his chances. He was fairly popular with voters, having achieved most of his campaign promises, including tax reform. Although his Freeway 77 road building-bond proposal was defeated, Hall had pushed through a successful education program.

Hall was considered likely for a second term until newspapers announced in May, 1973, that the governor had been under investigation by the Internal Revenue Service since 1971. In 1973, two state grand juries returned indictments against several of Hall's aides and supporters for alleged kickbacks from state building contracts. None of those indicted were ever convicted.

Above: Donna and George visit with Hollywood producer Al Ruddy and actress Kim Darby, right, at a special Hollywood world premiere of *True Grit,* an Oscar-winning John Wayne movie set in historic southeastern Oklahoma.

As usual, the 1974 campaign brought out thousands of volunteers, including some of the Nigh's neighbors on Picnic Lane. Left to right, Patty Bricker, Donna, George, and Martha Dickerson. Other Nigh neighbors active in the campaign were Bud Bricker, Bill Dickerson, Ken and Delores Carlson, and Jay and Jimmie Schick.

Facing page: George took time out from the 1974 campaign to make his annual appearance at Girls State. Standing, fifth from the right, is Susan Ferrell, the daughter of Don and Sally Ferrell. Tragically, Susan was one of the 168 victims of the Alfred P. Murrah Federal Building bombing in Oklahoma City on April 19, 1995. Courtesy Don and Sally Ferrell.

However, a federal grand jury began investigating the alleged kickbacks, an action that tainted Hall's re-election efforts.[1]

Oklahoma Attorney General Larry Derryberry also began a probe of the allegations.

In April, 1974, Derryberry asked the legislature to impeach Hall. However, a special committee of the House of Representatives found no evidence sufficient to warrant impeachment action at that time.

Hall was faced by two other strong Democrats in the 1974 primary. Second District Congressman Clem McSpadden of Oologah, a nephew of Will Rogers, and nationally-known rodeo announcer, was an attractive candidate who drew much of his support from members of the Oklahoma Senate, where he had served as President Pro Tempore.

The third major Democrat to make the run for governor in 1974 was David L. Boren, a six-year veteran of the Oklahoma House of Representatives. Boren, son of former Congressman Lyle H. Boren, who represented Oklahoma's Fourth District in the 1930s and 1940s, was unknown statewide before an 18-month tour of all 77 counties with his "Broom Brigade," signifying a new broom sweeping clean the state. Brooms posted in storefronts, sticking from car windows, and hoisted by supporters at rallies broadened the public's awareness of Boren and his desire for a clean start for state government.

Boren's campaign was similar to other Oklahoma campaigns that featured a highly-recognized symbol, such as George's later use of white hats, J. Howard Edmondson's "prairie fire," and Henry Bellmon's "Bellmon Belles."

Hall campaigned hard, stressing issues of education and prison reform. He brought five out-of-state governors to Oklahoma to campaign for him and received endorsements from major labor and education leaders. However, his administration had become unpopular and he ran a poor third in the August primary. McSpadden led the field, with Boren 13,000 votes behind. Hall did not take sides in the runoff which was won by Boren.

Promising to "sweep out the old guard," and refusing to take contributions from anyone but relatives and private citizens, Boren sailed to a general election victory over Republican challenger James M. Inhofe, a member of the state senate from Tulsa. When Boren later retired from public office to become president of the University of Oklahoma, Inhofe replaced him in the United States Senate.

Six days after Hall left the governor's office he was indicted by a federal grand jury on four charges of extortion and bribery. Although he claimed he was innocent and the victim of a conspiracy, Hall was convicted a year later for bribery in connection with investment of state retirement funds. He served 18 months in a federal prison and moved his family to California upon his release.[2]

In the lieutenant governor's race, George was unopposed in the Democratic primary but faced Republican Ralph E. Drews of Oklahoma City in the general election. George easily defeated Drews, 545,686 to 208,445. Although George had served with Governor Hall for four years, Hall's demise in the eyes of the public had no appreciable effect upon George.

Two weeks after the election, the names of convicted killer J.C. Fast, Jr., and George were again linked in state newspaper headlines. In 1963, during his nine days as governor, George had paroled Fast, convicted of killing the father of Oklahoma City banker J.W. McLean in Muskogee County 37 years before.

With Governor Hall out of state, George signed a pardon for Fast, causing the *Tulsa Daily World* to demand an explanation. The newspaper said, "The question is whether a lieutenant governor should make substantive decisions in the absence of an emergency merely because he has the opportunity while serving as acting governor."[3]

George defended his signing of Fast's pardon because the state Pardon and Parole Board and Governor Hall's legal advisor, Dan Rambo, had recommended it. George also pointed out that Fast was near 70 years old and almost totally blind.

George was particularly sensitive about rumors that had surfaced from time to time that he sold paroles for $500 each. George said, "I only sign the ones the governor's legal aide gives me. I have never initiated any action on pardons or paroles while acting as governor."[4]

Just before Christmas, 1974, George moved into the newly-renovated lieutenant governor's office on the second floor of the Capitol. The six-room suite was dubbed "Nigh's new playboy pad" by Republican G.T. Blankenship. George, recognizing that Blankenship was looking for an issue to assist his race for Republican state chairman, issued a brief, two-sentence statement, "G.T. Blankenship and I have been personal friends for years. I wish him well in his race for state chairman of the Republican party."[5] The two men have remained close friends.

Dean Gandy, a native of North Carolina, began driving George around the state in 1972 while working for the Oklahoma Tourism Department as a Midwest City High School student. George, as lieutenant governor, did not have a driver until Boren became governor in 1975. George once asked Gandy, "Can you drive me to Enid tonight?" The trip went so well that George asked Gandy to drive him to Cleveland the next week. Gandy thought George was kidding about Cleveland, Ohio. The next thing he knew he was in a state car driving George to Cleveland, Oklahoma. George was immediately impressed with Gandy who spent much of the next two decades on George's staff, including a stint as chief legislative liaison.

George's former office on the fifth floor of the Capitol was converted for use by the legislature. His new space, adjacent to the governor's office, was renovated at a cost of $18,320 in space previously occupied by staff members of the Oklahoma Department of Education.

George enjoyed a solid working relationship with Governor Boren who sought input from George regarding major appointments affecting tourism. Abe Hesser was named executive director of the state tourism department and Chris Delaporte was hired as director of the state parks division.

George and Donna's families turned out in great numbers for George's 1975 inauguration. Left to right, standing, George; Donna; Raphael Skinner, Donna's father; Jana Davis, Donna's niece; Mike Mashburn; Ann Davis, Donna's sister; cousin Helen Nigh; Alexis Rogers; Sam Nigh. Sitting, left to right, Georgeann Nigh; Ruby Skinner, Donna's stepmother; George's Aunt Bernadine and Uncle Sam Nigh; and Esther Nigh.

Right: Carl Clark became George's administrative assistant in the lieutenant governor's office. Clark later was George's chief of staff in the governor's office. The addition of Clark gave George a valuable link to the Oklahoma congressional delegation. Clark had previously served on the staff of United States Senator Fred Harris. Courtesy Fred Marvel.

Below: George's staff in the lieutenant governor's office and the tourism commission office. Left to right, Dean Gandy, Tom Grey, Mary K. Foster, Nancy Ivans, George, and Margaret Hall.

George, as chairman of the Tourism and Recreation Commission, hosted an annual state tourism conference and traversed the state and nation with his message about Oklahoma destinations. He developed, with Boren's approval, Youth Conservation Corps projects, utilizing federal money to provide employment for youngsters in state parks and recreation areas.

By 1975, the lieutenant governor had been assigned many additional duties and George presided over the state senate much less than his earlier years in office. However, he was available on occasion to break ties, a duty thrust upon the lieutenant governor by the constitution. When the vote on a bill allowing counties to round up stray dogs ended in a 24-24 tie, George was called to the floor. Learning of opposition from coonhunters who "thought the bill meant the end of Old Blue," George wisely left, saying, "I sure hope you get this worked out. But I've got a 2 P.M. meeting and have to run."[6] Newspaper reporter Howard Davis wrote, "Oklahoma is sure lucky to have in George Nigh a lieutenant governor who can think fast on his feet. Not all our public servants are quick enough to solve a constitutional crisis by simply walking out on it."[7]

The 1975 legislature appropriated $150,000 to the Tourism and Recreation Department to match local funds for such diverse events as the Kiamichi Owa-Chito Festival of the Forest at Beavers Bend State Park near Broken Bow and the cow-chip throwing contest at Beaver.

George had difficulty staying out of a fray between Boren and the legislature over state funding of such local events. Boren believed such events should be financed locally, not from state coffers. George, who was chairman of the Tourism Commission, supported the merits of local tourism events, saying, "Who can say that a cow-chip throwing contest at Beaver is not as great to them as the Stars and Stripes show in Oklahoma City?"[8]

George recognized that his efforts to boost tourism in Oklahoma were paying off. In 1974, 32 million people came to or through the state. There were 44 million visitor-days on lakes in Oklahoma operated by the United States Corps of Engineers. Seventeen movies had been made in the state during the first few years of the Tourism and Recreation Commission's attempts to lure movie makers. George told a chamber of commerce audience in Bartlesville, "You have to be proud when the top 10 metro areas in the nation are listed and Tulsa is ranked number two and Oklahoma City number nine as the best places to live. When you consider that Oklahoma's modern history is compressed into the lifespan of the memory of Oklahomans who are still living it is remarkable. I think the most dramatic change in our state is our people and their part in building a better Oklahoma."[9]

The role of the lieutenant governor was strengthened by a series of constitutional reforms successfully promoted in 1975 by Governor Boren. The state questions, approved by voters in a "Yes All Eight" campaign, made the lieutenant governor a member of the School Land Commission and Board of Equalization, while eliminating from the ballot the secondary offices of Chief Mine Inspector and Labor Commissioner, long the subject of criticism for becoming famous name races. Also, voters approved the elimination of the position of Commissioner of Charities and Corrections.

George, who intentionally did not participate in the Yes All Eight campaign because of the involvement of his office, applauded the approval of the state questions giving more power to the lieutenant governor. For the first time, the lieutenant governor had a say on setting property taxes and determining policy in the appropriations field. The equalization board decided how much money was available for the legislature to appropriate each year.

Under the constitutional change, George held a key position on the School Land Commission, setting policy on the leasing of thousands of acres of land owned by the state. The commission also made decisions on soil conservation and other practices involving the leasing to farmers.

The year of America's bicentennial celebration, 1976, was an active year for George. He appeared at dozens of bicentennial events. In February, while Governor Boren was in Washington, D.C., George proclaimed a day of prayer for rain in Oklahoma. A drought brought a constant threat of fire to homes, businesses, and wooded areas in the

George and Donna in their backyard at 8321 Picnic Lane in Oklahoma City. They described their home as "a great place to raise kids." An empty pasture across the road allowed Mike to have a horse. The pasture was owned by the Paynes, lovingly referred to as "Grandma" and "Pa-paw" by Mike and Georgeann.

state. George's proclamation read, "The strength of Oklahoma's economy depends largely on agriculture and much of Oklahoma's wheat crop has already been severely damaged and will be destroyed if rain does not fall soon. Oklahomans in times of great need have traditionally turned to God through prayer and sought His help and guidance." Oklahomans' prayers apparently worked. Within a week after the pray-for-rain proclamation, showers began to settle the dust of the parched earth.

In March, 1976, George told an audience in Guymon that tourism had become the third largest industry in Oklahoma, that "parks and recreational facilities are coming alive as Oklahoma emerges as one of the fastest growing tourism states."[11] George pointed to an article in *National Geographic* Magazine that said Oklahoma's license plates were wrong when they contained the words "Oklahoma is OK." The magazine said the license plate should read, "Oklahoma is Great."[12]

Also in March, George became one of the first public officials to endorse Democratic presidential hopeful Jimmy Carter of Georgia. George noted that Carter had outpolled Oklahoman Fred Harris in recent county Democratic conventions, saying "I am impressed with Governor Carter's experience as governor, his moderate position and his personal integrity. He can give this country the presidential leadership that we expect and need."[13] Carter went on to upset President Gerald Ford in the November general election. George's early endorsement of Carter led to a close relationship with the new president. That relationship brought unexpected federal funding later for the Centennial Expressway project in downtown Oklahoma City.

In May, 1976, in recognition of George's efforts to promote his home area of the state, the cities and counties of Kiamichi Country, in southeast Oklahoma, proclaimed June 11 as "George Nigh Day." Officials in McAlester, Wilburton, Hugo, Broken Bow, and Idabel rolled out the red carpet during the day-long celebration.

After United States House Speaker Carl Albert of McAlester announced he would not seek re-election in 1976, political prognosticators mentioned George as a possible successor. Even though George said he had no desire to go to Washington, the *Tulsa Daily World* reported, "A source close to Nigh said he has been thinking about it, particularly since receiving a deluge of calls after published reports he might be a candidate."[14] George was flattered by suggestions he would make a good congressman but he never seriously considered running for the Third District seat being vacated by his longtime friend and mentor, Albert.

In 1977, portions of western Oklahoma and many other states were again suffering drought conditions. Governor Boren appointed George to head a state drought task force to work with groups from other stricken states. George led the campaign for state and federal assistance for wheat farmers who not only were plagued by the lack of rain but by high production costs and low selling prices, resulting in an economic drought.[15] George was selected as chairman of the executive committee of the Western States Drought Task Force, assisting President Carter in development of plans for dealing with future droughts. George believed that it was imperative that states not wait to develop a plan of action until a drought became a disaster.

George, known forever in the public's eye for his youth, turned 50 in June, 1977. A huge birthday celebration was secretly planned for the south steps of the State Capitol. Attorney General Larry Derryberry, who served as master of ceremonies, wore undertaker's garb of a long black frock and a tall black stovehat and carried a shovel. Governor Boren designated the day "George Nigh Day."

Boren wore a black armband and heaped praise on George as "a wonderful man who has such a promising future behind him." Former House Speaker Carl Albert and dozens of state lawmakers and officials joined the crowd in singing "Happy Birthday" to the strains of a country and western band. A banner hung between two pillars read "Happy Semi-Centennial."[16]

Three dozen cakes fed the party-goers. One showed Nigh standing in a toilet. The lettering read, "Nigh is 50 and sinking fast." George surveyed the crowd, the cakes, and a collection of photos from his years in office and said, "I'm glad to be here. At 50 you're glad to be anywhere."[17]

Also in 1977, the people of Ponca City asked George and Donna to assist in fund raising activities to restore the Marland Mansion, the elegant home built by former Oklahoma governor and oil magnate

George escorts Lillian Carter, mother of the president, through a throng of well-wishers at the foot of the Pioneer Woman statue in Ponca City in April, 1979. Courtesy *The Daily Oklahoman.*

E.W. Marland. An annual Renaissance Ball was created, honoring an oil executive by induction into a hall of fame. Recognizing that the honor would most likely always go to a male, George and Donna suggested the presentation of an annual Pioneer Woman Award. The local Marland Mansion committee eagerly supported the idea and even authorized George and Donna to select the recipients of the award. In 1979, they chose Lillian Carter, the mother of President Carter and former Peace Corps volunteer.

The gracious Mrs. Carter stayed at the Skirvin Hotel in Oklahoma City the night before traveling to Ponca City. When George and Donna arrived at the hotel in the afternoon to pick up Mrs. Carter, she appeared in the lobby wearing a very wrinkled and damp evening gown. She related the story of bringing only one "outfit" from her home in Georgia and hanging it in the bath tub to rid it of wrinkles. However, the dress had fallen into the bathtub and was still wet. All the way to the airport "Miss Lillian," as she was fondly known to the nation, fanned her dress in front of the heater vents, attempting to dry the material. All the way to Ponca City in the private airplane of longtime friends Jerry and Vettye Morton of United Engines of Oklahoma City, Miss Lillian asked that the heat be turned on and continued her efforts to dry her gown. George assured her that "wet or dry" she fit into Oklahoma. He was right and she stole the evening.[18]

Miss Lillian's son, the President, was known for not drinking alcoholic beverages. At the mansion reception, George asked her if she wanted a drink, and quickly apologized, saying, "Oh excuse me, would you like a soft drink?" With a gleam in her eye, Miss Lillian told George, "Honey, you got the wrong Carter. I'll take a bourbon and branch water."[19]

Twenty years later former President Carter was invited to speak on the campus of Carl Albert Junior College in Poteau, Oklahoma. George and Donna were sitting in the audience when Carter spotted them and stopped mid-stream in his speech. He pointed to George and said, "There's George Nigh, my mother's favorite Oklahoman."[20] George says that to this day, from such a grand lady, that is as fine a compliment he could have.

Good Guy Nigh

The CIA probably will not classify the fact that George Nigh wants to be governor of Oklahoma as one of the best kept secrets of the year. In fact, it has been no secret that I've always wanted to be governor.

George Nigh

George's decision to run for governor in 1978 came after months of deliberation and waiting on two other candidates' decisions. The other candidates were United States Senator Dewey Bartlett and Governor David Boren.

Boren wanted to run for the United States Senate but did not cherish a head on race against incumbent Republican Senator Dewey Bartlett. Bartlett's health made the political picture cloudy. The former governor had been diagnosed with lung cancer in January, 1977. Two surgeries and extensive chemotherapy treatments weakened Bartlett, but many of his supporters thought he was strong enough to campaign for re-election.

On January 18, 1978, the dominoes began falling. Bartlett announced he would leave the Senate because of his fight against lung cancer. Boren telephoned George, who was in the middle of speech at the Hilton Inn West in Oklahoma City, and requested a quick meeting. Boren told George that he was running for the United States Senate.

Three days later, Boren publicly became a candidate for Bartlett's seat. Senator Bartlett lost his battle with cancer and died the following year.

No question about who John Reid was supporting for governor in 1978. Reid's license plate on his 1977 Toyota read "IM4NIGH." Reid, an Oklahoma City native, was hired by George in 1977 after submitting a near-obnoxious, yet eye-catching resume. George thought if Reid was that brazen he could handle public information in the lieutenant governor's office. Courtesy John Reid.

Donna was once again a faithful campaigner in 1978, reportedly drawing bigger crowds than George. Here she poses with Mrs. Ben Hill of Tulsa, the widow of a longtime Democratic legislator. Mrs. Hill served as a statewide official of George's campaign.

George's policy of not running against an incumbent governor would have forced him to run for re-election as lieutenant governor if Boren had chosen to run for a second term. However, Boren's decision to run for the Senate paved the way for George to run for governor and continue his life-long quest.

Before Boren decided to run for Bartlett's seat, George once again toyed with the idea of quitting politics. He believed that 1978 was the last time he could run for governor from his position as lieutenant governor. George reflected, "I could be a viable candidate in 1978, but not four or eight years later, should either Boren run for re-election or someone else become governor. If I served any longer as lieutenant governor, I would have been eternally tabbed as 'always the bridesmaid, never the bride.' "[1] At many functions, George was introduced as having been born lieutenant governor.

Before George had made a final decision to make a second run for the governor's office, he talked to Donna; Mike and Georgeann; his brothers, Bill, Sam, and Wib; his sister, Mary; and key supporters for all areas of the state. All agreed the time was right.

George again was the underdog in the race for the Democratic nomination for governor. Even before George announced, Attorney General Larry Derryberry, an Altus native and veteran of eight years in the Oklahoma House of Representatives and two terms as attorney general, had built a huge war chest to finance his campaign and had lined up support from many prominent Democrats and organizations who were uncertain what office George would eventually seek.

Derryberry had presumed that Boren would not seek re-election.With his head start, Derryberry had already locked up endorsements from the county officers association, the county superintendents association, the county commissioners association, the state labor organizations, vocational technical school leaders, the Oklahoma Wildlife Federation, and other politically active groups. In fact, the only major groups to support George were the informal association formed by the state's college and university presidents and the members of the Oklahoma Osteopathic Association.

George considered Derryberry an outstanding public official and his friend and regretted that they both wanted the same office at the same time.

The third candidate in the Democratic primary was another friend of both George and Derryberry, State Senator Bob Funston of Broken Arrow. Funston was well known in party and legislative circles, having served as state Democratic Party chairman.

To catch Derryberry, George decided upon a novel way to put his name on the ballot. He asked Jeannette Edmondson, the widow of for-

George and Donna and staff members pose with stacks of nomination petitions in July, 1979. Left to right, John Reid, Dean Gandy, Margaret Hall, Donna, Cindy Wegener, and Donna Dickerson.

mer Governor and United States Senator J. Howard Edmondson, to head a statewide petition drive for signatures to place George on the ballot. The method, which required signatures of two percent of the total votes cast in the previous general election, was allowed in the state constitution as an alternative to paying a cash filing fee, although only a handful of candidates had ever used it.

Jeannette Edmondson was the perfect person to be out front in the petition drive. After her husband's death, she and Donna had become close friends. George believed Jeannette and the Edmondson name would add a needed flair to his candidacy.

George's former landlady at the rooming house in Norman, Ma Richter, was the first to sign the petition in Cleveland County. It was Ma Richter who had told George 30 years before she would not have a quitter living in her house and who had taught him the words to "Life is Like a Mountain Railroad."

The campaign staff planned a public announcement of the success of the petition drive at a birthday rally at Chadick Park in McAlester, a few blocks from where George spent his childhood. Many press representatives from across the state were present when Jeannette and other campaign staff members declared the petition drive had reached, and exceeded, the required number of signatures.

There was much jubilation. However, later that evening, after the celebration ended, the staff discovered the original count was incorrect and that the effort was actually a few thousand signatures short.

George was visibly upset. He could imagine the fun the press and his opponents could have with this news. The next day an emergency meeting took place at the Nigh headquarters. Plans were laid to quickly and quietly make up the deficiency. With a concentrated effort, thousands of new signatures were obtained, without fanfare, within a few days.

When the petitions were filed, 72,000 Oklahomans had put their names on the line for George. But to prevent any chance of legal challenge, in case the new count was also wrong, George paid the customary filing fee and submitted the petitions to support his candidacy. George would not take a chance on his name not being on the ballot.[2]

Back in March, 1978, an incident at the State Capitol could well have spelled doom for George's candidacy. Governor Boren was in Washington, D.C., when 25 students from predominantly black Langston University decided to turn a peaceful sit-in into a blockade of entrances leading to the chambers of the House of Representatives.

The students insisted upon more funding for their school and apparently became dissatisfied with answers from legislators. Langston student body president William F. Strother led the demonstrators in taking over control of a corridor leading to the office of House Speaker William P. "Bill" Willis of Tahlequah. When Willis refused to talk further with the demonstrators, Strother said, "Then take us to jail."[3]

House members, especially Speaker Willis, were "incensed by this arrogance"[4] and demanded that George, as acting governor, take immediate action. Willis, who was separated from needed medication by the blockade, called George from the Speaker's desk and asked him to use state troopers to clear the chamber exits. Instead, George convinced student leaders to allow Willis's medicine to be delivered to him.

As there was no imminent threat that House members would be harmed, George moved slowly to avoid a violent confrontation. State troopers had reported to George the rumor that 1,000 demonstrators were gathered near the Capitol prepared to support the protesters. George believed the rumor was false, but directed troopers to check all major parking lots in the area that could accomodate that many people. As expected, the rumor proved to be untrue.

Behind the scenes, George desired to keep Governor Boren fully informed on events at the Capitol and telephoned Boren in Washington. After Boren was briefed, he expressed his full support of George's deliberate action, another example of their smooth and effective teamwork as governor and lieutenant governor.

George's patience turned out to be the best and wisest course of action. State troopers and other police officers, dressed in riot gear, covered all exits to the Capitol as George pleaded with the students to clear the aisle, allowing access to the House. When no one budged, George said, "You are forcing me to have you removed or arrested." [5] George told the students the choice was theirs, not his.

Eighty law enforcement officers began to methodically clear the halls and exits leading to the chamber. George's efforts were joined by Willis, speaking to the students one final time, pledging to work for more appropriations for Langston. The word from Willis and the threat of being hauled off to jail by George broke the sit-in. Only one student was arrested for slugging a state trooper.

Even though several House members chastised George for delaying police action, Governor Boren applauded George's handling of the crisis. George, rebutting his critics said, "Should I have called in storm troopers, cracked a few heads, and caused a race riot on national television?"[6] George had no desire to become the George Wallace of Oklahoma.

George's campaign team worried about fallout from the near riot of Langston students. Some newspapers questioned whether George was strong enough to lead the state. Other critics speculated that

George was dead as a candidate for governor. However, in retrospect, George apparently won support from John Q. Voter who appreciated his calm and deliberate approach that avoided major confrontation. Speaker Willis remained one of George's best friends and campaign supporters.

George went to work setting up a campaign organization. He was aided by excellent campaign treasurers, J.D. Helms and Bob Parks. Margaret Hall moved from the lieutenant governor's office to manage George's campaign schedule. Not every day was smooth. Margaret remembered when George called her at 5:00 A.M. from an Oklahoma City airport, asking, "Where's my plane?" George had arrived at the wrong airport. Across town, a supporter waited with his airplane idling, until George could be driven to the correct airport.[7]

Margaret, concerned about George flying with just any supporter who owned an airplane, developed her own screening system. When George handed her a piece of paper with the name and telephone number of a person who had offered the services of his airplane, Margaret carefully checked out the pilot and the type of airplane he or she flew.[8]

Meanwhile, Dean Gandy, Mary K. Foster, Cindy Wegener, Carl Clark, and John Reid held down the lieutenant governor's office until the campaign was up and ready to go. Then George's entire staff in the lieutenant governor's office was transferred to the campaign. Donna Dickerson, a neighbor from Picnic Lane, was employed as a secretary to work solely in and manage the lieutenant governor's office.

The separation of staff was yet another move by George to show voters that he would not use his position of lieutenant governor to assist his campaign. George even gave up his state salary and state car during the campaign. To this day George is convinced that giving up his salary did not gain him one vote but it at least made it a non-issue.

Robert White and Larry Wood were hired to direct George's campaign efforts. Other key people in the state headquarters were Jim and Madalynne Norick, Ted Combes, Carl Clark, Larry Brawner, Bob and Genny Carter, Shirley and Larry Cassil, Jack and Berma Craig, Jeannette Edmondson, Bill Crain, Del Cravens, Jim Echols, Bob and

Sharon Hodder, Delmas and Carol Ford, Bert Galloway, Ellen Garrett, Tom Kielhorn, Terry Linhart, Jay Mitchell, Crystal Mounts, Calvin and Mary Newsom, Steve Olim, Herb Pate, Sue Peck, Dan and Cindy Rambo, Pete Reed, Harold Rogers, Doug Sanderson, Bill and Marsha Shockey, Bob and Diane Wadley, Cindy Davis, Cindy Worley, Billie Worwag, Wayne Chandler, Bill and June Morgan, John Orr, Henry Roberts, Brad and Betty Ward, Norris and Betty Price, Pat Perry, Gary Jones, Sam Nigh, David Hudson, John and Shirlene Glenn, and Roger Sweeney.[9]

Early in the campaign, Derryberry labeled George as a good guy, too good to be a governor. Derryberry said, "If you want a good guy, vote for Nigh. If you want a strong governor, vote for me." The ploy worried George's closest advisors. In fact, George said, "It was eating our lunch."[10]

An emergency meeting was called. Afer a couple hours of discussion, George asked his campaign staff, "What's wrong with being a good guy? For 28 years I've been trying to build the voters' confidence by conducting myself in a manner of which they would be proud." Staff members agreed and pledged to make what was considered a negative a positive.

George recalled his first campaign, 28 years earlier, when his opponent in the House of Representatives race in Pittsburg County had said, "George is a fine boy and someday he'll be a fine man." In 1978, for a second time, someone was belittling him because he was a good person, a ploy that would surely backfire as it did in 1950.

As a direct response to Derryberry's charges, the good guy image became the Nigh campaign theme. The question arose, "What do good guys wear?" Thus came the now famous white hats, teeshirts, boots, and "Good Guy" caravans.

The first question of the new campaign theme was, "Where do Nigh's Good Guys get white hats?" The answer came from within the state campaign organization. George's state co-chairman, Pat Henry, and her husband, T. J. Henry, of Lawton, owned a chain of Gibson's retail stores and turned to their suppliers. The campaign staff was disappointed when they learned that white hats were produced seasonally. Assembly lines had been converted to make hats for other seasons. But Pat Henry would not be deterred. She asked a manufactuer, "How many hats do we have to buy to start up a new production line?" The magic number was 5,000, so that's how many hats the Nigh campaign ordered.

To establish a commitment to be made by supporters, the hats were not to be given away but sold to raise campaign funds. Henry flatly stated that any unsold hats would be retailed later in her stores in southwest Oklahoma even if took ten years to sell off the truckload of hats. She should not have worried because all of the hats were purchased by supporters within weeks. Hopes of campaign managers were buoyed by the fact that the 5,000 hats did not come close in meeting the demand of supporters who wanted to join Nigh's Good Guys.

The white hats became a symbol of George's campaign. Off went the business clothes and out came blue jeans, Nigh teeshirts, cowboy boots, and the Good Guy hats. In their new "uniforms" George and Donna and all the volunteers stood out at any political gathering.

It was a shrewd political maneuver that had a positive effect upon Oklahomans similar to that of David Boren's Broom Brigade four years earlier, when brooms, sticking out of car windows, reminded voters of Boren's candidacy.

Derryberry, age 39, was by far the best financed candidate in the election. The week before the August 22 primary, Derryberry reported contributions of $520,067, far ahead of George's total of $268,930.[11] Derryberry's fund-raising efforts were doubling those of George and his campaign.

Derryberry ran a classic high-visibility campaign, with hundreds of billboards and fence straddlers dotting the state. His heavy media budget financed a strong appeal to bloc voters. Derryberry won the backing of two additional strong factions, the political wing of the Oklahoma Education Association (OEA) and the leaders of the Oklahoma dry movement. In addition, his hard line on law and order won him support from many police and firefighter groups.

Funston provided the most provocative proposals of any of the three contenders, advocating liquor by the drink and pari-mutuel horse race betting. Funston also proposed that any future tax increase be submitted to a vote of the people, that current taxes be reduced by $23 million the following year, and that the state payroll be sliced by 10 percent.[12]

George based his grassroots campaign on support from rank and file voters and financial contributions from the business community. He limited cash contributions and announced he would report every single contribution, regardless of size, even though state law required only the reporting of contributions in excess of $200. George told contributors he wanted the whole state to know everybody who was supporting him financially. George said, “If you don’t want your neighbors to know you’re supporting me, don’t give me a penny.”

During 1978, as in all of his campaigns, George visited all of Oklahoma’s 77 counties to underscore his continued commitment to every section of the state. His campaign strategists developed a unique plan to prevent Derryberry from aggressively campaigning in eastern Oklahoma, where Democratic voters were concentrated, and the metropolitan areas of Tulsa and Oklahoma City. The Nigh forces launched an intensive campaign in Derryberry’s backyard in western Oklahoma. Jack Carter and Paul Davis stepped up activities in Comanche County. Supporters in Beckham and Kiowa counties increased their efforts on behalf of George. This additional Nigh campaign effort in western Oklahoma required Derryberry to spend more time and money in that part of the state to secure his home base, leaving less time for him to campaign across the state.

George stressed his 24 years of experience in state government and called for renewed efforts in economic development to combat what he believed were unacceptable rates of unemployment in Oklahoma. He called for stricter laws dealing with lawyer-legislators who practice before state boards and commissions, the reduction of classroom size in elementary schools, and beefing up of elementary counseling programs.

He was the only candidate in the race with a specific plan for improving Oklahoma’s highways, George told voters. He proposed spending nearly $27 million of new money in 1979 to update and repair the state’s aging road system. He also recommended $6 million in one-time grants of state money to cities and towns to help them repair winter-damaged streets. George knew from experience that the most frequent request a governor receives is for highway construction.

A solemn commitment was made to voters. No job, political appointment, nor stretch of highway would be promised until after the election. He even told his campaign staff members that their help in the campaign did not guarantee them a job in the administration.[13]

George was particularly disappointed that the OEA had not supported his candidacy, or at least remained neutral. As a former teacher, George was proud of his record of supporting a strong education program for Oklahoma. However, the OEA, based at least in part upon Derryberry's promise for a stronger teacher negotiations process in contract situations, backed the attorney general. Derryberry also won favor of the OEA for his support of proposals to permit teachers to retire with full benefits after 30 years, regardless of age, and to send most state funding back to local school districts with no strings attached.[14]

In addition to the endorsement, Derryberry had many fellow lawyers and now had some of the state's leading bankers behind him. But George had something probably more important. His 16 years of serving as lieutenant governor had led him to almost every local newspaper office in the state. One source said 213 of Oklahoma's 245 newspapers endorsed George.[15] Publishers remembered George's frequent visits to their communities and the good news he often brought about industrial development or tourism.

The man behind what Martin Hauan calls "a public relations miracle," the feat of getting so many of the state newspapers to endorse George, was Ben Langdon, himself a former publisher. Langdon button-holed colleagues in all 77 counties, asking for their endorsement of George.

Because both Derryberry and Funston were lawyers, George capitalized on the fears of many Oklahomans that a lawyer was the last person the state needed in the governor's mansion. The *Oklahoma Journal* asked, "Do you want a lawyer as governor? Half the Oklahoma Senate is now lawyers. Elect another in this race and lawyers would dominate the legislative, judicial, and executive branches. What then happens to the cherished divisions of power in state government? We think it would be too much lawyer control."[16]

Derryberry continued to hit hard, accusing George of carelessly granting paroles and pardons while serving as acting governor during absences of the governor. Derryberry charged that what he called "loose practices" on pardons and paroles were responsible for a rising crime rate, such as the well-publicized Sirloin Stockade murders in Oklahoma City.[17]

George criticized Derryberry's inactivity on utility matters during his eight years as attorney general and questioned Derryberry's promises to support binding arbitration and the right to strike by teachers in exchange for support of the OEA.

The primary campaign went down to the wire with most political experts predicting that George was the front-runner, but only by a razor-thin margin over Derryberry. Funston, one newspaper said, was the uncertainty in the race, and was sure to force a runoff between George and Derryberry.[18]

George listens to campaign chairman Loyd Benefield, left, during the 1978 race. Looking on are former Governor Raymond Gary and media expert Martin "Marty" Hauan, the only man in state history to serve as press secretary to two governors. Courtesy *The Daily Oklahoman.*

A wildly cheering band of Nigh supporters talked, sang, and danced at the Hilton Inn West in Oklahoma City on election night, August 22, waiting for George and Donna to arrive from Tulsa, where other supporters had gathered.

A hush fell over the watch party early in the evening when the crowd heard television reports of an attempt on Derryberry's life in Tulsa. A man fired red paint cartridges from a rusty pistol and splattered Derryberry's neck. Derryberry was not injured but his wife, Gale, was alarmed when she saw what looked like blood on her husband's neck.

Nigh supporters, wearing black and white teeshirts announcing "Nigh Time" crowded around television sets. When they learned Derryberry was safe, Nigh followers "reverted to their mood of jubilation."[20]

Supporters cheered when they saw on live television George and Donna, accompanied by three security guards, arrive at Will Rogers World Airport. Security for George and Donna had been increased after the Derryberry incident. A few minutes later, at 9:40 P.M., the 51-year-old lieutenant governor and his wife arrived at the hotel watch party.

As the votes trickled in from the nearly 3,000 boxes across the state, it was evident that the strategy had worked. George was piling up large totals in eastern Oklahoma. A four-piece band led nearly 500 supporters in several choruses of a campaign song titled "It's Nigh Time," written by campaign volunteer Dale Smith of Bartlesville.

George, always cautious about declaring a victory too early, a caution whispered in his ear by his lovely wife, told the faithful, "The returns show us ahead. But I'm not interested in the returns they're giving us now. I'm interested in the returns they're going to give us at one o'clock."[21]

As several men and women wearing cowboy hats adorned with Nigh buttons crowded closer to the stage, George thanked his supporters, saying, "Without you we'd be nowhere, and with you we're going everywhere."[22]

George needed one vote more than 50 percent to do what had never been done before in Oklahoma, escape a runoff. There was no doubt through the evening that George would have a sizable lead over Derryberry. However, avoiding a runoff was anything but certain.

At 2:00 A.M., when all of the more than 500,000 votes were counted, George fell only 621 votes short of a clear majority. He polled 276,910 votes to 208,055 for Derryberry. The 69,475 votes received by Funston denied George a clear win without a runoff. A headline in *The Daily Oklahoman* read, "Nigh So Close, But So Far Too."[23]

George had not expected to win without a runoff. He recognized that Funston would tally a reasonably good vote in Tulsa County from which he had served six years in the state senate. However, George surprisingly won Tulsa County and made a stronger than expected showing in Oklahoma County.

In the Republican primary, former University of Oklahoma running back Ron Shotts easily outdistanced Jerry Mash and Jim Head.

Remembering that Democratic disunity and in-fighting had cost the Democrats the governor's mansion in 1962, George approached Derryberry and asked him to drop out of the race to allow George's campaign kitty and effort to be spent on the battle against the Republican nominee. Derryberry angrily rejected the idea and suggested that George be the one to drop out. Looking back on the conversation years later, George regretted asking Derryberry to quit the race and fully understood why the request made Derryberry angry. George said, "I don't blame him. I should not have asked. He had the same dream I had. He had served the state well and it wasn't for me to make that suggestion." [24]

Derryberry came out swinging in the runoff. He said Nigh was too much of a good guy to run Oklahoma. Derryberry said, "Good guys can't cope with the problems of crime in the years ahead. Good guys can't deal with Judge [Luther] Bohanon [the Oklahoma City federal judge handling the volatile school desegregation and busing case]. And good guys can't handle the question of pardon and paroles."

Derryberry stepped up his attacks as he traveled the state. Speaking to about 50 people at a League of Women Voters candidate forum in Oklahoma City, Derryberry charged, "While George Nigh has been out cutting ribbons, we've been in court fighting the state's legal battles."[26]

Derryberry explained away George's big lead in the primary, conceding that George's thousands of appearances at graduations and civic clubs had made him a household name. Derryberry's campaign strategy changed dramatically during the runoff. Instead of Main Street tours and one-on-one campaigning, the attorney general relied heavily on television advertising and large group appearances.

On the other hand, George continued doing what had brought him large vote totals in the primary. He kept right on campaigning, as though he were in a tight race. He defended himself against a flurry of charges from Derryberry, but George refused to counterattack, instead emphasizing programs of economic growth, highway construction, and education. George believed Oklahoma voters would react positively to postive programs.

Derryberry bought time on local television stations in Ada and Ardmore, Oklahoma, and Fort Smith, Arkansas, and challenged George to a series of debates. George, having no control over the format of the debates, refused. However, George was pleased that Derryberry had issued the challenge, a sure signal to voters that the challenger believed he was losing. When it came time for the live telecast, Derryberry pointed to an empty podium labeled with George's name and lambasted George.

Martin Hauan, who managed George's media campaign, wrote of the debates, "Every question Derryberry got was right over the plate and he hit 'em out of the park. The attorney general proved he was unafraid of embracing mom, apple pie, and the flag. The sad thing was that everyone watching knew it was fake. The show was embarrassing to watch. Next day they were joking about the 'debate' in the capitol press room."

The *Tulsa Tribune*'s Richard Tapscott said, "It may be the first debate between a candidate and empty chair when the empty chair won."[28]

By the end of the runoff, Derryberry had spent more than $700,000 in his run for the governor's mansion, a record in state political history to that point.

During the final week of the runoff campaign, George and Derryberry met head on in debates in Tulsa and Oklahoma City. In

Campaign brochure used to convince voters to stamp George's name on the 1978 Democratic runoff ballot.

Tulsa, George was grilled by Derryberry about pardons and paroles. However, a similar attempt in Oklahoma City was thwarted by the moderator of the program who refused to let Derryberry proceed, contending it was a violation of previously agreed upon rules.

In the Nigh camp there was concern about the debates. As an attorney, Derryberry was a natural presentor. George's ability was in speaking, not debating, so the mission given George by his campaign staff was simply "not to mess up."

State newspapers agreed that Derryberry came out of the debates with a slight edge, but it was apparent that Derryberry "had not scored decisively enough to have a significant impact upon the race."[29] George's strategists were pleased.

All of Derryberry's criticism of George's granting of 2,300 paroles, his role in the state lodge controversy, and in a dozen other areas, apparently fell on deaf ears among Oklahoma voters. As returns were posted on large blackboards in front of county courthouses in rural Oklahoma, and as computers in Oklahoma and Tulsa counties spat out results, it was obvious that George was scoring a knockout punch.

Watch parties in both Tulsa and Oklahoma City swelled with supporters as the night wore on. An *Oklahoma Journal* reporter described the scene at the Hilton Inn West in Oklahoma City, "Supporters sipped soft drinks and munched popcorn awaiting Nigh's initial appearance and some tapped their shoes, while others chanted 'Nigh,

Nigh, Nigh.' "[30] Supporters sporadically trumpeted whoops and waved placards throughout the evening as vote totals marched across six silent television screens.

With Donna, Mike, and Georgeann at his side, George declared victory at 10:09 P.M. in the south ballroom of the Hilton Inn West. He accepted the Democratic nomination and assured the crowd that he had talked to both Derryberry and Funston and both had pledged their full cooperation in his run against the Republican nominee. George was not the first Nigh to declare victory that night. At 9:00 P.M., Donna had told a reporter, "Yes I will predict a victory. I was the first to announce he was going to run. So leave it to a wife to open her mouth. Yes, I'm predicting a victory."[31]

Smothered in congratulatory hand-pumping and back-slapping accolades from the white-hatted gathering, George credited his win to teamwork, saying, "We're a team. And I want to thank my teammates and partners individually. And get 10 days rest." After pausing for effect, George continued, "following the November election."

The runoff totals showed George scored a convincing statewide victory. He carried 56 of the 77 counties and won by more than 74,000 votes, 269,681 to 197,457. Derryberry's strongest showing of support was in his native western Oklahoma. George carried the urban areas of central and eastern Oklahoma by a large margin. The head-off-Derryberry-at-the-pass strategy won again.

With the Democratic nomination for governor secure, George rested only briefly, preparing for the race of his life.

Good Guy vs. Nice Guy

By George, it's time we begin
With a guy like Nigh
We know we can win
We're having a high time
We're making it Nigh time
By George, it's Nigh time... let's win!

FROM "IT'S NIGH TIME," THE CAMPAIGN SONG WRITTEN BY DALE SMITH

THE TONE OF THE GENERAL ELECTION battle was set by *The Sunday Oklahoman* on September 24. State Capitol reporter Mike Hammer dubbed the campaign "Good Guy vs. Nice Guy." Hammer called George the Good Guy, writing, "He wore a white cowboy hat throughout most of the campaign, signifying his role of being a good guy." Shotts, according to Hammer was the Nice Guy. Three independent candidates, Floyd Shealy, an Oklahoma City volunteer corrections organization director; Jim McCuiston, an Oklahoma City family counselor; and Billy Joe Clegg, a Midwest City minister, had little impact upon the race.

"I will not sling mud, make personal attacks on Nigh, or run a negative campaign." With those words, Shotts, a handsome football star from Weatherford, began his general election campaign for governor the day after George's victory over Derryberry in the Democratic primary. However, Shotts said he would scrutinize George's record of 24 years in state government and "point out deficiencies to the people."[1] The scrutiny soon turned to mud.

Shotts, an easy-going, soft-spoken, husky man whose face was not marred by his years on the gridiron as a star for the University of Oklahoma, was an avowed conservative. He was 32, a veteran of four years in the Oklahoma House of Representatives, and had run an admirable race for a seat on the Oklahoma Corporation Commission two years before. He lost to Jan Eric Cartwright but polled the most votes ever by any GOP candidate for state office.[2]

Battle lines in the race for the governor's mansion were drawn in the opening days of the campaign. Shotts said Oklahoma needed a "new face" in government.[3] Shotts immediately accepted offers from two television stations in Tulsa to debate George and said he was willing to discuss issues with George anyplace, anytime.[4]

George realized it was going to be a long election campaign when Republican state chairman Rick Shelby criticized George for taking a few days off with his family after the runoff. George and Donna were invited to a weekend retreat in California. Shelby said, in fake shock, "I find it absolutely incredible that George Nigh would urge all Oklahoma Democrats to work to make sure he gets elected, while he heads for a vacation in sunny California. He's vacationing. . . with a movie star while, as usual, he leaves the work and tough decisions to someone else."[5]

The Nigh for Governor state headquarters in 1978 was in a shopping center at Northwest Tenth Street and Meridian Avenue in Oklahoma City. Courtesy John Reid.

Donna was an integral and irreplaceable part of the 1978 campaign. Martin Hauan explained, "Donna often got more notice than George. George has been some places so often, he is old hat. Not Donna. She has a lively personality and can and will speak on the issues. She was also blessed with the livest-wire sidekick around, Shirley Cassil [Donna Nigh's campaign aide and later personal assistant]. . . Like Donna, you can see in her face what she thinks. I promise you this pair made votes wherever they went."[6]

George remembered Donna's impact on the campaign, "She's an issue person more than a tea-sipper. We had people on the caravans who would rather go with her than me. We had press asking to go with her. She's strong, knowledgeable, discussing issues from my vantage point but not afraid to come right out with how she feels." [7]

George never forgot the hard work of his campaign volunteers. An example is Glenda Carlile who worked in the "Friends of George" office. Years after the 1978 campaign, Glenda was installed as president of the Auxiliary to the American Osteopathic Association at the group's annual convention in Anaheim, California. George and Donna showed up at the installation as a complete surprise to Glenda who said, "We had never had a governor appear before. George was his usual wonderful speechmaker self and regaled the audience with stories such as how smart they were to have elected me since I came from a state in the middle of the country and anytime anyone needed me all they had to do was call my husband who could stick a stamp on my forehead and ship me off to them."[8]

Tom and Glenda Carlile and Terry and Connie Nickels were just two of many osteopathic physician families who actively participated in the campaign. In fact, Bob Jones, the executive director of the State Association of Osteopathic Physicians, and his wife Gayle, were major players during the race and later on in the administration.

Near tragedy turned into at least one vote for George on a campaign swing through western Oklahoma. Don Price of Midwest City was driving the campaign van for Donna when the engine exploded and the van caught fire. Don's clothing was also on fire and campaign workers rolled him around in the stubble of a wheat field beside the road. Unfortunately, the field caught on fire. Donna flagged down a passing motorist to take Don to a nearby hospital, while other workers stayed behind, using their hats, campaign signs, and anything they could find to beat out the flames.

Actually, the flames were fanned and spread by their actions. A sizeable portion of the the wheat farmer's land was burned off. The campaign worried about what would be said of the damage caused.

The following week, a local newspaper carried a letter to the editor. It said, "I wasn't sure who I'd vote for until the other day I passed a van parked beside the road with big George Nigh signs. All of Nigh's workers were out in a field trying to beat out the flames with campaign signs. A candidate whose people are that concerned about others gets my vote."[9]

Neither George, nor anyone in the campaign, ever told the newspaper how the fire began.

The men who "Won the West." Left to right, George, his brother-in-law Jack Davis of Dallas, Texas, Norris Price of Del City, and George's brother Sam of Norman. The three accepted the challenge to coordinate western Oklahoma for George's election as governor in 1978.

George's campaign was shored up by hundreds of dedicated workers slapping fence straddlers on lonesome barbed wire fences in western Oklahoma, delivering yard signs in metropolitan areas, and transporting billboard-size signs from the state headquarters in Oklahoma City to destinations all over the state. In Caddo, in southern Oklahoma, George's local campaign manager was none other than the widow of his former foe, Cowboy Pink Williams.

An Athletes for Nigh team, including football and golf stars from the University of Oklahoma and Oklahoma State University, was formed by Pete Reed of the campaign staff. In naming the group, George hoped to not fumble the occasion as Shotts did earlier when he announced the formation of a group called Athletes for Shotts. Several of the appointees disavowed membership because they did not support Shotts whose aides had failed to confirm their sentiments. Instead, they supported George.

Among the athletes active for George was University of Oklahoma quarterback and later Republican Oklahoma fourth district Congressman J.C. Watts.

OSU golf coach Mike Holder and National Football League official Don Porter made George's team along with football players such as Jim Weatherall, Albert Chandler, Tinker Owens, Richard Mildren, George Cumby, Reggie Kinlaw, and Mike Babb.[10]

George also formed special campaign groups of supporters who were doctors, lawyers, and college students. Virtually every campus in the state had a "Students for Nigh" organization.

Newspaper publisher Larry Ferguson of Pawnee, a veteran hard-nosed Republican, and later Minority Leader of the Oklahoma House of Representatives, threw his support behind George and served as statewide chairman of the Republicans for Nigh committee.

The Nigh team blanketed Oklahoma. George went one way while Donna went the other, covering the state with the Nigh message. Every three or four days the two Nigh caravans met up for a joint rally.

After an October campaign swing to Miami, in northeast Oklahoma, George had a good feeling, for the first time the feeling he was going to win. He participated in a street festival in Miami and people crowded around him, seeking his autograph and wanting photographs taken with him. That night George came home and told Donna, "I'm gonna win. I can tell by the way people reacted to me today."[11]

George tried his best to keep the campaigning positive, discussing issues such as his proposed restoration of the full federal income tax credit on state income tax returns, phased in over four years; increases in education funding; and major advances in Oklahoma road construction.

However, issues waned as mudslinging began. Shotts accused George of soliciting $200,000 in contributions from lobbyists during a meeting of the Oklahoma Society of Association Executives at the home of member Leo Cravens and his wife Lee Ann. Shotts charged that 50-ticket envelopes were passed out to lobbyists for the upcoming $100-a-plate Nigh dinner.

The reception at Cravens home certainly touted George's candidacy, although the event's stated purpose was to honor George who was a founding member and the very first president of the professional group.

Shotts' attacks on George were graphic and personal. Shotts said, "This clarifies the close association between George Nigh and lobbyists. Even a champion hunting dog, if it gets enough ticks sucking its blood, won't be able to hunt. I'm afraid Nigh's association with lobbyists will weaken his ability to operate independently as governor."[12]

Shotts slammed George for waiting three days to answer his charges about the fund raising methods. However, George told a news conference that he waited until he could assimilate all the facts and respond correctly. Cravens was out of state and George in fact had no knowledge of Cravens' fund-raising efforts.

Shotts later recanted part of the story because newspaper reporter Jack Taylor of *The Daily Oklahoman* discovered that tickets were passed to lobbyists at other times.[13]

Loyd Benefield, George's official campaign manager, came to George's defense in regard to the uninteresting issue of lobbyists raising money for George, and for that matter, for his opponent. Benefield, an Oklahoma City lawyer, when asked by a reporter what role lobbyists had played in the election effort, said, "I don't think they played any role. They haven't influenced me. However, if I were a lobbyist, I would try to get in good with all the candidates and tell my clients I knew the candidates personally. What's wrong with that?"[14]

Polls showed that voters cared little about the flap, which only made good copy for newspapers and radio and television stations.

Donna's operation of a mail order gift shop came under attack a few weeks before the November election. Earlier, Donna had formed "George and Donna Nigh Inc." when George was thinking about leaving politics. The shop sold moderately priced items, mostly made in Oklahoma.

Shotts accused George of twisting arms to influence lobbyists to buy gifts from Donna's store, a charge flatly and firmly denied by George and Donna. It was the lowest time in Donna's life. Reporter Jack Taylor, sat outside the campaign office daily demanding a list of her customers and their accounts. She steadfastly refused.[15] Some political experts believed many women voters resented the stalking of Donna and signed on with the Nigh bandwagon. The governor's security treated Taylor as a stalker.

Two weeks before the election, polls published in metropolitan newspapers showed 67 percent of the voters surveyed favored George over Shotts. However, the barrage of charges from Shotts and a series of anti-George editorials in *The Daily Oklahoman* eroded George's lead.

The critical editorials reached a new high, or low, depending on the politics of the reader, on Thursday before the November 7 election. The newspaper, in a front page editorial, accused George of covering up the facts of the fund raising event allegedly involving lobbyists. The editorial said, "After a long career on the public payroll and an associate of the lobbyists, Nigh has shown clearly he has learned well how to try to pull the wool over the eyes of the public... Ron Shotts has shown he trusts the voters enough that he doesn't need to spoon feed them only what he thinks will help him. What clearer choice could Oklahomans have next Tuesday?" [16]

The same issue of the newspaper reported George's support slipping in the fourth and sixth congressional districts. Straw polls showed George falling from 75 to 55 percent in Jackson County and

Shotts increasing a two-point lead to a eleven-point margin in Woodward County.[17]

Both George and Shotts sparred over their campaigns' connections with former Governor David Hall. Shotts' press secretary, Pam Holliday, claimed five of Hall's former advisers, Dan Rambo, Robert White, Bill Crain, Bob Burns, and Larry Brawner, were active members of George's inner circle. Carl Clark, George's press secretary, countered with the fact that Hall's former press secretary Mike Williams, and his wife C.J. Murphy, were directing Shotts' media blitz.[18]

Rambo and Crain were members of Hall's staff and White headed up the Office of Economic Opportunity. Crain had actually moved to George's campaign after assisting Funston's effort in the primary.

Shotts' point was that he believed the "old guard" that had run government during the Hall administration was back at the top of George's campaign, citing George's visit with Hall on the California mini-vacation after the runoff. In truth, George and Donna had dinner with the Halls during the California trip but polticial strategy was not discussed. It was the first time George had seen or talked to Hall in three years.

George finally had enough of the mudslinging and ripped Shotts in a press release that was still warm with George's anger. George said, "Not only is my opponent engaging in last minute smear attacks but in this case they are quite hypocritical. I believe the voters are tired of desperation attacks by a man who's running a losing race."[19] George also charged that *The Daily Oklahoman* was engaging in character assassination and of doing Shotts' "dirty work."[20]

Angered at their seemingly personal attacks on Donna, George said, "Their front page editorials, their cartoons, and Jack Taylor's articles are an obvious element in my opponent's campaign. They are doing his mudslinging for him. Therefore, I refuse to answer any further questions from Jack Taylor or *The Daily Oklahoman*."[21]

George and his top aides worried as polling results showed the race getting closer. A poll released by *The Daily Oklahoman* on Friday before the election indicated that George's once seemingly safe lead of 34 percent in Tulsa County had been whittled to 18 percent. However,

George strongly believed that voters would see through the smear attacks and rely on his record of long service with never a hint of scandal.

George's analysis of the impact of the newspaper editorials, an analysis given 20 years after the election, was that the newspaper campaign against him seriously eroded his voter base from five weeks before the election until 10 days before election day. At that point, however, George believed voters saw the editorials as "overkill" and any erosion of support ceased and in fact, had turned with the swing back in his favor.[22]

The Saturday edition of *The Daily Oklahoman* contained a front page editorial entitled "Hall Rerun," charging that George's campaign was "riddled with supporters and cronies of ex-Gov. Hall." The newspaper asked, "Does this mean that Nigh will raise state taxes more than any other administration? Hall did. Does this mean Nigh will load the statehouse with his old 'friends' and waste money again?" [23]

Frosty Troy, editor of the *Oklahoma Observer,* spared no choice words in chastising *The Daily Oklahoman* for what he called an attempt to destroy George, his family, and the Democratic Party. Troy wrote, "Edward L. Gaylord, editor and publisher of *The Daily Oklahoman* and *Times,* hung like a piece of rotten meat around the neck of Republican Ron Shotts, who was never sufficiently conscious-stricken about it to at least hold his nose." [24]

The *Tulsa World,* along with more than 200 other state newspapers, including Oklahoma City's other major newspaper, the *Oklahoma Journal,* endorsed George over Shotts. The *Purcell Register* wrote, "Ron, all the mudslinging did was damage your credibility. . . Voters are not going to stand for a candidate who resorts to such political mudslinging and 'hatchet-man' techniques. They smell of a desperate candidate who will stop at nothing to scandalize his opponent."[25]

The *Anadarko News* said, "Nigh won't punt on first down." "George Nigh gets our nod," said the *Clinton Daily News.* The editorial continued, "He can win without being obligated by promises to any special group or individual, because of the successes resulting from his leadership in attracting tourists and new industry to the state, because he likes people-all kinds of people-and because of the down-to-earth way he relates to western Oklahomans, especially the farmers and ranchers."[26]

The *Henryetta Daily Freelance* supported George, opining, "We emphatically believe that George Nigh has done more for Oklahoma than any other official elected to a statewide office. He is one of us. He isn't crippled by special interest 'strings attached'... He is realistic, practical, sensible, and responsible."[27]

"When you add up all the pluses, it looks as if George Nigh has to come out on top," said the *Checotah Democrat.* The *Daily Ardmorerite* in Ardmore wrote, "Nigh is so definitely the best choice for governor, we are glad to recommend him to all voters."

George's stand against strikes by policemen, firefighters, and teachers drew praise from the publisher of the *Pauls Valley Daily Democrat,* who wrote, "Teachers must be in the classroom, police on the beat, and firemen always ready to answer the alarm."[29]

An exclamation point to the many newspaper editorials came from the *Oklahoma Eagle* in Tulsa. The *Eagle* editorial said, "We think George Nigh is best suited to lead the state at this time. Events are moving so fast, and the problems and solutions so complex, that to entrust the governor's chair to an unknown quantity is counter-productive."[30]

Aware that voters were tired of negative campaigning, George spent the final days of the campaign desperately trying to stay positive. While his state headquarters issued position papers on certain issues, George talked to the people about increasing tourism and the state's economic growth. He pointed with pride to his work in tourism, noting that Oklahoma's tourism industry had grown the previous seven years from $400 million to $2 billion annually. George reasoned that economic growth would bring pollution-free industries to the state and increase state revenues.

Two days before the election, *The Sunday Oklahoman* made a final stab at undermining George's chances of becoming the first lieutenant governor to ever be elected governor of Oklahoma. A front page cartoon showed George telling funny stories and talking in "generalities," rather than facing the state's problems and issues. The cartoon was

This Jim Lange cartoon appeared after George was elected governor in 1978. Courtesy *The Daily Oklahoman.*

strategically placed under a large headline that read, "Nigh Lead Over Shotts Softens in Survey." Numbers from the newspaper's survey in 18 counties showed George leading Shotts 55 to 41 percent, down substantially from two weeks before.[31]

State Election Board Secretary Lee Slater predicted that 700,000 Oklahomans would go to the polls on election day. However, good weather and the hot rhetoric of the closing days of the gubernatorial campaign brought 801,190 voters to the ballot box.

Shotts took an early lead for the first three hours, fueled primarily by quick tabulation of votes from Oklahoma County. However, as results began pouring in from George's strongholds in southeast, northeast, and southwest Oklahoma, Shotts' lead shrank steadily. Even while newscasters were reporting Shotts in front of George, vote results called in by volunteers from county courthouses in rural Oklahoma to the Nigh headquarters convinced George he would win. As usual, George knew he would win even before the press did.

Shortly after 10:00 P.M., the state saw what George's campaign staff already knew. He took over the lead and never relinquished it. By 10:40, Shotts conceded defeat and a giant roar arose from the Nigh watch party at the Hilton Inn West.

George and Donna waited in the hotel suite of Jeannette Edmondson until he believed the time was right to appear at the watch party. When the victory was secure, and true to his pledge not to promise any jobs before the election was over, George turned to Jeannette, and asked, "Will you be my secretary of state?" When Jeannette nodded her acceptance, George had filled the first of many positions in the new administration.

George and Donna, now the victors, appeared before a sea of white hats.When the cheering died down, George thanked his supporters. "This state belongs to each of us," he said, "As governor of Oklahoma, we are going to continue to be a people's administration as we were a people's candidate." [32]

George did not ignore the editorial campaign of *The Daily Oklahoman*, saying, "I believe we should do something positive every day. Tomorrow I'm going to get my copy of *The Daily Oklahoman* and I'm going to frame it, not because of the headlines that say I won, but because that will be the last *Oklahoman* ever delivered to my doorstep."[33] The crowd of several thousand went wild.

Early the next morning George, wide awake with anticipation of seeing his victory prominently reported in a banner headline in the newspaper, went outside his home to look for the *Oklahoman.* It never came.

In the loud throng of victorious Nigh supporters was Tulsa businessman Julian Rothbaum. George tapped Rothbaum on the shoulder and asked him to serve on the University of Oklahoma Board of Regents. Even before the thrill of election night victory had subsided, George was at work filling important posts in his administration. He wanted to hit the ground running.

The final, official vote tally gave George a 35,000 vote victory over Shotts, 402,240 to 367,055. The three independent candidates garnered less than 10,000 votes among them. George carried 51 counties. He lost Oklahoma and Tulsa counties but more than made up the difference in Little Dixie and other Democratic strongholds.

George's polltaker during the election was Tom Kielhorn. When all the votes were counted, Kielhorn had predicted the outcome within one-tenth of one percent. Kielhorn, who then became the state's best-known pollster, told George, "Tonight, you have made me an expert and made me money."[34]

George spent $890,000 in his successful bid for the governor's mansion, nearly $400,000 more than Boren spent running for the same office four years before.[35]

In other state elections, Democrat Boren overwhelmingly defeated James Inhofe for the United States Senate seat vacated by Senator Bartlett; Democrat State Representative Spencer Bernard won the race for lieutenant governor; Republican Tom Daxon won the state auditor and inspector's job; Jan Eric Cartwright, a Democrat, was elected attorney general; and Democrat Leo Winters won the state treasurer's race.

In order to buy billboard space cheap and in the right locations, the Nigh campaign had to sign long-term contracts which ran after the election. Donna suggested putting the word "Thanks" over the original billboards.

When the election night celebration was over, George and Donna went home. Donna kicked off her shoes, savoring the reward of years of campaigning and working toward the highest office in the state. George, however, reminded Donna that they needed to be up early the following morning because he had a million things to do before the legislature convened in January. "George," Donna said quietly, "tell me, when does all the fun start?"

George was up early the next morning, meeting at several offices around Oklahoma City, talking about selection of a staff and the preparation of a budget. Governor Boren gave George space in his office and a second-floor Capitol conference room for use by his transition team.

George appeared briefly before the House Democratic caucus to pledge a partnership between the two branches of government. He told members of the House, where he first served as an elected official 28 years before, "I didn't want my first day to go by without visiting you."[36] A newspaper reporter observed, "Wearing black pants, a polka dot shirt opened at the neck, and a black and white sport coat, Nigh received a perfunctory standing ovation when he entered the House chamber."[37]

All news of the day after the election was not rosy. Newly elected Speaker of the House, Representative Dan Draper of Stillwater, announced he would oppose George's campaign promise of restoring the federal income tax credit on state income tax returns over a four-year period.

George received a call the day after the election from a strong supporter who wanted to serve on the OU Board of Regents. When George told him that the position was filled, the supporter said, "I thought you said you would promise no one a job or appointment until after you were elected." George reassured his friend that he had kept that promise, that the offer to Rothbaum was made after George was declared the winner. The supporter laughingly said, "I saw you talking to Julian last night. I should have talked to you first."[38]

George replied, "Be patient. I'm going to be around a long time." Later, Mickey Imel became the second Tulsan to serve as a Nigh appointment to the OU Board of Regents.

AT LAST

Perhaps the best thing Nigh has going for him is that apparently his desire to succeed as governor is not based on any aspiration for higher office. If he continually strives for compromise, it will be a reflection of his nature, not some ambitious drive.

OKLAHOMA MONTHLY MAGAZINE

BY DECEMBER, 1978, George had surrounded himself with a loyal and proficient staff. He decided to serve as his own chief of staff. Carl Clark was selected as press secretary. Former commissioner of public safety Robert Lester, Oklahoma City attorney David Hudson, Enid accountant Robert Parks, Robert White, Dean Gandy, and John Reid were named administrative assistants. Former State Senator Robert Wadley of Claremore and former State Representative David Hood of Oklahoma City were picked by George to handle relations with the state senate and house of representatives.

George gave his office finance manager Robert Parks the same single admonition he had given Parks as his campaign treasurer, "Keep me out of jail." It was the only instruction ever given Parks. To assure the integrity of his staff, George required each person to provide a financial statement with a detailed source of income. The financial information was sealed without anyone reading it and would be opened only if the integrity of a staff member was questioned. None of the financial statements were ever opened.[1]

George wisely added a special touch to his staff with the appointment of Sam Hammons as administrative assistant. Hammons had been in the inner circle in Governor Boren's office, a connection George thought important as the baton of power was passed to him from Boren. Many members of state boards and commissions, by law, contained members appointed by Boren and Hammons' presence gave them a natural connection to the new Nigh administration.

George experienced the rigors of a new governor-elect, with slots still open in his staff, no permanent office, and meeting with legislative leaders to introduce programs that the governor wanted. He often worked into the wee hours of the morning to outline programs and ideas that would be the subject of briefings with legislative leaders the following day.

In December, for the second time in his life, George was told by a sitting governor that he was resigning. Governor Boren told George that he wanted to resign as governor early to take his United States Senate seat so as to not lose valuable seniority to other freshman senators.

Boren resigned at one minute before midnight on January 2, 1979. Constitutionally, George, at that moment, became governor. However, he was not sworn in until January 3.

George decided to hold his swearing-in ceremony outside Oklahoma City so it would not overshadow his planned inauguration on the State Capitol steps five days later. It would be the first time a governor was sworn in outside the capital of either Guthrie or Oklahoma City.

George chose Tulsa as the site for the ceremony to emphasize that Oklahoma had two great major metropolitan areas and to express his appreciation to Tulsa County and all of Green Country, in northeast Oklahoma, for being so good to George in the campaign. Many of his supporters and financial backers had come from that section of the state. George's reception there was similar to the enthusiastic support he received in his home area in McAlester and all of Little Dixie.

George also specifically wanted to honor former Governor and United States Senator Dewey Bartlett by taking the oath of office at Bartlett Park in downtown Tulsa.

The exact site of the swearing-in ceremony in Bartlett Park was selected for a humorous reason. During the campaign, on a day the thermometer topped the century mark, George was handing out cards in the park when he was approached by a lady who obviously supported his opponent. She caustically said, "It will be a cold day in Tulsa before you are ever governor." George stood on the same spot and told onlookers, "It is and I am."[2]

Well-wishers crowd a downtown Tulsa park to watch George sworn in for his second term as governor, a five-day term that followed the early resignation of Governor David Boren who had been elected to the United States Senate.

On January 8, 1979, after serving in Oklahoma's number two office for 16 years, George was sworn in as governor a third time, but this time for a full four-year term. He had become the state's first three-term governor and the first chief executive to succeed himself. As Donna looked on, George was sworn in by longtime friend and Oklahoma Supreme Court Justice Ralph B. Hodges of Durant. Courtesy *The Daily Oklahoman.*

About 1,000 people gathered in sub-freezing cold to watch United States District Judge Allen Barrow administer the oath to George. Donna stood beside George as he raised his right hand and repeated the oath of office before a bank of radio and television microphones.

In a 20-minute, light-hearted acceptance speech, George poked fun at the brevity of this term as governor, the shortest in history.[3]

Unlike his first term as governor, the nine days after the resignation of Edmondson in 1963, George's second term was uneventful. George used one of the days of the short term to move his family into the mansion. As was the custom, very little state-owned furniture was in the official residence and the Borens had moved their personal belongings from the mansion. George said, "It's kind of a shock to walk into the mansion and not have a bed." George's new staff presented a king-size brass bed to George and Donna, a welcomed house-warming gift.

Inaugural day, January 8, 1979, began with a prayer breakfast from 8:30 to 10:00 A.M. Then George, Donna, Mike, and Georgeann gathered in the governor's office with other state officials waiting to be sworn in.

George delivered his inaugural address, not from a prepared text, but from strategic cryptic notes on his left hand. George had for many years written key words on his hand to refresh his memory when he stood before audiences. While waiting to be escorted onto the inaugural platform on the south steps of the State Capitol, George peeled off his black leather glove to reveal yet another set of notes for his inaugural speech.

George and Donna were the final persons to walk down the steps. George was dressed in a black business suit and black patent leather cowboy boots that glistened in the sunshine.

George came to the governor's office with definite ideas and plans for Oklahoma's future. He introduced those ideas to the people of Oklahoma in his inaugural address. An estimated 2,000 persons stood in bright sunshine but chilling 15-degree temperatures as 51-year-old George took over the reins of the state he first served 28 years before as a young legislator from Pittsburg County.

George told the inaugural crowd, "We want a people's administration. I want progress, better services, better government. But I want the hallmark of our administration to be honesty and integrity." [4]

George and Donna danced the night away at the inaugural ball at the Oklahoma City Myriad Convention Center. Floyd "Red" Rice's band was one of three musical groups for supporters who paid $5 each to attend the "people's"event.

The rat-a-tat-tat of helicopters landing outside their bedroom window awakened George and Donna in the middle of the night for their first few nights in the mansion. George discovered that the helipad on the mansion grounds was being used to transport patients from outlying communities to nearby University Hospital. George telephoned Department of Human Services Director Lloyd Rader with the request to build a first-class landing port for helicopters at

University Hospital, to shorten the emergency trip. Within two days, Rader's employees had constructed a fully-equipped, lighted helipad, complete with windsock. It was the beginning of a statewide medi-flight program in which all hospitals were asked to designate a landing spot for helicopters.

Oklahoma's economy was booming as George assumed the reins of state government. Both historic staples, agriculture and petroleum, were profitable beyond all predictions. A meat shortage had shot cattle prices to a handsome high. Crop failures overseas and massive grain sales to the Soviet Union also drove wheat prices in Oklahoma to a record high. Money flowed freely from banking institutions to farmers and ranchers who bought new and more expensive machinery. Farmers were as anxious to spend money as the bankers were to lend it.

Even more impressive was the state's booming oil and gas industry. The 1973 Arab-Israeli War, and short supplies of oil because of cuts in production by the Arab-led Organization of Petroleum Exporting Countries (OPEC), sent Oklahoma oil men scurrying back to the oil patch, drilling new wells and reworking old ones. The price of crude soared from $12 to $35 per barrel. Historians Danney Goble and David Baird wrote, "Oklahoma oilmen rarely bothered even to sleep. Old rigs pumped around the clock, sucking up crude oil almost as fast as its price was rising. New wells dug deeper and deeper, tapping pools that never would have been profitable at the old price level.[5]

Because of the bursting economic growth, state revenue coffers were full and overflowing, putting George in the enviable position of not having to worry about asking the legislature for a tax increase to finance the growing state government.

George had many friends in the legislature and wanted his relationship with the solons to be a partnership. His theory was, "The only way to be a partner is be friendly with the House and Senate. It's important to get along. I make recommendations but if the legislature doesn't like 'em, they don't pass 'em. I work on what I think is best as long as there's a chance to pass it but I don't get mad every time some-

Right: The Governor's Art Gallery was created in 1979 in a room adjacent to the Blue Room on the State Capitol's second floor. The gallery was the result of George's idea to display works by Oklahoma artists. Eventually, hundreds of thousands of visitors enjoyed the gallery each year. Here Oklahoma Arts Council chairman Martin Hagerstrand of Tahlequah holds the ribbon for Donna and George to cut at the official opening in November, 1979.

Above: George used his power as governor to support Oklahoma art and artists. Left to right, Ben DiSalvo, director of the Oklahoma Arts Council; artist Enoch Kelly Haney, later a state senator from Seminole, with his painting *Mark of the Knife;* George; and Oklahoma Adjutant General Robert Morgan. Courtesy Betty Price.

Leaders from Oklahoma were the first to be invited by President Jimmy Carter to the White House in February, 1979, in a series of presidential meetings with state government officials. Left to right, Nigh aide Sam Hammons; State Senator Jim Lane of Idabel; Representative Vernon Dunn of Loco; Representative Cleta Deatherage of Norman; State Senator Gene Howard of Tulsa, President Pro Tempore; Representative Dan Draper of Stillwater, Speaker of the House; President Jimmy Carter; Donna; and George. Courtesy The White House.

body disagrees with me. Where the public's concerned, you might be politically better off being at odds with the legislature. I try not to be."[6]

Retiring House member Mandell Matheson, a former State Capitol newspaper reporter, said George needed to show the legislature that he could be tough, saying, "The one thing Nigh will have to do to deal effectively in the legislature is at the outset show an ability to get down nose to nose with them and slug it out on vital issues. What's going to happen is that people in the legislature will expect a push-over but will find that he's a lot tougher than they think. He's a very determined man. He makes up his mind and he sticks with it."

George, ever the detail man, organized the governor's office as he had the lieutenant governor's office. Every shelf in storerooms was labeled. He even labeled the shelves in the medicine cabinet in the personal bathroom adjacent to the governor's formal office with appro-

Members of George's staff help raise money during Festival '80, the annual telethon of the Oklahoma Educational Television Authority, which George strongly supported. Longtime Executive Director Bob Allen remembered that George taped tourism training programs for broadcast on OETA at 6:30 P.M. on designated nights in 1973. One evening that year, during OETA's live broadcast of the Watergate Committee hearings, presidential counsel John Dean was just sitting down to testify as George's taped program interrupted with the opening, "Hi, I'm George Nigh." OETA received hundreds of complaint calls. One of George's most ardent supporters, Juanita Kidd, served for 16 years on the OETA Board of Directors. In 1985 George led the effort to name the entrance to the OETA studios in Oklahoma City the "Juanita Kidd Courtyard." After George retired as president of the University of Central Oklahoma, he hosted an OETA series called *Oklahoma, Yesterday, Today, and Tomorrow,* vignettes of interesting Oklahoma stories coordinated by producer Pam Henry. Courtesy OETA.

priate tags for "toothbrush," "aspirin," and "razor." On evenings Donna was out of town, George stayed at the office late, occasionally reorganizing the desk and bookshelf of his executive secretary Margaret Hall. George's theory was, "if you don't know what is supposed to be in the desk, you won't know what's missing."[8]

Once when Donna was out of state George rearranged furniture on the first floor of the governor's mansion. As Donna's secretary, Shirley Cassil, arrived for work, she exclaimed, "This will never do!" George reminded Shirley that he was the governor and he lived there and could move the furniture wherever he wanted. Shirley said, "Well Donna won't like it." When Donna returned, she proved Shirley right. Donna said, "This will never do!"

George eulogized former Governor Dewey Bartlett in the State Capitol rotunda after Bartlett's death in 1979. Later, at George's suggestions, the plaza at the state headquarters of the Oklahoma Department of Vocational Technical Education was named the "Dewey F. Bartlett Plaza." Courtesy *The Daily Oklahoman*.

Above: George and Donna welcome Vice President Walter Mondale during a 1979 Mondale visit to Oklahoma City. Courtesy The White House.

Right: John Reid, left, became George's press secretary during his tenure as lieutenant governor. Reid knew George so well that he generally could predict what George's response would be to almost any question, even before the question was asked. Courtesy *The Daily Oklahoman.*

George slipped into a routine. He arose at 5:30 or 6:00 A.M., worked an hour before breakfast, conducted a top level staff meeting at the mansion from 8:00 to 9:00 A.M., and then was escorted by a state trooper to his office in the Capitol. Telephone calls, appointments with supporters, filling appointment to boards and commissions, and meetings with legislators filled his day. He usually left the office about 6:00 P.M. and then, five evenings or so a week, attended social functions, political gatherings, ribbon cutting ceremonies, civic events, and legislative dinners. On rare nights when no outside appearance was scheduled, he had dinner at home with his family and worked in his mansion office. He had a grill installed at the mansion so he could play chef, but he could only grill hamburgers.

George proudly opened the governor's office to the public once a month. He described his first term as a "people's administration," proving his point by making himself available to anyone and everyone who came to his office at the appropriate time set aside each month.

Especially time-consuming in his first few months in office was the laborious task of bringing balance to the many boards and commissions of which the governor appoints members. He was sensitive to proper representation for women, minorities, the handicapped, the young, old, and the urban and rural constituencies in Oklahoma.

"Outstanding" was the word George used to describe the 1979 legislature which appropriated $1 billion for state spending, the first time a budget had exceeded that high water mark. Even though the legislature cut taxes by $15 million, experts predicted state income would be higher the following year, because of the good economy. George patted legislators on the backs as they ended the session. He was convinced that a good legislative-executive relationship was possible if the three C's were used—conflict, cooperation, and consensus.[9]

Other observers were not quite so complimentary about the success of George's first session of dealing with the legislature as governor. Journalist David Fritze, writing for *Oklahoma Monthly* in June, 1979, said, "Very little of substance was accomplished this session. Looking at some of the legislation, perhaps it was a blessing in disguise." [10] Fritze was referring, among other things, to national media attention given a bill by Representative Frank Shurden of Henryetta to authorize castration of sex offenders. The measure failed in the House of Representatives by only three votes.

Other politicians called it a "lackluster" session, especially for supporters of the Equal Rights Amendment (ERA). A bill which would have allowed Oklahomans to vote on the controversial amendment died before it ever made it to the floor of the House for a vote.[11] George and Donna both publicly and privately supported the ratification of the ERA. They hoped Oklahoma would be the state to put efforts to ratify the ERA over the top.

During debate on the ERA, the National Organization for Women (NOW) sent representatives to assist in lobbying members of the legislature. George got into hot water when he arrived for a meeting in his office where the women were seated. George said, "Hello, girls!" and was berated by the NOW officials for the next 30 minutes. George called the national NOW headquarters and requested that the lobbyists be recalled, saying, "We want to win this issue with Oklahomans, not with people from other states. Their attitude and the attention that these women will draw will hurt us." The ERA never received approval of enough states to become part of the federal constitution.

The fight for the tax cut was a classic among Oklahoma political battles. George found an ally in his push for slicing taxes in Senate President Pro Tempore Gene Howard of Tulsa. On the other side of that battle was House Speaker Dan Draper of Stillwater who adamantly opposed any tax reduction.

George threatened to veto appropriations bills sent to him because of inaction by the House on the tax cut bill. George specifically looked at areas of appropriations bills that contained the $20 million necessary to give taxpayers the break he had promised during the campaign. Draper threatened to override the vetoes, an almost impossible task because of the three-fourths majority required. George's bi-partisan support in the Senate and the presence of 26 Republicans in the House assured his veto would be sustained.

In a rare move, *The Daily Oklahoman* cast its lot on George's side, and against Draper. The newspaper editorialized, "Oklahomans... will applaud his courage in going to the mat with... Draper over the related issues of tax reduction and no new taxes. The governor is leading from obvious strength in stating, clearly and unequivocally, that he will stand firm on his campaign commitment for an income tax reduction of at least $20 million."[12]

George scheduled two tough speeches on May 16. The first was to a throng of 14,000 Oklahoma school teachers gathered at the state fairgrounds in Oklahoma City for the annual meeting of the Oklahoma Education Association. The teachers were strongly against any tax cut, afraid that money for the reduction in taxes would come from cuts in state education aid.

Under a hot sun, fueled by dry, gusty winds, George told the teachers he had no apologies for the proposed state tax cut. Unruffled by frequent catcalls, taunts, and boos, George said, "I've heard you crying out. But I cannot forget my commitment to the people of Oklahoma."[13] George was jeered when he suggested that teacher salary increases be kept in line with federal guidelines asking for a seven percent limit on pay hikes. When George finished his speech, teachers rose to their feet and shouted, "Teacher power!"[14]

While speaking, George noticed a solitary figure standing just away from the crowd. It was Norris Price, State Director of Civil Defense, who said, "I just thought you ought to see a friendly face."

Angry teachers followed George to the State Capitol for his next speech of May 16, a planned address to a joint session of the Oklahoma legislature. Caravans of teachers filled the south steps of the Capitol and the House gallery as George prepared to speak. George made the extraordinary move of requesting time to speak to Senate and House members because of his strong belief that a tax cut was necessary. George spoke briefly, but with passion, saying, "The time is right. The people expect a tax reduction. The people deserve a tax reduction."[15]

The Daily Oklahoman again supported George, saying, "Whatever else Oklahoma's demonstrating school teachers might think about Gov. George Nigh, they'll have to admire him for maintaining his composure and not wavering in his tax-cut position in the face of an overwhelmingly hostile audience... He kept his priorities straight, reminding the teachers... that he is committed to eliminating a 'tax on a tax.' "[16]

The newspaper slapped at the OEA, writing, "The OEA lobby always insists teachers are just as concerned about improving all-around educational funding, not just their salaries. If that is so, why are the teachers not praising Nigh for including in his $43 million increase for common schools more money for textbooks, school libraries, elementary guidance counseling and programs for gifted and talented children and the handicapped at home?"

In the end, George and the Senate won over Draper and the House. A compromise restored the full deduction for federal income taxes on state income tax returns. However, a surtax on higher incomes and a five-cent per pack hike in cigarette taxes, offset the reduction in revenue from the elimination of the "tax on a tax."

Other significant accomplishments of the legislature during George's first year at the helm were a bill to allow counties to vote a county fuel tax, a bill authorizing the State Board for Property and Casualty Rates to hire auditors to check insurance company rate increase requests, and legislation designed to offset expected natural gas price increases due to federal energy legislation.

George described his first six months in office as "just terrible, but wonderful." He loved being governor but it was a traumatic experience to move his family into the mansion, hire a staff, move into a new office, balance the state budget, work with the legislature, try to formulate major policy for Oklahoma, and fill dozens of vacancies on the more than 200 state boards and commissions.

The second half of George's first year as governor began triumphantly. A special session of the legislature appropriated $120 million in capital improvements over four years. The program was the largest in state history to be passed without aid of the sale of general obligation bonds.

Interim studies, suggested by George and authorized by the legislature, began on issues facing the state in agriculture, corrections, education, energy, federal funding, the handicapped, law enforcement, and water.

George launched unprecedented moves to work toward better coordination of the cumbersome state government. He hosted a meeting with directors of the approximately 250 state agencies and invited the 2,000 members of state boards and commissions to a conference at the Myriad Convention Center in Oklahoma City.

Also in July, George reorganized his staff, appointing Carl Clark as chief of staff. Promoted to senior administrative assistants were Margaret Hall, Sam Hammons, David Hudson, Bob Lester, Bob Parks, Bob Wadley, Larry Brawner, Del Cravens, Jim Echols, Dean Gandy, Ben Langdon, and Betty Ward.

Administrative assistants on the staff were Shirley Cassil, Bill Crain, Retha Duggan, David Hood, Richard Mildren, Jay Mitchell, Bill Morgan, Paul Patton, Pete Reed, John Reid, Harold Rogers, Doug Sanderson, and Cindy Worley. The governor's office had 43 employees, four more than in the previous year.[18]

Oklahoma Monthly Magazine analyzed George's staff, writing, "No... youthful zeal surrounds senior staff people. With few exceptions, Nigh's chief aides are middle-aged and older... Nor does the governor's office appear to be racked with jealousy, a sure sign that eager people are trying to gain ground and influence." [19]

Oklahoma Monthly described Carl Clark as the most trusted "good guy," although observing, "Clark has a tough time communicating with a daily press which needs to be humored." The magazine called Wadley "the most visible member of Nigh's inner circle," Hood "ostensibly the perfect complement to the conservative Wadley." Wadley and Hood were George's liaison with the Senate and House, respectively.[20]

Margaret Hall was described by the magazine as "Nigh's unflappable executive secretary, whose duty it is to schedule engagements for a governor who likes to remain visible." The article also called Margaret "an attractive designer-clothed woman" who served as "a Nigh gatekeeper who is said to possess many of the governor's instincts. You don't sneak past her."[21]

David Hudson and Larry Brawner were George's legal advisers. Hudson was a well-regarded chain-smoking Oklahoma City lawyer who was an expert in municipal finance. Brawner had worked for Governor Hall and the state Department of Consumer Affairs.

Wayne Chandler, a popular black former school administrator and state government official, became an integral member of George's staff. Chandler, who became the highest ranking black state official,

George and Will Rogers, Jr., look at a display commemorating the 1979 centennial of the birth of Oklahoma humorist Will Rogers. Courtesy Fred Marvel.

was instrumental in getting George and Oklahoma City black newspaper publisher Russell Perry, who had not supported George, together. Chandler said, "I need to get my two friends together." Perry became a strong Nigh supporter and later served as Oklahoma Secretary of Commerce.

Sam Hammons, the holdover from the Boren administration, was George's energy advisor. Bob Parks, a certified public accountant and former vice president of St. Mary's Hospital in Enid, was the expert on budget matters. Parks and George had met years before in the Jaycees. Ed Pugh joined the staff as an administrative assistant. Bob Lester, described as "all whiskered and wise," at age 68, was a valuable member of the staff. He had served state government well as commissioner of public safety and chairman of the board of affairs.[22]

Because Hood was battling leukemia, Dean Gandy, dubbed by the press as "Disco Dean," replaced Hood as George's link to the House of

Representatives. *Oklahoma Monthly* said of Gandy, "The slick and well-tailored Gandy caught Nigh's attention at... tourism where he worked part-time during college... As executive assistant to Nigh, he does everything from cleaning the governor's swimming pool to putting out policy fires."[23]

Observers generally liked George's staff which was cordial and approachable. Senator Rodger Randle of Tulsa said, "I can't think of a single instance when the Nigh people didn't keep their word."[24]

George learned early in his political life that keeping your word is critical to success in government and politics. He often was criticized for taking too much time to make a commitment. However, George reasoned that if he was to err, he should err on the side of correctness rather than quickness. The gubernatorial staff was given the same admonition.

George was proud of his first year appointments. He closely screened supporters to match up their expertise with membership on boards and commissions. He appointed, as promised on election night, Jeannette Edmondson as secretary of state. George also selected Norma Eagleton of Tulsa as the first woman to serve on the Oklahoma Corporation Commission.

Living up to his reputation of making friends of his enemies, George appointed former Democratic primary opponent Bob Funston as executive director of the Oklahoma Department of Economic and Community Affairs, later reorganized into the Department of Commerce. George explained the appointment, saying it was not a payoff for Funston's support in the general election, but was a payoff for Funston's organizational ability. George had been impressed with Funston's knowledge of Oklahoma's business and economy and his demeanor during the primary.

George won future votes during summer camp exercises of the Oklahoma Army National Guard at Fort Chaffee, Arkansas. As Commander in Chief he was reviewing the troops standing in the hot July sun, and was instructed by Oklahoma Adjutant General Robert "Bob" Morgan to order "Pass in review" upon his introduction. Recognizing that the national guardsmen and hundreds of family members had already stood in the sun too long, George shocked military commanders when he strode to the microphone, making his shortest speech ever, and loudly said, "Dismissed." An appreciative roar went up from all areas as guardsmen and family members ran toward each other. George had remembered his Navy days of the agony of standing, waiting to pass in review. That memory served him well.[25]

With the legislature in adjournment, George spent much of his time returning to the state's 77 counties to thank supporters and listen to their problems and solutions for state government. In October he stumped the state in opposition to State Question 539, a Republican sponsored constitutional amendment to cut the state income tax by $132.5 million. George argued that the large tax cut would make a donnybrook of the budgeting process and would create chaos in appropriations. Oklahomans followed George's lead and rejected the proposed amendment. George was in favor of a tax cut, just not this particular one, at this particular time.

In November, 1979, George endorsed the re-election bid of President Jimmy Carter. George made the announcement nine days before First Lady Rosalyn Carter appeared in Oklahoma City for a $50-a-plate dinner and $250 per person reception at the Skirvin Hotel to raise funds for the Carter campaign. George and United States Senator David Boren were co-hosts of the event.

George sat down for an extensive interview in December with Ed Montgomery, a reporter for *The Daily Oklahoman*, for a look back at his first year in office. George called the cabinet approach in management of state agencies a major advance. George said his goal was to continue to "keep a steady hand at the wheel of Oklahoma."[26]

THE FIRST FAMILY

The mansion belongs to all the people, not just the first family.

DONNA NIGH

WHILE GEORGE was working on his relationship with the diverse membership of the Oklahoma legislature, Donna was settling down in a new home, the 51-year-old governor's mansion on Northeast 23rd Street, one block east of the State Capitol.

Early Oklahoma leaders had envisioned a real mansion, a $200,000 showplace, for the state's chief executive and family. However, the 1913 legislature balked at such a lavish expenditure to build a home for the governor. Another 14 years passed until the 1927 legislature pared down the original idea and appropriated $75,000 to build a 19-room house. Governor Henry Johnston and his family moved into the official residence in September, 1928. The legislature gave Mrs. Johnston another $25,000 to furnish the mansion.[1]

When the Nighs moved into the mansion in January, 1979, none of the original furniture remained except for a hall tree on the second floor landing. Former governors had been required to provide their own bedroom and living room furniture so the sprawling mansion was basically empty when George and Donna surveyed what would be their home for the next eight years.

The mansion needed rewiring, new carpet, energy efficient windows, and sandblasting of the Indiana limestone exterior. Donna always liked to point out that the mansion and George were born the same year and that she "had to have the mansion sandblasted." She also gave George a 1927 radio and never fails to mention that she had it rewired.

Life in the mansion for the Nighs was far different than life in their Picnic Lane home by Lake Overholser in west Oklahoma City. Mike had graduated from OSU and moved away. One of the major changes that required adustment was the Nighs' relationship with friends who could not, or would not, just drop by. Guards, a high fence, and a break-neck pace kept friends away.

Donna decorated the mansion with antique chairs and tables she rescued from Capitol storage rooms and personal furniture she brought from their Picnic Lane home. Then, as a people person herself, invited all of Oklahoma to visit. Going against advice to open the mansion for public visits, Donna instituted a weekly open house, Wednesday afternoons from 1:00 to 4:00 P.M. Hostess-guides were volunteers, primarily from Democratic Women's Clubs across the state. Longtime friend Mary Newsom coordinated the open houses.[2]

Donna was excited about opening the three-story home to the public, saying, "The mansion belongs to the people of Oklahoma. We want to make sure it's accessible to the public."[3]

The weekly opening of the mansion was a first for the state. Mrs. Johnston Murray had periodically welcomed visitors in the early 1950s and Shirley Bellmon had occasionally hosted county receptions for supporters and friends. However, no previous first lady had ventured a weekly opening, especially of the entire mansion including the private living quarters. By 1982, 20,000 people annually visited the mansion.

Donna never feared that opening the mansion to as many as 3,000 people on Wednesday afternoons would interfere with family life for her husband, daughter, and cocker spaniel, Susie.

At first Donna stayed at the mansion and greeted every guest. In time, people wanted to stop and talk to her, holding up the line of visitors, sometimes in inclement weather. After a few weeks, at the request of the volunteer hostesses, Donna ran errands away from the mansion during open house time.

Donna was proud of the pieces of Oklahoma history she publicly displayed in the various rooms of the mansion. In a curio in the foyer were mementos or items owned by each of the state's former governors, including Governor William J. Holloway's gavel, Robert S. Kerr's Bible, David Boren's broom, and even a memento of the Nine Days of Nigh. In the official dining room was the silver punch bowl from the USS *Oklahoma*, sunk at Pearl Harbor December 7, 1941. Throughout the mansion, to encourage appreciation of the state's artisans, their works were hung. The collection grew as the Nighs' scheduling secretaries encouraged civic clubs and organizations to which the governor or first lady addressed to break tradition. It was suggested that, rather than the presentation of a certificate or plaque, the Nighs be presented a piece of local art to display in the mansion. This plan complimented the Nighs' desire to promote Oklahoma artists and began the George and Donna Nigh Art Collection that was eventually displayed in the Donna Nigh Gallery at the University of Central Oklahoma.

To make the Oklahoma governor's mansion more family-friendly, a swimming pool, in the shape of the state, was added. The $25,000 necessary for the pool's construction came from private funds. Loyd Benefield of Oklahoma City and Julian Rothbaum of Tulsa headed a fund-raising effort which was limited to $250 per individual. An Oklahoma City newspaper columnist wrote, "We're glad George is not the governor of Rhode Island. All we would have is a hot tub at the mansion." Note son Mike Mashburn taking advantage of the Oklahoma sun.

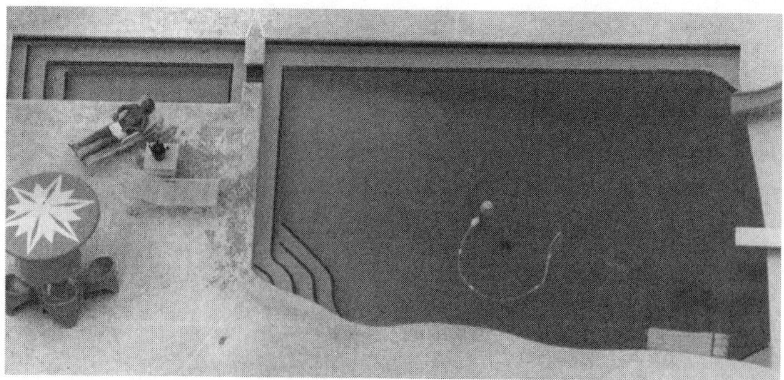

After living in the mansion for one month, Donna described her new home to a newspaper reporter as "cold and drafty, but very livable and something nice we should be proud of."[4] The second floor, with its five bedrooms, became the family's home. The third level, built as the state ballroom, was available for large gatherings and dinners. One of the upstairs bedrooms was converted into a family room for family privacy.

Isolation was a problem for Donna living in the mansion. Her new home was miles from former neighbors and shopping areas. With a house always full of people she realized, "The days of running around in your nightgown and barefooted are over."[5] Constant security was also a new, bothersome fact of life. Every piece of mail received at the mansion had to be tested for letter bombs. Donna could not drive her own car and the constant presence of a security guard when she left the mansion was cumbersome. Guards were with her while she shopped for clothing and even when the family attended church. Always one to see the positive side of a situation, she commented, "There's one good thing. I've got four state troopers back in church."[6]

Donna believed her first obligation, after being a wife to George, and mother to Mike and Georgeann, was her full-time job as Oklahoma's First Lady, overseeing the mansion and the three-member domestic staff. She said, "I must be the right kind of help to George." However, Donna wanted to have her own life also, to be casually independent, saying, "I don't want to depend on George for everything." She simply wanted to be Donna.[7]

In the beginning, Donna, who had always cleaned her own house and cooked the family meals, thought taxpayers' money was being squandered by hiring cooks and cleaning staff at the mansion. It was not long until she changed her mind. She said, "Sometimes we have 20 for breakfast, 40 for lunch, and 80 for dinner. I felt like I was running a catering service. There is no way I could have done it by myself." [8]

Doretha Hays, hired at the mansion during the Boren administration, became a valued friend and helper for Donna. Doretha, who had three daughters herself, became a valued family member and a second mother to Georgeann. Doretha knew what to expect from visitors coming to the mansion. Donna called her a "nurturing woman."[9]

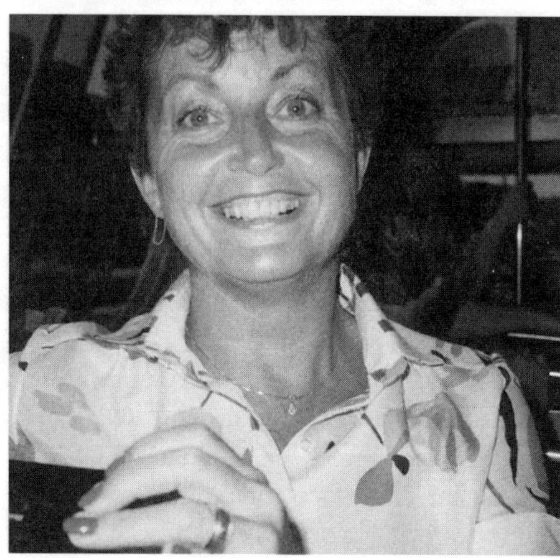

Shirley Cassil was hired as Donna's assistant. Donna and Shirley had been close friends for many years since Capitol Hill High School days. Donna depended upon Shirley for everything from keeping up with correspondence to having a faithful travel companion.

Coincidentally, Doretha was originally from McAlester and, as chief maid, cooked most normal meals for the first family. Donna saw no reason to hire a full-time cook because she and Doretha cooked breakfast for as many as 20 legislators for George's Monday morning legislative breakfast. If more than 20 came to the mansion for a meal, it was catered.

The love and respect for Doretha was dramatically shown in 1995 by members of four first families for whom she worked who spoke at her funeral. Governors Nigh, Boren, and Walters, and First Lady Cathy Keating all spoke of Doretha in glowing terms.

Donna's first luncheon as the new first lady was anything but peaceful. For some unknown reason, fire alarms began blaring during the luncheon. No fire was found but huge, red fire trucks sat strategically placed around the mansion for the remainder of the meal and into the afternoon.

Early in the new administration, George and Donna hosted a press luncheon at the mansion. The preview luncheon was scheduled at noon to kick off the Wednesday open houses that were to begin at 1:00 P.M. After members of the press were seated, there was a late arrival, whom no one recognized. George asked press secretary John Reid which radio station the man represented. No one knew. Turns out the man was not a member of the press, just a visitor who had arrived early for open house scheduled for later in the day. Since he had arrived at 12:15 security guards thought he was a reporter and escorted him to the third floor luncheon.[10] After the meal, George stood at the door of the state ballroom, shaking hands as the guests departed. As he was pumping the governor's hand, the unknown guest whispered encouraging words to George, "Thanks for the meal. You'll have a lot more people next week at open house, especially when I tell my friends that there is also a free lunch."[11]

One of Donna's first actions as first lady was to meet with Department of Public Safety officials to remove practices in the state's driver education and testing program that discriminated against the handicapped. Being the wife of the governor allowed Donna to access any state official she desired, and her kind, informed approach to problems brought results and gains for handicapped services and programs. She served as chairman of the Mothers March on Birth Defects and chairman of Oklahoma's Cancer Fund drive.

Donna saw her role as first lady as an opportunity to further programs to serve Oklahoma's handicapped citizens. Years before, at the request of Governor Bartlett, during tours of state facilities, George and Donna visited the three state schools for the developmentally disabled. After seeing conditions at Pauls Valley, Enid, and Sand Springs, Donna resolved to dedicate her public work for these special Oklahomans with special needs.

Donna, while touring the state school at Pauls Valley, remembered the very moment that she fell in love with the children. She was concerned that they might be forgotten by state government. Even though she was busy with carpools, Parent Teacher Association (PTA) projects, and other mom chores, Donna joined the Oklahoma Association for Retarded Citizens (OARC), eventually serving as vice president of the organization.

In 1968, Donna began volunteering at the Dale Rogers Training School, a home for the the developmentally disabled, in Oklahoma City. She changed diapers, cleaned bathrooms, and cheerfully took on

In 1996, both houses of the Oklahoma legislature honored Donna for her leadership in programs for the developmentally disabled. In this photograph, Donna addresses the House of Representatives as House Speaker Glen Johnson, Jr., looks on. Earlier, State Senate President Pro Tempore Stratton Taylor praised her contribution to so many Oklahomans.

any assigned task. As her children grew older, Donna spent more and more time volunteering at Dale Rogers and in Special Olympic events and activities.

Donna actively sought information about treatment and assessment of developmentally disabled citizens. She recognized that while institutions may be necessary for a small percentage of the disabled population, there was a desperate need for group homes, or an viroment other than nursing homes, often the only available residence for developmentally disabled men and women past the age of 18.

"Ninety percent of adult mentally retarded patients end up in nursing homes," Donna said, "I just don't think that's where they belong."[12] Ultimately, Donna's personal lobbying of the legislature resulted in the creation of a series of state-funded community residential group homes as an alternative to placing developmentally disabled citizens in nursing homes. Donna's lobbying efforts were carried out while she helped prepare and serve breakfast to legislative leaders at the mansion on Tuesday mornings during the session.

Many citizens were fearful of group homes planned for their neighborhoods. Donna appeared at zoning board hearings and did what she could to allay fears.

The cost of housing a developmentally disabled person in a group home was estimated to be half the cost of institutionalizing the same

Donna Nigh, a classy first lady of Oklahoma, was comfortable in her role as wife, mother, and advocate for the state's developmentally disabled population.

Donna fell in love with Oklahoma's developmentally disabled children during a visit to state institutions during the administration of Governor Dewey Bartlett. She spent much of her public life after that trip pushing programs to improve their lives. Here Donna poses with some of her friends at the 1999 opening of a new group home in Bartlesville.

person. To live in a group home, a person had to be at least 18 years old and capable of being employed, either in a sheltered workshop or in private business.

In recognition that this new program for Oklahoma was a direct result of her personal effort, the program was named the "Donna Nigh Group Home" project by the Department of Human Services.

In a magazine interview, Donna called the developmentally disabled her "friends." She said, "I love them. They have so much love to give. We've made it too easy to institutionalize these people and a lot of them have a contribution to make." Her goal was to "make as many of the disabled as independent as possible."[13]

In 1983 Donna was chosen by the Commission on Developmental Disabilities of the United States Department of Health as Oklahoma's "Volunteer of the Year."

The following year hundreds of Donna's friends established the Donna Nigh Foundation to provide funds to supplement the needs of Oklahoma's developmentally disabled. The formation of the foundation was a surprise announcement at Donna's 51st birthday party. By this time 24 group homes had been established in communities around the state and Donna was receiving national attention for her work.

John Orr was the first chairman of the foundation. Executive board members were Major General Richard Burpee, Commander of the Oklahoma City Air Logistics Center; Dr. Jean Cooper of the Oklahoma Department of Human Services; Vaughndean Fuller, Tulsa homemaker and civic leader; John Harrison, a retired Oklahoma City television station public affairs director; Patricia Hefton, Oklahoma City homemaker and civic leader; J. D. Helms, Oklahoma City attorney; Bob Jones, executive director of the Oklahoma Osteopathic Association; Duncan businessman M.J. Lewis; civic leader James A. Mueller of Oklahoma City; Robert D. Parks of Oklahoma City; Southwestern Bell division president John R. Parsons; Medford banker Joseph Reed; Tulsa oil man Julian Rothbaum; and Tulsa civic leader Patricia Wheeler.

A black-tie dinner at the Vista Hotel in Oklahoma City benefited the Donna Nigh Foundation to the tune of $50,000. Donna declared the purpose of her effort was simple, "To make life just a little more enjoyable and a little more meaningful for some of the 90,000 mentally retarded citizens of Oklahoma."[14]

The establishment of the Donna Nigh Foundation won praise from the the *Tulsa World*. An editorial stated, "One of Oklahoma's most pressing needs has been group homes for the adult developmentally disabled. Until recently, the state offered no facilities or system of care for these people." The story continued, "Great strides have been taken in the past two years, and First Lady Donna Nigh can take much of the credit...Oklahoma's first lady was in Tulsa this week to remind us again of something we know but can't bring ourselves to do anything about. Namely, that something must be done to provide homes and modest supervision for mentally retarded adults."[15]

In September, 1984, Olympic gymnast Bart Conner performed at a fund-raising event for the Donna Nigh Foundation. The night was appropriately dubbed "A Salute to Donna Nigh." In October, George signed a gubernatorial proclamation creating the Governor's Task Force on Mental Retardation, bringing together parents of retarded citizens and representatives of the legislature, nursing homes, group homes, the Department of Education, and the Department of Human Services, to make "a strong commitment to provide for the needs of the mentally retarded."[16]

Later, under the leadership of close friend Geneva Sarratt of Edmond, a garage sale at the governor's mansion netted more than $20,000 for the foundation. Clowns, soft drinks, ice cream, beer, popcorn, peanuts, and cotton candy were free for a $25 gate admission. Once inside, buyers were faced with table after table of Nigh mementos cleaned out of closets and drawers. Bud vases, teeshirts, and the keys to two Oklahoma towns, Broken Arrow and Woodward. Good Guys white hats and belt buckles brought $25 each. Merle Swineford of Laverne paid $75 for an Indian headdress. Someone bought an orange divan and carted off state seal wine glasses for $2.50 each.[17]

Donna continued her efforts to help Oklahoma's developmentally disabled through the years, culminating in her appointment by President Bill Clinton in 1997 to the President's Committee on Mental Retardation.

Other programs in which Donna was involved included preschool immunization campaigns and legislation to require approved car seats for children. Her favorite project, however, was an annual Easter egg hunt for blind children. Held on the mansion grounds, Donna hosted students from the School for the Blind in Muskogee and other public and private schools and institutions serving blind children. Costumed characters such as Mr. and Mrs. Easter Bunny were on hand to assist the children. Huge baskets of candy, cookies, and toys were given to the children.

With the help of the Pioneers, a group of retired employees of Western Electric, blind children hunted for plastic eggs that contained beepers. All the children, including those who had partial sight, were blindfolded to make the egg hunt fair. Sights such as children scampering around the governor's mansion lawn in search of beeping eggs filled Donna's bright blue eyes with emotion and made a deep impact upon her life and her sense of doing something good for the people of Oklahoma.

Donna and George had to make time to be alone. They exercised regularly together, played tennis, and swam. Sundays were set aside as family and church day at Council Road Baptist Church where they both taught Sunday School and were advisors to the Senior High Fellowship group.

Being governor and first lady presented a personal problem at church. The Nighs had reservations about having security guards with them as they prayed and worshiped in the same pews with the same people they had been with for years. Many, such as David and Millicent Gillogly, had been actively involved in the campaign.

About the time George decided to request that no security be assigned during church services a visitor approached George with a request that he sign his parole. The worshiper had attended church on three consecutive Sundays with plans to appeal to George.

Commissioner of Public Safety Paul Reed insisted that the first family be provided security. A compromise was reached when a plan was approved for state troopers active in their own local churches to attend services in civilian clothes at Council Road with the Nighs.

None of Donna's jobs was more important than being a mother to Georgeann, who turned 14 just six days after her father was inaugurated as governor in January, 1979. Donna laughingly predicted the difficulties Georgeann would encounter as a teenager in the governor's mansion, "She's worried when she gets old enough to date, her dates will be afraid to come meet her daddy and the security guards, too."[18] Donna said that her goal was to make Georgeann's life as near to normal as possible, although both she and George recognized the near impossibility of achieving that desire.

Georgeann was a spritely blonde, an eighth grader at Western Oaks Junior High School near the Nigh's former home in Oklahoma City just across from Lake Overholser. She was a straight-A student who had proved her excellence in athletics since elementary school. She played guard on three basketball teams, was a top-notch softball player, played piano, and was a member of her school's pep club.

Even the move into the governor's mansion did not reduce the frequent trips to basketball gyms and softball fields to watch Georgeann play. The first addition to the mansion grounds was a basketball goal.

At first, Georgeann resented her father being governor. She had been moved into a neighborhood where she knew no one, at an age when neither she nor her school friends could drive. The sudden change disoriented her and some people treated her differently after the election. In her first two years in the mansion, Georgeann often disappeared into her room, referred to by her parents as "the hole."

In an attempt to enable Georgeann to visit with more of her friends, George and Donna bought a condominium in Hefner Village in northwest Oklahoma City, close to Putnam City North High School. The idea was to make it easier for friends to drop by after school and on weekends. However, the experiment for the first family was short-lived. It was impossible to maintain two residences in the Oklahoma City area. They never had the right things at the right place at the right time.

Wednesday tour days at the mansion interfered with Georgeann's private life. Often she forgot what day it was. She recalled, "So I'd pull on my swimsuit and get all greased up to lie out by the pool. Twenty minutes later I'd open my eyes and look into the faces of 25 first

Georgeann, left, with college roommate Keli Satterlee at Oklahoma State University.

Georgeann excelled in athletics, especially softball. From an early age, she loved softball. George and Donna spent their vacations following Georgeann to softball tournaments.

Georgeann grew into a beautiful young lady and attended college at Oklahoma State University.

graders." On another occasion, Georgeann was trapped in her room, half-dressed, while a group explored the mansion. There was no lock on her bedroom door, causing curious visitors instinctively to attempt to see what was behind the closed door. Donna had to rescue Georgeann.

Soon Georgeann felt better about her life in the governor's mansion. Several of the younger members of her father's staff took on the role of big brothers and even became Georgeann's advocate in parent-child issues. Once during a University of Oklahoma football game in Norman, aides Dean Gandy and John Reid handed a note to George, pleading for a car for Georgeann's 16th birthday. The governor gave her a choice, a used car at 16, or a new car when she graduated from high school. Georgeann chose instant gratification, and took a used Chevrolet rally sport Camaro. Only then was Georgeann allowed to drive across town to Putnam City North High School, a far better course of action than riding to school in an old, unmarked highway patrol car, driven by a state trooper, and at Georgeann's insistence, being let out a block from the school.[19]

To be able to stay closer to her school friends, Georgeann had chosen to attend high school at Putnam City North. Because the Nighs lived outside the Putnam City school district, and paid transfer tuition, Georgeann had a choice of which high school in the district to attend.

Donna was the primary disciplinarian for Georgeann even though George was the more conservative parent, grudgingly giving in to requests for a telephone in Georgeann's room and allowing her to wear makeup and have her ears pierced.

"Dad was a pushover," she said, "He was philosophical. If I was told to clean my room, and I didn't, he couldn't just spank me. He made it worse by saying, 'Why did you not clean your room? Is it because you forgot or because you chose to be disrespectful and disobedient?' "[20]

Mopeds were a Christmas gift so Georgeann and her friends could ride on the expanse of open land behind the mansion. Often her best friends stayed overnight in the mansion and George and Donna hosted parties for Georgeann's fellow students. A pinball machine was

George gets a hug from Georgeann during a 1981 basketball game in Stillwater between Putnam City North and Stillwater. George and Donna worked basketball and softball games into their busy schedule to perform what they considered to be their most important task, raising their daughter. Courtesy *Stillwater NewsPress.*

installed in the mansion basement, another attempt to make the mansion livable and enjoyable for their teenage daughter and her friends.

In August, 1979, the family attended a week-long Amateur Softball Association National Junior Girls' Fast Pitch softball tournament in Freeport, Texas. George was chosen honorary mayor of the tournament and watched Georgeann's team slug its way to a third-place finish.

Georgeann's involvement in softball translated into proud parents who learned the sport well and became one of its biggest supporters. They became active in a successful effort to convince the Amateur Softball Association to locate its national office and hall of fame in Oklahoma City.

Georgeann developed close friendships with security and household staff at the mansion. If her mother and father were away on official business, Georgeann often went to the guard shack and watched television with security officers on duty.[21]

Georgeann threw herself into competitive athletics, excelling in fast pitch softball. When she graduated from Putnam City North High School in 1983, she turned down an athletic scholarship in favor of enrolling at Oklahoma State University in Stillwater, following in the footsteps of her brother Mike.

Of her father, Georgeann said, "He's one of my favorite people. He's very fair minded, honest, very aware of being fair. He's good at managing situations, telling me over and over again, 'Don't sweat the small stuff.' He's a peacemaker and a peacekeeper."[22]

Georgeann called her mother "quite determined." "She could have been anything she wanted to in life," Georgeann said, "but she chose to drive a van and carry my friends and me around to softball and basketball games. She was always there for me."[23]

Being the daughter of the governor had its low moments. After an anonymous bomb threat during debate over Oklahoma's beer-drinking age in 1982, she had to stand outside the mansion in her bathing suit for hours while officers searched the executive residence. She had to change her private telephone number after reporters discovered the number and called her in the middle of the night asking for her father. When an anonymous caller threatened to kidnap Georgeann, security guards took the threat seriously.

College life at Oklahoma State University, where she roomed with high school friend, Keli Satterlee, was near normal for Georgeann. She reflected, "In Stillwater, three-fourths of the people don't know who I am. And if they do, they see me eating lunch in the cafeteria and with my hair frizzed, and realize right away that I'm just like everybody else." [24] An exception to her anonymity was on the first day of a political science class when the professor called the roll and asked, "Georgeann Nigh, surely you're not really the daughter of the governor?" [25]

Georgeann had to learn to overlook comments from spectators when she came to bat during softball games. It was not uncommon for someone to yell, "Hey, tell your dad to give teachers a raise."

Georgeann met Gordon Whitener during her final year in college. They were married a year later. Georgeann gave birth to Macy Nigh Whitener on August 10, 1991. Georgeann and Whitener were later divorced.

Mike Mashburn did not move to the mansion initially with George, Donna, and Georgeann, having earlier left the nest after graduating from Putnam City West High School in 1970. He graduated from Oklahoma State University with a B.A. degree in marketing.

"Daddy George" and "Mama Donna," proud grandparents of Macy Nigh Whitener, daughter of Georgeann.

The Nighs and their "famous" dogs in front of their home on Picnic Lane before moving into the governor's mansion. Left to right, Mike, Georgeann, Donna, and George.

The relationship between Mike and George improved dramatically after Mike graduated from high school. In the early years of George and Donna's marriage, Mike reacted adversely, although normally and predictably, to George's authoritative role as stepfather. The normal parent-teenager conflicts over curfews and "hanging out" were magnified by George's conservative rules and disagreements over the use of Mike's car.

By the time George was elected governor, Mike, at age 26, lived in an apartment in Oklahoma City and worked with his father, J.W. Mashburn, in the construction business.

In December, 1981, Mike married Mara Kerr, the daughter of Mr. and Mrs. William G. Kerr of Norman and granddaughter of the late United States Senator Robert S. Kerr. Mike and Mara were married in the Blue Room at the State Capitol, a marriage referred to by *The Daily Oklahoman* as "a Sooner version of a royal wedding."[27] A reception at the governor's mansion followed.

Mike and Donna, 1999.

Mike Mashburn's four children. Top, left to right, Graycen and Ayla. Front, left to right, Chase and Berry.

Eighteen months later on July 15, 1983, Mike and Mara were blessed with the birth of a seven pound eight ounce daughter, Ayla Mashburn, in an Oklahoma City hospital. A second child, Graycen Mashburn, was born May 3, 1985. Graycen was named after maternal great grandmother, Grayce Kerr, the wife of Robert S. Kerr.

After the divorce of Mike and Mara, Mike moved into the governor's mansion.

In June, 1987, Mike married Rebecca Sue "Suzy" White and presented two more grandchildren to the former first family. Berry Mashburn was born January 24, 1989. Chase Mashburn was born November 1, 1990.

Being in the spotlight as the first family of Oklahoma gave George and Donna opportunities to comment on each other's characteristics. Donna refuted rumors that she was the boss of the house. She told the *Tulsa Tribune*, "Anybody who really knows George Nigh knows that is not true. He is one of the most forceful people I've ever met. I can't think of a single time when I've ever changed his mind." Donna disclosed that George was happiest when he was with hundreds or thousands of people.[28]

When asked about her husband's strengths, Donna said, "He's the same every day. He's fair to everyone, thoughtful, there are no quick decisions. I have never seen him be unkind or disrespectful to anyone."[29]

Boom Times Continue

I've come to Oklahoma to see how you do it.

President Ronald Reagan

In 1980, while Oklahoma's government coffers were filled to overflowing with increased revenues, there still existed problems in Oklahoma's future.

George believed that water problems would become as critical in the next decade as energy problems were in the 1970s. He asked both public and private agencies and corporations to work toward a statewide water plan that produced more water for arid western areas of the state and better water distribution systems in the east.

George tried to build a consensus for a water plan. He called a statewide conference of hundreds of members of local soil conservation and water districts and civic leaders from all corners of Oklahoma. Addressing the conference at Oklahoma City's Lincoln Plaza Hotel, George began by saying, "I want to be governor of all of Oklahoma but your great differences makes it impossible to serve all. You are too divisive."

Then he made a surprising announcement to the hundreds of Oklahomans who were his guests, "I'm leaving now but I want you to stay, close the doors, and reach a consensus, and then give me your advice."

After much discussion, the conferees huddled and unanimously passed a resolution that simply said to George, "Do something." The vote was a reflection of the tremendous confidence people on all sides of the controversial water issue had in George.[1]

A second major problem was that county governments were strangling because of chronically limited revenues. George, House Speaker Dan Draper of Stillwater, and Senate President Pro Tempore Gene Howard of Tulsa called for increased funding to prevent some overburdened counties from going broke.

A third concern was the skyrocketing costs of highway construction. While other state revenue sources were increasing, the flat 6.58 cents-per-gallon motor fuel tax, one of the lowest in the nation, had leveled off after declining during the energy crisis when drivers cut back on miles driven. George warned legislative leaders that unless the state dipped into the general fund to supplement the motor fuel tax, Oklahoma would face a rapid deterioration of its aging state highway system. George firmly believed that the infrastructure at the local, state, and federal levels, needed to be updated and expanded. He especially targeted bridges on Oklahoma roads and highways.

The state badly needed improvements in existing mental hospitals and money for construction of group homes and other facilities for handicapped children and adults. Federal lawsuits similar to the one that forced costly prison improvements were threatened unless the legislature acted quickly to fix the problem of the underfunding of mental hospitals.

George called the condition of the state merit system, once the pride of reform, "deplorable and archaic." His mini-cabinet listed the merit system as the number one problem in state government. George succinctly stated his opinion of the merit system, "There has been no job reclassification in the 20 years since we created the system." He explained, "We've had a system where we hired someone and guaranteed he couldn't be fired, but we didn't have a system that trained, evaluated, and promoted people." He promised, "We are going to develop a system that helps state employees help themselves and we are going to reclassify every job."[2]

George's lofty goal of restructuring the state merit system was approved by legislators, prompting Frosty Troy, editor of the *Oklahoma Observer,* to write, "George Nigh will be remembered for the most massive up-grading of the state's work force ever undertaken. It was long overdue. The turnover in state government passed the 40 percent mark last year, costing taxpayers millions." Troy continued, "It was Nigh who came up with the idea of a massive reclassification of the entire workforce—more than 35,000 employees. Because of his determination, classified employees won an average pay increase of more than 15 percent."[3]

After 80 days of committee meetings, hearings, and political wrangling, the 1980 legislative session ended on June 16, 1980. It was the shortest session since 1974, but a mid-season recess made it seem long. Lawmakers went home for 25 days in April and May after a district court ruling threw a shadow over $100 million in income tax revenue.

One of the most far reaching actions of the 1980 legislature was the transfer of University Hospital in Oklahoma City to the Department of Human Services (DHS). The hospital, along with nearby Children's Hospital, which had been transferred to DHS during the Boren administration, had suffered financially for years. University was renamed Oklahoma Memorial Hospital. The transfer was a turning point financially for the state-run hospital that provided much needed care to thousands of indigent Oklahomans.

These actions and others later in his administration set in concrete the foundation for George's mission of developing a world class health center in Oklahoma City.

While the legislature was in recess in May, George traveled to McAlester for the dedication of a national guard armory in his name. The armory, home to the Oklahoma Army National Guard's 45th Military Police Battalion, was a 1937 structure that had been rebuilt at a cost of $335,000. Major General Robert Morgan, state adjutant general, joined other military and civilian officials to officially open the George Nigh Armory as part of an elaborate Armed Forces Day celebration. George joked about an Army facility being named after a former Navy seaman.

He told the audience that he had broken a family tradition, "My grandfather, my father, and my three older brothers all joined the

Army, but I joined the Navy because they kept their ships so clean. Of course, I found out who keeps them clean!"[4]

The armory was named for George as an expression of appreciation that during his tenure as governor, most state armories were updated and two new ones were constructed.

In recognition of those who served their country, all existing state veterans centers were renovated and a new facility to serve veterans was built in Claremore, another example of the effort to make all state services more accessible to every area of the state.

George called the legislative session "the most productive for the people" in his 26 years in state government. In the final hours of the session, George told lawmakers, "We end this session with the continued wisdom of the previous. Another tax cut, a strong cash reserve, expanded people-oriented programs of state government, and a substantial cash carryover for insurance as we look to the future."[5]

George praised Senate leader Gene Howard for promoting legislation to exempt utility bills from the state sales tax and House Speaker Dan Draper for enactment of a five-year, $54 million rural bridge improvement program.

George singled out Senator Rodger Randle of Tulsa and Representative Jim Fried of Oklahoma City for their leadership in bringing about what he called a "much-improved program" for public schools, vocational technical education, and colleges and universities.[6]

George was acutely aware that the bullish state of Oklahoma's economy and the continuing wave of prosperity allowed him to increase programs and agencies in which he believed. Oklahoma was the most fully employed state in the Sunbelt and ranked in the top ten of the fastest growing states in the nation. Agriculture, energy, manufacturing, and tourism were growing beyond the national average. George said, "Oklahoma's time has come, it's the place for the 80s!" George believed that if the economy remained strong, state government could afford "some of the icing on the cake that we've been looking at for years but haven't been able to afford."[7] George particularly wanted to upgrade the infrastructure.

Oklahoma was still entangled in the thicket of trying to comply with sweeping directives of United States District Judge Luther Bohanon to reform the state's penal system. Oklahoma's prison population was exploding, rising an average of 50 inmates per month. With federal court mandates on inmate space, health, and safety minimum standards in force, the state either had to find alternatives to incarceration or plan to build a new 600-inmate prison each year for several years.

George had called on the legislature to appropriate additional funds for the corrections system, but it fell mostly on deaf ears. George said, "Prisons appropriations were not politically sexy." In fact many candidates openly attacked those who supported penal reform.

George had refused to criticize Judge Bohanon during the gubernatorial campaign, even though some advisors thought such lambasting would win votes, and showed up in Bohanon's courtroom after he was elected to promise the state's best effort to comply with orders for improvement of prisons.

George was nervous sitting on the front row of the courtroom waiting to testify before Judge Bohanon. As he was called to the witness stand, he was bent over tying his shoe. Startled, George, with all eyes on him, pulled so hard tying a knot that he broke his shoelace, providing a moment of mirth for the serious-minded participants of the litigation.

As the clerk began to administer the oath, Judge Bohanon interrupted, "You don't have to swear in the governor." Lou Bullock, the attorney for inmate Bobby Battle who had brought the historic lawsuit, objected. Bullock strongly pointed out that all witnesses needed to be sworn in. Judge Bohanon retorted, "We all know George Nigh doesn't lie and doesn't need to take an oath. Mr. Bullock, do you have any more objections?" Bullock promptly replied, "No, sir." Department of Corrections board chairman Denny Hopkins of Woodward told reporters, "The personal reputation of Nigh was the best thing going for Oklahoma's case."[8]

The Daily Oklahoman asked, "How much is enough?" In an editorial commenting on hearings in McAlester at which state officials told

Judge Bohanon of actions the state had taken, the newspaper said, "Nobody knows the eventual price tag to taxpayers for the building and operating of the kind of correctional institutions that will satisfy Bohanon's personal criteria for protecting the constitutional rights of convicted felons. Six years after he issued his mandate for prison reform, we still don't know."[9]

Bohanon was satisfied with George's testimony and plans to construct two new medium security prisons and conversion of one of the facilities at McAlester into a maximum security prison. However, the judge believed the state fell short in availability and quality of mental health care for inmates and the degree of continuing legal aid the state must provide to persons convicted of crimes. *The Daily Oklahoman* editorial said, "And from some of the bleeding hearts at the hearing, it seems that access to law books and help from inmate clerks is not adequate. They would have a staff of lawyers on hand to assist convicts."[10]

The federal lawsuit concerning Oklahoma's prison system was destined to continue until 1999, a quarter of a century after it began.

In July, 1980, "the pulses of oil and gas wells were throbbing with growing rhythm across the state of Oklahoma."[11] The state's share of a bursting oil market was pouring into the state treasury, creating the largest surplus in state history.

"The state of the state is great!" George declared to a July 1 meeting of 500 members of state boards, commissions, and advisory groups massed at the Myriad Convention Center in Oklahoma City. It was the same theme of George's state of the state message six months before, at the opening session of the legislature. George likened the position of Oklahoma in mid-1980 to the position of Oklahoma City on April 23, 1889, the day after the first Oklahoma land opening. He said, "Oklahoma City was a spot on the prairie when the gun sounded to start the run. The next morning it was a city of 10,000 people. We're virtually at the next morning of a new run in Oklahoma." [12]

George pointed with pride to the condition of the state treasury; a $100 million surplus compared to a $3 million surplus at the end of a fiscal year just five years before. At his request, the legislature left unappropriated $60 million to be carried over to the next fiscal year.

The surplus became a "rainy day fund," a state savings account that proved valuable in later years as legislators looked for sources of emergency funding. The rainy day fund was one of George's proudest achievments. "It won't always be this good."

In an interview at the end of December, 1980, George self-evaluated the first half of his term as governor. He estimated he had completed 95 percent of the program he had promised during the 1978 campaign. He spoke of his pride in his campaign to increased industrial development, especially outside the metropolitan areas, and his efforts to assist local governments.[13] "There are 77 counties."

In early 1981 George announced his plan for the first session of the 38th state legislature. Riding on a wave of a projected surplus of $326 million, George proposed $80 million in tax cuts, on top of the $90 million of tax reductions over the previous two years; one-time capital improvements; and a new emphasis on economic development. He told *Oklahoma Business* Magazine, "Only if you keep the state's economy growing will we continue to have growth monies. If the economy dies, then you cut back on roads, schools, and other government services. If the economy grows, you can add to, and supplement these services."[14]

Oklahoma Business credited George for Oklahoma's rosy economy, saying, "One of the major reasons for this healthy state of affairs and record state revenues is the pro-business attitude of Nigh. Since his days as Lt. Governor he has been a strong booster of industrial and tourism development. He recognizes that a gainfully employed population and a profit-oriented business environment generates the tax dollars needed to fund quality government services."[15]

The magazine pointed to George's leadership on a regional and national scale. He was on the executive committee of the National Governors Association, chairing the subcommittee on oil and gas; was the lead energy governor for the Southern Governors Association; a member of the executive committee of both the Southern Growth Policies Board and Council of State Governments; and chairman of the Ozarks Regional Commission, a six-state economic development organization that funneled federal grants to local units of government. He wanted Oklahoma's point of view enhanced.

As 1981 began, George announced plans to restructure the state Industrial Development Department into a Department of Economic Development. His stated objective was to expand the market place for Oklahoma and to increase state assistance to existing Oklahoma companies. He said, "'Too long we have neglected the people here in Oklahoma in going out and selling new companies. We always gave the break to a new firm that would move in, often competing with existing businesses. We have an obligation to help Oklahoma firms while continuing to solicit new business nationally."[16]

George attempted to take politics out of water development. Since statehood, little had been done to bring leaders of water-rich eastern Oklahoma to the same table to talk about water development with representatives of dry western regions of the state. George de-emphasized talk of water transfer, opting instead to help local communities increase their bonding capacity to facilitate construction of new water treatment plants and expansion of distribution systems.

Of the political pulse of water development, George said, "If anybody pushes for water transfer and makes it their first priority, they are going to lose the whole water plan. On the other hand, if you realize that water transfer might be a part of an overall water plan into the next century, and you approach it from this standpoint, many things can be accomplished as you strive for a solution."[17]

The brevity of the 1980 legislative session did not carry over to 1981. Limited to 90 legislative days, the legislature had to recess four times in 1981. The first recess was called May 29 as a cooling off period after a conservative coalition of Republicans and dissident Democrats blocked passage of several appropriations bills. Legislators returned and recessed three days later after deciding there remained too much paperwork while the number of days they could legally meet was dwindling. A major challenge to ending the session was squabbling over congressional redistricting, a constitutionally-mandated responsibility after each federal census.

At George's insistence, taxes were slashed again. Ending state and city sales taxes on prescription drugs was expected to save $12 million annually. Another $18 million would be saved by a new law reducing the state inheritance tax and eliminating the state gift tax[18]

George signs a 1981 law requiring judicial and citizen review of Oklahoma's foster care system. Looking on are the bill's co-authors, Representative Cleta Deatherage (D), left, of Norman, and State Senator John McCune (R) of Oklahoma City. George signed into law a series of statutes known as the "Victims' Bill of Rights," legislation setting up a victims' compensation fund and creating victim-witness coordinators in district attorney offices. George encouraged bi-partisan legislation. Courtesy *The Daily Oklahoman.*

When the legislature finally adjourned in July, it had appropriated a state record $1.7 billion, $400 million more than the previous year. Record amounts were handed out to almost every state agency, including $162 million to the state highway department, that provided $10 million for restoration of the Chicago, Rock Island, and Pacific Railroad line through the state. This was a new endeavor.

A most unusual yet signficant achievment of the administration was the saving of railroad rights-of-way in many areas of Oklahoma. Oklahoma Railroad Association Director John Kyle reported that during the Nigh years, more than 600 miles of rail was purchased at a cost of $23 million. These purchases prevented the abandonment of sections of rail that allowed continuing service critical to moving farm and manufactured goods to market.[19]

One of the bills in the legislative hopper that died in the 1981 session was the annual attempt to ratify the Equal Rights Amendment to the federal constitution. Even though George personally supported ratification of the amendment to guarantee equal rights for women, he evaluated any hope of Oklahoma ratifying the ERA as "slim." When George's prediction drew the ire of the Oklahoma Women's Political Caucus, headed by Wanda Jo Peltier, he issued another strong statement of support. Noting George's position, *The Daily Oklahoman* correctly predicted it was twilight time for the ERA, editorializing, "From the increasing desperation of its supporters, one gathers that fact has begun to sink in. If they couldn't win ratification of the requisite number of states in nine years, their chances of picking up the necessary three more states by next June 30 are just about what the governor said they were." [20]

Although both George and Donna lobbied hard for the amendment, it fell one vote short in the legislature.

Reform of county government was on the minds of George and members of the Oklahoma legislature as 1982 dawned. The largest single case of public corruption in the nation's history, a county commissioner scandal, shocked Oklahoma in 1981. The scandal ended with 230 convictions or guilty pleas, including 110 against commissioners alone. Equipment suppliers were caught giving elected officials money under the table in 60 of the state's 77 counties.

The commissioner probe began in 1974, headed by assistant United States Attorney William "Bill" Price, who with assistance of the Federal Bureau of Investigation and Internal Revenue Service, uncovered elaborate kickback schemes. From May to December 1981, more than 70 county commissioners resigned because of the probe.

George responded to the sweeping investigation of county commissioner corruption by appointing a 36-member Oklahoma Task Force on County Government. The task force submitted its recommendations in a November 23, 1981, report, charging that county commissioners were not accountable to anyone for many of their actions. The task force suggested electing commissioners on a countywide basis, rather than by districts as had been the law since statehood. The report also proposed creating three full-time professional county officers in the areas of highways, purchasing, and administration and the hiring of a county administrator to handle the business side of county government. Another sweeping recommendation was to consolidate the offices of county treasurer and assessor and abolish the offices of county surveyor, county school superintendent, and county court clerk.[21]

Faced with severe opposition to the task force report from county officials, George developed his own agenda of reform. He picked proposals from the task force report and others from suggestions placed on the table by a joint legislative committee. George recommended the creation of a county purchasing officer; a requirement for counties to use the state central purchasing system for large items such as road graders; a requirement that all county officers participate in training programs; a reduction of the maximum amount of purchase that could be made without advertising for bids; funding the district attorney's office from state funds rather than from the county budget; and strengthening the state's grand jury system.[22]

The final reform legislation looked very much like George's proposals. Some state laws were changed and new ones passed. Possibly the most far-reaching law that resulted from the county commissioner scandal was the authorization of multi-county grand juries that could cross county lines to investigate criminal activity. That investigation tool has been used many times since 1982.

The 1982 legislative session began with legislators looking at a $236 million surplus up for grabs in the appropriations process. Oklahoma's booming economy was fueled by taxes from natural gas and crude oil running 30 percent ahead of collections the previous year.

In his state of state message to the legislature in January, 1982, George cautioned legislators not to spend all the extra money, instead suggesting that solons carry over $100 million. George announced his top priority for the year was the development of a statewide water plan. George was concerned about studies that predicted that Oklahoma's main water aquifer, the Ogalala formation, in the northwestern part of the state, would be depleted by more than 50 percent in 40 years, leaving 330,000 acres in the crop-heavy Panhandle too dry to cultivate.

Of George's proposed budget for the following fiscal year, *The Daily Oklahoman* said, "Nigh surely must be the envy of nearly every other governor in the country. Being able to preside over the annual dispensation of a constantly increasing state till is a heady experience few politicians ever get to enjoy... There was, indeed, something for just about everybody in his blueprint of how the state should spend the bonanza of growth revenue."[23]

In April, George joined Tulsa area legislators working on a law creating the University Center of Tulsa, an innovative higher education center that provided public education for college juniors and seniors, and graduate degrees, for the first time in Tulsa. Tulsa was the largest metropolitan area in the United States without a public institution of higher learning.

Forbes Magazine interviewed George in May for a feature story on Oklahoma's government surplus. George said the huge surplus was "a reverse *Grapes of Wrath*." *Forbes* wrote, "His once dusty state, whose drought and crop failures pushed Okies westward during the Depression, now has an unemployment rate of 4.8%, tied for lowest with Wyoming."[24]

One of George's most personally satisfying appointments came in 1982. Alma Wilson, a native of Pauls Valley, was named as the first woman to serve on the Oklahoma Supreme Court. George already

George with Oklahoma actor Ben Johnson at the Oklahoma premiere of the movie *Dillinger,* filmed in Oklahoma. Courtesy Fred Marvel.

Three giants of Little Dixie. Per capita, no other Oklahoma town matches McAlester in the production of government leaders. Gene Stipe, left, has served in state legislature longer than anyone in American history. Carl Albert, center, rose through the ranks of the United States House of Representatives to become Speaker, holding the highest post ever for an Oklahoman in the federal government. George served as governor of Oklahoma longer than anyone else. George and Stipe spoke at Albert's funeral, broadcast nationally on C-SPAN in January, 2000. George summed up the tribute: "This pint-sized coal miner's son became a giant who cast a long shadow that reached from Pittsburg County to the Arkansas and Texas borders and eventually . . . to the borders of the world. Carl Albert would want us to be ever mindful of the challenge of his life's motto 'There is no greater job in the world than representing the people.' "

had established himself as a governor who gave women an equal standing in state appointments. In addition to Secretary of State Jeannette Edmondson, George had appointed Norma Eagleton of Tulsa to the Corporation Commission; Tulsan Mary Warner to the Board of Public Affairs; Betty Ward of Bartlesville as State Education Council director; and Cindy Rambo of Norman as director of the Department of Economic and Community Affairs.

George had appointed women to serve as the majority on the board of regents of the Oklahoma College of Osteopathic Medicine and Surgery in Tulsa. Some of his other major appointments of women were Bertha Parker of Tahlequah, Transportation Commission; Tulsan Augusta Mann, Pardon and Parole Board; Loretta Jackson of Chickasaw, Banking Board; and Zula Bay of Oklahoma City, State Board for Property and Casualty Rates.

There was much speculation in the press as to whom George would appoint to the state's highest court. When House Judiciary Chairman, Representative Robert Henry of Shawnee, went to George's office to support Wilson's candidacy, George said, "Line up with all the others. Alma Wilson apparently has lots of friends." Wilson eventually rose to Chief Justice of the Supreme Court. Upon her death in July, 1999, at age 82, George called Wilson "a grand lady."[26]

The Alma Wilson appointment was a shining example of George's stated purpose of making sure that all aspects of Oklahoma would be represented by his appointments. Freda Diane Deskin, writing about the Wilson appointment in her 1993 Ph.D. dissertation at the University of Oklahoma, said, "Nigh meant equal representation, not only race and gender, but age, geographical area, rural and urban, Democrat and Republican. . . He wanted to underscore the reality that all people, regardless of where they live or what they do had a role and voice in Oklahoma."[27]

Deskin related a story of Nigh looking hard at the Commission on Children and Youth and discovering that youth had no representation. Deskin wrote, "He appointed the first 18-year-old in state history to an official state commission."[28] The high school student later became chairman of the Commisison while attending OU.

Billboard, a mega magazine in the music and entertainment industry, featured Oklahoma in July, 1982. The article called George "a press agent's dream. handsome, personable, intelligent, a frustrated horn player who probably turned to politics because a four-year term beats a one-night gig."[29]

Billboard applauded George for promoting Oklahoma artists by quadrupling the appropriation to the Oklahoma Arts Council and making the walls of the State Capitol open to anyone with talent. George had tapped the artistic experience and ability of Betty Price to feature artwork of Oklahomans in the Capitol, with money from the sales going to the artists.

George was credited with bringing movie and television production to Oklahoma. The *Billboard* special quoted Mike McCarville, Governor Dewey Bartlett's press secretary, and later a popular talk show host at KTOK Radio in Oklahoma City. McCarville told the magazine, "It was 1968 and he really beat the drums to get a movie. He got a production that nobody ever mentions. It was *Two Lane Blacktop,* not a raging success, but it was filmed in Oklahoma. It's one of the best things he ever did, developing a commission to go after movies."

In an August, 1982, poll in northwest Oklahoma City's newspaper *Friday,* George was voted as the most powerful person in the state, edging out Edward L. Gaylord, publisher of *The Daily Oklahoman.* United States Senator David Boren was number three in the poll, followed by House Speaker Dan Draper, Congressman James Jones, and oil man Dean A. McGee.[31]

Oklahoma turned 75 years old in 1982. George chose Oklahoma City banker Jack T. Conn to head a Diamond Jubilee Commission which oversaw nearly 1,500 projects to celebrate the state's birthday. Lee Allan Smith and Bill Thrash produced a November 13 Diamond Jubilee production showcasing Oklahoma talent at the Myriad Convention Center in Oklahoma City. On November 16, the first statehood day was reenacted in Guthrie, culminating in a lavish Inaugural Ball at the Scottish Rite Temple in Guthrie. George played the role of Governor Charles Haskell in the reenactment on the steps of the Carnegie Library in Guthrie where Oklahoma was born.

Above: George prepares to announce the Oklahoma vote for the presidential nomination to the Democratic National Convention at Madison Square Garden in New York City, August 13, 1980. The results of the Oklahoma caucus are neatly printed on George's left hand. One of the persons receiving votes was Oklahoma Congressman Tom Steed of Shawnee who had remained in office because he wanted to serve another term in Congress while George was govenor. At the convention President Jimmy Carter received the nod of an overwhelming majority of Oklahoma's delegates.

Below: Linda Rosser and George admire the permanent marker on the State Capitol grounds that celebrated Oklahoma's Diamond Jubilee in 1982. Courtesy *The Daily Oklahoman.*

Three governors of Oklahoma chat during a 1982 Diamond Jubilee celebration. Left to right, Raymond Gary, George, Henry Bellmon. Courtesy Fred Marvel.

Running For Re-election

In the management of the campaign against George in 1982, we set an Oklahoma record; we lost all 77 counties.

Tom Cole,

campaign manager for George's opponent

At the end of 1981, George's thoughts turned to re-election. Problems with prison overcrowding and the county commissioner kickback scandal had made him tired. He was a happy family man who considered the fact that his daughter Georgeann was growing up and maybe he would have more time for her if he was not governor. Also in the back of George's mind was the fact that the only two governors who tried to succeed themselves, Dewey Bartlett and David Hall, had failed.

When Donna pointed out that Georgeann would be graduating from high school and moving on to college the next year anyway, George decided to run again. He and Donna totally refuted rumors that Donna was against the re-election bid. George said, "She's the most supportive wife a guy could have."[1]

George Nigh's life has been full of firsts, youngest legislator, youngest lieutenant governor. It was a natural progression in his career for George to attempt to become the first governor in state history to be reelected, a feat made possible by a constitutional amendment in 1966.

Left unanswered was the legal question of whether or not the five-day term George served at the end of the Boren administration counted as a term. If it did, he had already served two consecutive terms and was not eligible to run for re-election. Fortunately, the potential problem never came up, even though a possible court battle was discussed by George and his staff. One plan was to have George resign as governor for the last day of his first full term, allowing the president pro tempore of the state senate to succeed him. That move technically would have allowed him to serve as governor again.

A Friends of George organization was created months before George made any public announcement of his intention to ask voters for a fourth term as governor. He had raised more than $300,000, much of it, said *Oklahoma Observer* editor Frosty Troy, coming from "fat cats in the Republican Party." Troy cited pre-election reports from a $1,000 per person fund-raiser at the Oklahoma City Golf and Country Club, attended by some of Oklahoma's foremost Republicans such as Oklahoma Gas and Electric president James G. Harlow, Jr.; Sylvan Goldman, one of the state's richest men and inventor of the grocery shopping cart; banker Jean I. Everest; Coors beer baron C. Richard Ford; oil man John Kirkpatrick; Stanton L. Young of Oklahoma City; and industrialist Bill Swisher, who had served as a high-ranking fund raiser for George's GOP opponent, Ron Shotts, four years before. Swisher, out of deep respect for the results George had accomplished in his first term, became an avid supporter and campaign worker in the re-election effort.[2]

It was Swisher who referred to George as the best governor Oklahoma City ever had.

With an admonition to "Let's keep a good thing going," George officially announced for re-election on March 5, 1982. At a State Capitol news conference George said he would run on his record of achievement "where all voices have been heard." He pointed to major strides in transportation, health, mental health, corrections, education, and aging programs. George said, "As we chart Oklahoma's course for the eighties, I want to be part of it."[3]

With a positive theme, "Good Guy... Good Governor," George limited his campaigning during the remaining months of the legislative session to two dozen fund raising appearances.

On July 10, George and Donna hosted a campaign kickoff and fourth annual Nigh Good Guy's Reunion at the amphitheater at the Oklahoma City Zoo. In vintage Nigh fashion, George was dressed casually in a short-sleeved shirt, navy blue shorts, and tennis shoes. Campaign supporters dusted off their white hats and converged upon the zoo by the hundreds. A rock band, square dancing, balloons, soft drinks, and ice cream made the kickoff feel more like a family reunion than a political function.

Four of George's staunchest supporters for re-election. Left to right, Delmas Ford of Midwest City, Julian Rothbaum of Tulsa, Norris Price of Del City, and Jim Clark of Tulsa.

When George approached the amphitheater stage at the Oklahoma City Zoo to officially announce for re-election in July, 1982, he rode a white horse, symbolizing the continuation of the good guy theme.

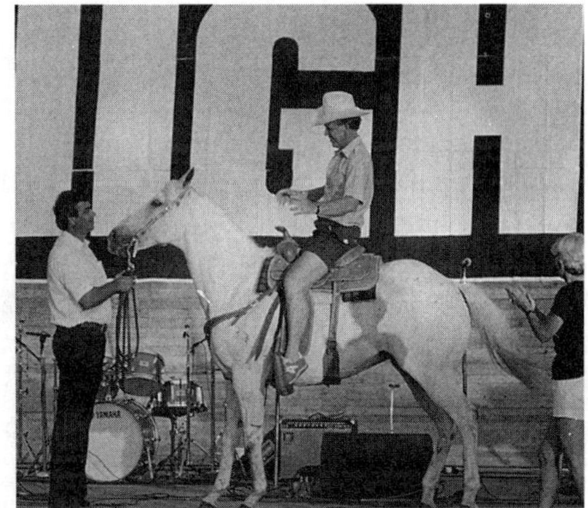

George was delighted with legislative funding for two major higher education projects. George appeared at a Blue Room ceremony with University of Oklahoma President William Banowsky, left, and Oklahoma State University President L. L. Boger, to announce a new energy center for OU and an agriculture center for OSU.

To top off the evening, a dunk tank was set up, giving youngsters a chance to throw softballs to dunk Nigh supporters who wore bumper stickers containing the names of George's two Republican opponents, Tom Daxon and Neal McCaleb.

George pointed to 16 tax reductions in his first full term as governor as absolute proof that his leadership was best for Oklahoma. He said he had appointed more women and minorities to important positions than any previous governor, had successfully promoted economic development, had helped elderly citizens by helping remove the states sales tax from prescription drugs and removing three-fourths of the state inheritance tax. George also cited improvements in road construction, increased spending for common schools, higher education, and the vocational-technical education system, and programs designed to help the handicapped and the Veterans Centers.

George recognized that the oil and gas industry in Oklahoma was largely responsible for the glut of money in the state budget. He said, "There is not a governor tonight in this country who literally would not change places with the governor of Oklahoma. Our challenge is to keep it like that."[4]

George became an invisible candidate in the Republican primary. Daxon, elected four years previously as state Auditor and Inspector, and McCaleb, the minority leader of the state House of Representatives from Edmond, largely ignored each other in campaign speeches. Instead, they both attacked George. Once again, the Good Guy image came under attack.

McCaleb did not mince words, calling George "Ole Marshmallow Nigh, a nice guy but not a governor." McCaleb, whose great-grandfather, a Chickasaw Indian, came to Oklahoma on the Trail and Tears, did not soft-pedal his views on the state of the state. He said, "George Nigh is totally ineffective. He will avoid controversy. This state needs a governor that can take the political heat along with the adulation."[5]

Daxon, who raised substantially more Republican primary money than McCaleb, based his attacks on George on his private polls that he interpreted as indicating George's widespread support was not solid, and that with the right money and media package George could be defeated. Daxon admitted there was no groundswell to throw George

The Oklahoma Human Services Commission voted to name a state of the art rehabilitation center in Okmulgee the "George Nigh Rehabilitation Center." Left to right are George, State Senator Bob Miller, and State Representative Glen D. Johnson, Jr. During his two terms as governor, George emphasized social services programs. He established the nation's first Office of Handicapped Concerns, appointing legally-blind Ernest Simpson, Norman, as director. He commissioned studies to make Oklahoma's parks, turnpike and highway rest stops, and other state facilities accessbile to the disabled. He had remembered how bad the conditions were at University Hospital when his mother was hospitalized there years before. Her nurses were so underpaid they often asked his mother if they could have food leftover from her meal. George asked DHS Director Lloyd Rader to take over the hospital and appointed a committee to bring nursing and mental health components into the OU Health Sciences Center, so all state-owned programs could be centrally located and controlled efficiently.

out of office. However, he predicted, "I can win by getting myself known. The people want a younger man, new blood, and someone who will represent all the people." This was a strange twist, someone was attacking George for being too old.[6]

George deftly balanced his job as governor with a rigorous campaign schedule. Bright young Nigh aide, Michael Clingman, engineered a massive information gathering project which proved vital to the campaign. Clingman asked the state agencies to prepare a detailed report on the Nigh administration's accomplishments. These reports became press releases and media packets and as source material for campaign speeches as George traveled to every county to remind the people what his administration had done for them.

Two weeks before the primary George was verbally jabbed by Daxon and McCaleb for his aggressive highway construction program. The Republican candidates scoffed at the Northwest Passage project, a six-year plan to upgrade OK-3 from Oklahoma City to Boise City in the Panhandle. George worked a miracle to win support of highway commission members from several districts to develop the long-range project to improve the Northwest Passage. In previous administrations, highway projects were traditionally limited to one county or one area represented by a single highway commissioner.

The Northwest Passage project covered 353 miles from the State Capitol to the Oklahoma-Colorado line—the longest stretch of continuous highway improvement in the nation's history announced at one time.

Interestingly enough, McCaleb, while serving as director of the State Highway Department, lobbied the legislature for tax increases, explaining that "my tail lights burn brighter than my head lights."

In early August, George hosted the nation's governors at a meeting of the National Governors Association (NGA) at Shangri-la on Grand Lake in northeast Oklahoma. The *Cherokee Queen* was the flagship of a flotilla of boats carrying the governors. Abe Hesser, director of the Oklahoma Tourism and Recreation Department, arranged the conference. Secretary of Interior James Watt and Secretary of Agriculture John K. Block headlined the group of federal officials who met with

In 1982, as part of Oklahoma's 75th year of statehood, George officially opened the Hall of Governors, a display of busts of Oklahoma's governors.

governors to discuss critical problems facing the nation. NGA officials said the Oklahoma meeting was the organization's best ever.

George's opponent in the Democratic primary was Blanchard businessman Howard Bell, 58, a political novice. He was swamped in the August 24 primary, George gathering about 80 percent of the Democratic vote, 379,301 to 79,735.

More than 5,000 supporters celebrated the primary election victory at Oklahoma City's Sheraton-Century Center Hotel, chanting "Four More Years." Madalynne Norick, the victory party decorator, supervised volunteer crews all day to set up a western store-front decor that served as a backdrop for a buffet line of tacos and barbecued ribs.

George claimed victory less than two hours after the polls closed. With Donna at his side, George told the cheering throng, "The record will show that no administration has ever equaled the Nigh administration when it comes to education, tax cuts, the water bill, and the push to save railroads in western Oklahoma."[7]

Pat and Joe Fallin, members of Special Oklahomans for Nigh, told reporters that George had done more for Oklahomans with disabilities than all previous governors.[8] When asked what his proudest accomplishment was, George often replies, "Special needs for special people."

In the Republican primary, Daxon outdistanced McCaleb two-to-one, and immediately launched attacks on George. Daxon, who personally opposed pari-mutuel betting, accused George of straddling the fence on the issue. Daxon's deputy campaign manager, Tom Cole, said the low voter turnout in the primary showed George's support was soft and that Daxon's hopes were pinned upon apathy. More than 200,000 fewer voters had gone to the polls in the 1982 primary than four years before.[9]

Cole had run the numbers. Republicans composed about 27 percent of the Oklahoma electorate. But, Cole predicted, if only 32 percent of the registered voters went to the polls in November, and a higher percentage of Republicans voted, as statistics showed, the GOP chances were greatly enhanced.[10] George laughed and asked "Did they actually pay for that analogy?"

George's general election campaign was based upon the theme of continuity—"Keep a good thing going." Though Oklahoma employment was dropping off slightly, it was still high. The energy business had begun to slump but state tax collections were at all-time highs, allowing new money to be pumped into highways, education, mental health, and other areas of the government often ignored in the past.

George's campaign organization was comprised of many veterans of his earlier races. George identified 1,000 key people in the state. Campaign workshops were scheduled. In Clinton, regional coordinators Merle and Barbara Swineford and Denny and Marion Hopkins, and Custer County campaign manager Wayne Salisbury, were responsible for turning out more than 100 people to a workshop, an indication of the excitement about George's re-election effort.

Former Oklahoma City State Representative Hannah Atkins, later Oklahoma Secretary of State and a presidential appointee to the United Nations, and Erna Winters, northeast Oklahoma City civic leader and a member of the governor's staff, co-chaired a group called "Blacks United for Nigh." The organization generated excitement for George's re-election bid among leaders of the African-American community. Years later Erna and George, in the same year, were among the five national winners of the Martin Luther King, Jr. Award.

At the state campaign headquarters, volunteers manned banks of telephones trying to identify supporters throughout the state. Direct mail brochures were loaded onto pickup trucks for the short trip to the Oklahoma City main post office. Campaign treasurer J.D. Helms stayed up late at night recording the record contributions that flowed into the state office. Helms and Bob Parks observed that raising money on a record was far easier than raising money on blind faith.

George and Donna traveled in caravans in late September and October, going in different directions to blanket the state with the Nigh message. Rallies were held in each of the congressional districts. George capitalized on his incredible name recognition, a result of his crisscrossing the state for 30 years. *The Daily Oklahoman* reporter Mike Hammer accompanied George on one swing through southwest Oklahoma and wrote, "the Democratic governor is taking no chances that apathy will wreck his re-election bid. He performed the political rituals making speeches, shaking hands, signing autographs, and even kissing babies." [11]

An overwhelming majority of Oklahoma's newspapers repeated their 1978 endorsement of George. The *Perkins Journal* said, "Nigh is responsive to the people's needs. He is a man that's easy to talk with and he listens. His experience, knowledge, and wisdom is unequaled in Oklahoma history. He is the man of the hour." The *Duncan Banner* defended George's reputation as a nice guy, saying, "It's refreshing to find someone in politics who is a nice guy." The *Daily Ardmoreite* cited George's long experience as a plus for Oklahoma, "It gives him good judgment on what is feasible to attempt and what is not... He initiated a Total Oklahoma program, aimed at greater economic development and more jobs in all 77 counties."[12]

On September 11, George announced a five-year, $38.4 million program to upgrade US-81 from border to border. He was joined by gubernatorial aides, campaign staff members, and local campaign coordinators on a trip to Enid, Chickasha, and Duncan to announce the project. US-81 stretched 277 miles from Grant County in the north to Jefferson County on the Oklahoma-Texas border.

By early October, 1982, private polls showed George with a large lead over Daxon in all sections of the state. Daxon removed six employees from his campaign payroll, ceased polling operations, and made other moves to lower the cost of his election effort.

As the election neared, more newspapers endorsed George. The *Beaver Herald Democrat* said George had been the "best friend the Oklahoma Panhandle has ever had and the folks out here should remember it." The *Bartlesville Examiner-Enterprise,* in heavily Republican Washington County, wrote, "Through George Nigh's hard work, Oklahoma's natural and man-made attractions have developed into one of the country's finest recreation and tourism programs." The *Lawton Constitution* said that in George Oklahoma taxpayers had "a friend in the mansion."[13]

Elk City publisher Larry Wade, a strong supporter of Larry Derryberry in the 1978 primary, threw his full support behind George in 1982. Wade editorialized, "George Nigh has shown many people that he is tougher than some imagined. He has stood firm on a statewide water development program, the long term result of which may be the most important step being taken in Oklahoma government in this era." Wade reminded readers that many jobs in western Oklahoma were preserved by George's efforts to save railroad service. Wade said, "Not because of his political strength but because of his personal qualities and leadership, which he has so well exhibited, we support George Nigh for re-election." [14]

The enthusiasm of most of the state's newspapers for George's re-election was met by a series of prominently placed editorials in *The Daily Oklahoman*, strongly calling for George's defeat. Almost daily, the newspaper viciously attacked George. In an October 17 page-one editorial, the newspaper said, "Nigh's latest political ploy is pitiful, his election-eve call for legislative action next year to repeal the sales taxes on funerals and insulin for diabetics. That is Nigh's version of tax relief, a feeble proposal indeed when compared with Republican Tom Daxon's call for a real tax cut of 15 percent across-the-board reduction in state income taxes." Commenting on George's charges that the Daxon income tax cut would break the state financially, the editorial charged, "The governor obviously does not have his finger on the public pulse... The only way for Oklahomans to get any real tax relief and put an end to the state's wild spending spree is to elect Tom Daxon as governor."[15]

In October, George dropped a bombshell on the press, announcing he had chosen former Republican governor and United States Senator Henry Bellmon to replace retiring State Welfare Director Lloyd Rader. After 31 years at the top of state government's largest agency, Rader was calling it quits. George reached Bellmon by telephone while Bellmon was at a meeting in Denver, Colorado. Shocked by the proposition that he, as the state's first Republican governor, serve in a Democratic administration, Bellmon told George he would think about it and talk further when he returned to Oklahoma. Bellmon wrote in his autobiography, "The notion... potentially the state's most explosive political position... was at first illogical."[16]

Assured that he would have a free hand without political interference, Bellmon accepted the job. He had worked with Rader for many years and was aware that Rader believed someone of Bellmon's stature could lead the welfare department, newly named the Department of Human Services, out of troubled times. The agency had been named as the defendant in several lawsuits.[17]

The Daily Oklahoman, even though a rabid supporter of Bellmon, called George's appointment of Bellmon "a transparent but typical political ploy...to enhance his re-election campaign against hard-charging Tom Daxon." The editorial continued, "It represents an attempt to gloss over the eternal mess at the Department of Human Services with the veneer of Bellmon's residual prestige." [18]

Closer to election day, *The Daily Oklahoman* stepped up its criticism of George. On October 31, the newspaper got personal, "Nigh makes a good public appearance, tells funny stories, and will travel anywhere to cut a ribbon or make an after dinner speech... Four years of Nigh's non leadership have proved he lacks the skills to be an effective governor. More than a quarter century on the public payroll had turned him from Boy Wonder to Old Guard... Oklahoma has suffered the past four years. Industry no longer seeks out our state to locate plants and create jobs."[19]

The constant, daily attacks on George's ability weighed heavily upon him and his family. Even though he knew his polls showed he would win by a large majority, the barrage by editorial writers for *The Daily Oklahoman* hurt George deeply. He arose before everyone else at the governor's mansion to read, and hide the newspaper. If Donna asked him what the newspaper said that morning, George said, "Oh, nothing. It's just politics."[20] Donna remembered the repetitive volleys from the newspaper as "like a year of diarrhea."[21]

Calling George an ineffective leader, *The Daily Oklahoman*'s editorial headline on October 29 read, "It's Nigh time to retire George." The day before the election, the newspaper attack was harsh:

> Since 1954, there have been only two real losers—David Hall and George Nigh. And at least Hall was effective, albeit a crook. You have to go all the way back to Johnston Murray in the early 1950s to find a governor who was less of a leader than Nigh. Nigh has waved a white flag in the war on crime. Rapes and murders continue as victims fall prey to freed convicts under Nigh's loose parole policies. Oklahomans have a chance Tuesday to return competence to the governor's office by electing Tom Daxon... Oklahoma voters have made good gubernatorial choices in Gary, Edmondson, Bellmon, Bartlett, and Boren. We can correct one of our rare mistakes by electing Tom Daxon tomorrow.[22]

Other newspapers in Oklahoma tried to explain the editorial policy of *The Daily Oklahoman.* The *Beaver Herald Democrat* wrote, "Whether you take newspaper editorials seriously or with a grain of salt, the latest crusade by *The Daily Oklahoman* to keep Gov. George Nigh from being reelected is becoming one of the most talked-about aspects of the campaign. The *Oklahoman* is alone on this one."

The *Purcell Register* said, "*The Daily Oklahoman* tried to defeat him four years ago but the editorials and cartoons did not work. They won't work this time as the citizens of this state have confidence in George Nigh. He has done an excellent job as governor. He has shown that he cares for Oklahoma. He loves this state and has thousands of friends in all 77 counties who are busy working for his re-election. Yes, Mr. Gaylord, we agree Oklahoma voters have a clear choice. But it's easy to make that choice... George Nigh!!!" [23]

Oklahoma voters were not swayed by negative newspaper editorials or negative campaigning. On November 2, more than 900,000 Oklahomans went to the polls and gave George a 200,000-plus-vote victory over Daxon, 548,159 to 332,207. Independent candidate Allah-U Akbar Allah-U Wahid, a non-factor in the race, received 2,764 votes.

As in previous elections early returns showed a neck-and-neck race, but George was elated when he received the traditional telephone calls from every county courthouse, including word from Fairview that he had carried Republican-dominated Major County. This was the only county that J. Howard Edmondson had lost in the 1958 general election. En route from a watch party in Tulsa to the airport for the trip to the victory party in Oklahoma City, George turned to Donna and said, "We've won Major County. It's going to be a landslide."[24] With Major County in tow, George carried all 77 counties, the first and only gubernatorial candidate to ever accomplish that feat.

The thousands of Nigh faithful gathered in the South Ballroom of the Hilton Inn West Hotel, awaiting arrival of their hero. The John Arnold Band of Norman played country music for two-steppers and toe-tappers, in the middle of hundreds of white hats. Food and soft drinks were plentiful. By the time George and Donna arrived at the victory party at 9:30 P.M., the election was over. Daxon's campaign had been left in shambles. George called the easy victory "humbling and

After the 1982 election, Donna's father, 80-year-old Raphael Skinner, fell ill and moved into the governor's mansion. Donna's mother had died years before. George converted one of the mansion's upstairs bedrooms into a rehabilitation room for his father-in-law, shown here between his daughters, Ann Davis, left, and Donna. George moved a desk into the room where he worked every evening after dinner. Even though his father-in-law could not communicate, George would lift him from his bed and place him in a recliner near his desk as he worked on state business.

gratifying." He urged Oklahoma to move forward, to diversify its economy. George said, "The best thing I can do is to be the type of governor you expect me to be."[25]

In the final analysis, Republican pollsters and campaign gurus misinterpreted the mood of Oklahomans and George and Donna's statewide political strength. The campaign organization they had built over nearly a 30-year period remains unmatched. George and his finance committee raised $1.3 million, the first time in Oklahoma history a gubernatorial campaign had topped the million dollar mark.

Daxon had campaigned on a theme of less government and lower taxes. However, that theme did not play well in most sections of the state. *The Daily Oklahoman* reporter Mike Hammer, in an analysis, said Daxon misread Oklahomans' wishes for the state to provide more

On January 1, 1983, George and Donna rode in "the surrey with the fringe on top," part of Oklahoma's float in the Rose Bowl Parade at Pasadena, California. The float was sponsored by the Farmers Insurance Group. A man in the crowd along the street yelled, "Governor Nigh, you signed my parole!" Courtesy *The Daily Oklahoman.*

and better services, especially roads. Hammer wrote, "The people of Fay and Thomas, in Dewey and Custer counties respectively, would have tied Daxon to the narrow bridge spanning the South Canadian River, the narrow bridge they want rebuilt and widened because they fear a school bus may one day be crushed by an oil field truck." Hammer continued, "Or the people of Oologah, in Rogers County, would have ridden him out of town on a rail because they demanded of Nigh a new bridge over the Caney River to Collinsville because of several road deaths there. Or the people of Boswell, in Choctaw County, would have laughed him out of town. They want a county road to link U.S. 70 with State Highway 7."[26]

George Nigh had done what no other Oklahoman had ever done. He had been elected to successive terms as governor.

The Daily Oklahoman mellowed with an editorial headline, "George Did It Again!" Admitting that pre-election polls predicting George's relatively easy win were right, the newspaper said, "The governor has every right to be elated at his smashing 63 percent victory. . . Nigh will begin his second term with an impressive reservoir of good will and the support of a resounding majority of Oklahomans. *The Oklahoman* joins them in wishing him success in tackling the tough problems that must be resolved if Oklahoma is to continue moving ahead."[27]

Penn Square and Beyond

Lord, give us one more oil boom. We promise not to screw this one up.

1983 BUMPER STICKER

GEORGE'S SECOND FULL TERM as governor of Oklahoma began with two pieces of bad news. One was personal. Donna's father died the day before the January 10 inauguration. Donna and her sister, Ann Davis, insisted the inaugural activities go on as planned.

The other parcel of bad news was the unexpected depth of the slide in the economy. State revenue collections had dipped in recent months, resulting in George's call for a freeze on the hiring of state employees and projecting major reductions in state agency budgets for the next fiscal year. He sadly said, "The ship of state is aground financially."

Against a backdrop of a growing economic slump, George reminded listeners to his inaugural address that times in Oklahoma had been worse before. He recalled the pioneer traditions of barn and church raisings. He said, "I call on the people to participate in the world's largest barn raising in the Oklahoma tradition of helping your neighbor, of caring and sharing."[1]

Inauguration day began with a prayer service at the Council Road Baptist Church in Oklahoma City conducted by their pastor and friend, Wendell Estep. The sermon was delivered by another family friend, Dr. Ponder Gilliland, pastor of Bethany First Nazarene Church.

After an open house at the governor's mansion, the day's activities ended with a gala inaugural ball at the Myriad Convention Center. The Red Rice Orchestra and John Arnold Band provided continuous music. To celebrate his victory in all 77 counties, 77 trombones led the big parade, playing "76 Trombones." The trombone ensemble was composed of one high school trombone player from each county and was directed by Dr. Irv Wagner of the University of Oklahoma.

Hundreds of Oklahomans helped make the inaugural activities a success. Committee chairmen included Dr. William Horton, Reverend Wendell R. Estep, Jack T. Conn, Major General Robert Morgan, Lou Kerr, and Madalynne Norick. From the governor's office, serving as liaison to the inaugural committee, were Carl Clark, Mary K. Foster, J.R. McClanahan, Pete Reed, Betty Price, and Paul Pearson.

On inaugural day, the *Tulsa World* called George "a nice guy and a good governor." The newspaper's editorial page said, "One popular perception of Nigh is that of a nice guy who has parlayed that image into a successful career. While that is an indisputable fact, it also is true that Nigh's administration has so far been marked by a practical, non-confrontational approach that has had remarkable success." 2

After the inaugural activities, George began the difficult task of mastering a plan for the state as gloomy economic predictions appeared in newspapers and on radio and television. The boom was over, economists said, and tough times lay ahead.

George is sworn in for his second full term as governor of Oklahoma. Donna, saddened by the death of her father the day before, looks on. Courtesy *The Daily Oklahoman.*

Oklahoma's non-farm wage and salary employment had peaked at 1,244,100 in May, 1982. The active drilling rig count, an indicator of oil and gas activity in the state, was at an all-time high. Mercedes-Benz and Rolls-Royce dealers were breaking sales records. Oil companies spent millions for "executive gymnasiums, hot tubs, and helicopter pads."[3]

The boom had excited bankers and investors across the nation. Penn Square Bank, located in a northwest Oklahoma City shopping center, became a symbol of the exuberance and lax banking practices that permeated many oil hungry banks. Penn Square Bank provided a back door for large banks to participate in the oil and gas producing frenzy. Hundreds of millions of dollars changed hands, sometimes agreements were scrawled on cocktail napkins.

Then the bottom fell out. A sustained drop in energy prices, with resulting bankruptcies in the petroleum and contract drilling industries, caused Penn Square Bank to fail. In domino fashion, larger banks, such as Continental Illinois Bank, which got involved with more than $1 billion in loans, folded. Many of the nation's banks, large and small, were injured by the reverberating failure of Penn Square.

Other factors doomed the Oklahoma economy. Historians W. David Baird and Danney Goble observed, "When meat prices crested the hill and started slipping downward, ranchers rushed to get their

Donna enjoys a greeting card during the celebration of her birthday in 1983. Left to right, Robert White, legal counsel Bob Renbarger, Hannah Atkins, Charles Henry, Donna, and George.

George and Donna meet with Vice President George Bush at Kennebunkport, Maine, in 1983. Courtesy The White House.

cattle to market. More cattle at the sale lots meant lower prices, lower prices meant cutting back herds, cutting back herds meant even more beef for sale, and that meant lower prices."[4]

Falling oil prices had a direct, catastrophic effect upon Oklahoma's state government budget. Each reduction of $1 a barrel in the price of crude oil meant a $10.7 million drop in tax collections and another $143 million in pre-tax income for state producers.[5]

George had based his budget submitted to the legislature on $31.76 a barrel oil. However, by the time the legislature convened in January, 1983, oil had dropped to $29 a barrel, and would plummet even farther, to $9. State budget director J.I.M. Caldwell burned midnight oil to provide current figures for George and legislative leaders. Often the numbers changed daily, with the downward trend of oil prices on the world market.

The original budget had suggested that a $50.6 million cut in state agency appropriations would be necessary. George had already declared an emergency and forced state agencies to trim spending by 5.5 percent the previous November and 12.7 percent in December.

With a stern warning that "all pet projects had gone out the window," George told lawmakers that the financial crisis was not just belt-tightening, "it was a fast." He said, "If we have cutbacks, all Oklahomans should be given the opportunity to participate equally."

Oklahoma's problems were not confined to money issues. The legalization of pari-mutuel gambling, authorized by voters in 1982; demands for greater funding of education; and a federal court order to reduce prison overcrowding faced George and the legislature.

George suggested $37 million be spent to build new prison space. Others wanted to go with cheaper alternatives. State Senator Rodger Randle of Tulsa unveiled a 12-point plan to reduce overcrowding by using inmates for public works projects, establishing county-operated regional jails, and better use of existing alternative sentencing.[6]

Budget cuts became monthly priorities for state agencies. In January, 1983, agencies absorbed a 11.9 percent cut, followed by 10 percent cuts in February and March, and a 25 percent reduction in April. George asked the legislature for a $1 million emergency fund to help agencies facing acute shortages.

In the midst of this budget crises, George worked with legislative leaders to create the Oklahoma School of Science and Mathematics (OSSM), an innovative approach to train some of the state's brightest high school students in a special, residential school in Oklahoma City. Much of the legwork on the OSSM, pronounced "awesome," project was performed by Dr. Carolyn Smith, the governor's education coordinator.

In 1999, Marilee Jones, dean of admissions at the Massachusetts Institute of Technolody called OSSM, "a national resource producing young people who will be among the leaders of the next generation."[7]

Above: George signed legislation making Indian Blanket the Oklahoma official wildflower. Left to right, State Senator Billie Floyd of Ada, co-author of the bill; Betty Price, executive director of the Oklahoma Arts Council; George; Abe Hesser, executive director of the Oklahoma Department of Tourism and Recreation; Senator Enoch Kelly Haney of Seminole, co-author of the bill; and Professor Doyle McCoy of East Central Oklahoma State University in Ada. Price helped George dramatically improve state government's role in promoting the arts. Since Price's days as a fill-in secretary in George's office, she had sparked George's interest in the arts. One of George's cherished accomplishments in his first year as governor was to increase state spending for the arts. HB 1143 was signed April 17, 1979, increasing program funding for the Oklahoma Arts Council by 95 percent over the previous fiscal year. Price later became executive director of the Oklahoma Arts Council.

George congratulates Oklahoma City book store owner Jim Tolbert as a winner of the Governor's Arts Award, a tribute established to honor business leaders for strong support of the arts in Oklahoma.

The expected topic of tax increases rose to the surface during the 1983 legislative session. However, George strongly objected, wanting to ride out the tough times. Talk of raising taxes was placed on the back burner, even though Senate President Pro Tempore Marvin York of Oklahoma City predicted that Oklahoma would be in trouble by the end of the year.

George sparred with the legislature over several issues. His promised veto of a bill by House Speaker Dan Draper to allow cities to set the age a person could purchase 3.2 percent beer spelled doom for the measure. Draper led forces in a House committee to kill two bills, supported by George, to raise the beer-drinking age from 18 to 21.[8]

Lawmakers failed in an attempt to override George's veto of a bill that would have given the legislature authority to appropriate federal block grants to state agencies. The measure would have greatly decreased the governor's influence on how federal funds were spent in the state.

These and other battles between the governor and the legislature were hardly ever partisan in nature. Instead, they were grounded in an elementary and traditional debate between the legislative and executive branches of government.

The 1983 session was not without merit. A major change was made in Oklahoma's banking structure, permitting multiple ownership of banks by holding companies and branch banking. Legislation passed to authorize counties to levy a sales tax of up to two percent.

Legislators also pushed through a bill providing a surcharge on unemployment insurance, a move necessary to guarantee the solvency of the state unemployment fund.

The Department of Human Services was the focal point of disputes between George and the legislature. Interim DHS director Henry Bellmon drew fire from legislators when he began trimming programs to cope with falling revenues. The Whitaker Children's Home at Pryor was closed. More than 200 employees in the DHS-run teaching hospitals were laid off. The state senate blocked a move to furlough DHS employees to meet budget cut mandates.

Senate Democrats and George battled over a permanent director of the sprawling DHS. Senators wanted former Ada state senator

George Miller, a longtime assistant to Lloyd Rader. George and Bellmon wanted Robert Fulton, chief counsel of the United States Senate Budget Committee, who Bellmon had enticed to come to Oklahoma to help him write a comprehensive plan to save money in the DHS budget. George won. The Human Services Commission selected Fulton to replace Bellmon. This was a bittersweet victory for George because of his longtime friendship with Miller.

George called the legislature into special session in September, 1983, to appropriate monies to rebuild the Conner Correctional Center at Hominy that had been badly damaged in a riot, blamed on overcrowding resulting from double celling of inmates and a heat wave that flared tempers. George and corrections officials had asked for $5 million but lawmakers cut the figure in half, denying funds to rebuild the prison's law library and banned the hiring of an outside architect to draw up new plans.[9]

The Penn Square Bank failure created problems for Oklahoma's image. Jay Casey, who headed the state's economic development efforts, described the problem in blunt terms, "There was this image after Penn Square that 'they'll woo you and screw you in Oklahoma.'"[10] Casey recalled companies that he and his staff had been working with to convince to move to Oklahoma suddenly were turned off after Penn Square Bank's failure. Texas, traditionally a competitor for industries locating in this region of the country, turned the Penn Square Bank debacle in their favor, pitching prospective companies with "Do you really want to locate in Oklahoma?"

In addition to the image problem for Oklahoma economic development, Casey's state agency budget was reduced as a result of falling revenues. The promotional theme changed from "Energetic Oklahoma" to "Productive Oklahoma."

Oklahoma was not alone in experiencing fiscal crisis. *U.S. News and World Report,* in May, 1983, reported that 38 states had cut spending in fiscal 1983 and several more states were mulling over options to cut state services. Ten states, according to the magazine, had passed income tax hikes in the previous six months, another 13 had increased sales tax, 12 had boosted gasoline taxes, and 4 states had hiked cigarette taxes.

George was interviewed for the *U.S. News and World Report* special report. He pointed out that Oklahoma's drop in oil and gas exploration had fallen from 900 drilling rigs to 200, resulting in the loss of thousands of jobs. He promised to veto any tax increase passed by the legislature, at least until projections could be made on future revenues. In explaining the budget crunch, George answered, "The energy boom couldn't last forever. But revenues have fallen deeper and quicker than we anticipated. The rise in unemployment cut our income-tax collections. The state's portion of sales taxes is down 100 million dollars so far this year when compared to last year."[11]

By July, 1983, the freeze imposed by George seven months before on state hiring had startling results. The freeze had reduced total state employment by 2,041, including 1,253 fewer employees at the state's colleges and universities.

In August, 1983, George called for the sale of Fountainhead and Arrowhead lodges at Lake Eufaula, the same lodges he had helped create during his nine days as governor 20 years before. The state had never been able to service the $9 million loan that made possible the construction of the lodges. The agreement with the federal government was that payments would be required on the loan only if the lodges made a profit. They did not.

The lodges had served their purpose, creating jobs and development in counties surrounding Lake Eufaula which experienced unemployment rates of 13 to 20 percent in 1963, a bleak condition that made possible the original federal government intervention. George predicted that moving the lodges to the private sector would continue to promote economic development for the Lake Eufaula area.

In September, 1983, when George's staff began working on the fiscal year 1984 budget, a $90 million shortfall in revenue was projected for the remainder of the current fiscal year. Predicting that the 1984 legislature would have $250 million less to appropriate than the previous year, budget director J.I.M. Caldwell said Oklahoma was in trouble. The previous legislature balanced the budget by tapping several state savings funds for about $200 million. Those funds were depleted.

A national recession was in full swing as unemployment hit record highs. Talk of tax hikes in Oklahoma surfaced again. *The Daily Oklahoman* encouraged George to "Hang In There, Governor," in an editorial applauding George's stance against raising taxes.[12]

However, every time budget officials laid reports of new income projections on George's desk, the news was worse. Tax collections continued to decline. George believed he had no choice but call a special session of the legislature to deal with the festering problem. Senate chief Marvin York told reporters that unless higher taxes were enacted, 5,000 teachers, 3,000 college instructors, and 83 highway patrolmen would lose their jobs. That statement drew ire from *The Daily Oklahoman* which called it "a blatant, despicable scare tactic."[13] The newspaper suggested putting a tax hike to a vote of the people, rather than having the legislature address the problem of falling revenues.

Just before Thanksgiving, George announced a sweeping $654 million tax increase plan to make up the $219 million shortfall for the last seven months of the present fiscal year and create reserve funds. Among the recommendations were:

1. A one-year, two-cent hike in sales tax, to raise $179 million;
2. Remove the sales tax exemption from beer and cigarettes, to raise $7 million;
3. Increase the gasoline tax 4.42 cents a gallon, to raise $33 million.

George also proposed a one-cent permanent sales and use tax and an increase in liquor taxes.

George opened the special session of the legislature on November 28, 1983, with a frank admonition, "You have a terribly difficult choice to make. I've made mine. I asked for this job as you asked for yours." In his opening speech, George lambasted Edward L. Gaylord, publisher of *The Daily Oklahoman*, for editorial opposition to the Nigh tax plan. George said, "I think the proudest moments of my life are those times that I read the editorials and become more and more convinced that the people know that Eddie Gaylord does not own George Nigh. He never has, he does not now, and he never will." George's comments drew thunderous applause and a standing ovation.[14]

As in the past, other state newspapers had a kinder response to George's predicament. The *Tulsa World* said, "Nigh has decided to face the unpleasant reality of a state financial crisis. He is to be congratulated for grasping this painful reality." The Tulsa newspaper did not necessarily like a tax hike, but recognized that some adjustment of revenue was probable.

House leaders tried to put off the inevitable, calling for a ten-day recess to consider a tax increase. However, the Senate would not agree to a delay because many House members were predicting no tax increase could be passed because members' mail was running 10-to-1 against any increase. On November 30, both houses of the legislature gave up and adjourned.

George called it "one of the bleakest days in state history." Senator Gene Stipe of McAlester blamed the House for "taking the easy way out and going home." [16] However, F.M. Petree of Oklahoma City, co-chairman of a quickly-formed anti-tax increase group known as the Taxpayers Survival Team, called the aborted special session one of the "brightest days in history."[17]

A prominent member of the Taxpayers Survival Team was publisher Leland Gourley, in the past one of George's staunchest supporters. However, Gourley parted with George's call for a tax increase because he believed some state agency directors were attempting to frighten taxpayers into a tax increase. Gourley said, "It borders on the criminal the way they are trying to scare employees into believing they are going to lose their jobs."[18] Gourley stated that the $240 million shortfall in the state budget was only five percent of the state's total expenditures, an amount that could easily be "cut out in fat and waste." [19]

After the public outcry against new taxes, George issued a 30-day freeze order on state spending. A team, consisting of Delmas Ford, director of the Office of Public Affairs; state finance director J.I.M. Caldwell; and state personnel director Jim Thomas, reviewed 3,000 requests from state agencies. The panel delayed $8 million in purchases in its first three days of existence. George's emergency order directed that only life, health, and safety items were to be bought and all spending, hirings, and promotions had to be reviewed by the three-member team. Gubernatorial aide Carl Clark was assigned the task of coordinating the massive review.

Food and medicine orders for hospitals and institutions were honored immediately. A request for the Department of Transportation to repair one of its trucks was rejected. So was a request for recreational equipment for state prisons.

George proposed that state workers take an unpaid day furlough in agencies that did not have sufficient monies to meet its payroll. As part of the deal, George agreed to give up 10 percent of his salary for each month that state employees had to sacrifice.

The drumbeat for new taxes continued in Oklahoma as George, House Speaker Jim Barker of Muskogee, and Senate chief Marvin York of Oklahoma City all agreed that taxes must be raised. As the 1984 legislative session opened, the question was by how much?

George scaled down his original tax hike package to $431 million, to be financed by a smaller increase in sales and fuel taxes. Slowly but surely, many Oklahoma taxpayers, aware that oil prices continued to drop, recognized the need for both cutting the fat out of government and raising revenue by a tax increase. Legislators had gotten that message from constituents at home during December before convening in January.

Historians Baird and Goble characterized the mood in the Oklahoma oil patch, "Oklahoma oil men gave up their dreams of forty and fifty dollars a barrel. Instead they suffered nightmares as crude prices slipped down an oily slope past thirty-five, past thirty. The rout was on. In a matter of weeks crude prices fell from $27 to $13. Developers suddenly wondered what they would do with all those empty homes. . . Car dealers took back their fancy cars...Jewelers shipped Rolexes back to Switzerland. . . Coupled with the scandals surrounding the state's athletic programs and the county commissioners, they contributed to an atmosphere of psychological gloom."[20]

Nowhere was the mood gloomier than in George's State Capitol office. He was in his sixth full year as governor. He had seen the best, and now the worst of times. It had frankly been easier being governor when huge state surpluses were available for popular and needed programs. The financial crisis had placed the heavy burden of tough-times leadership squarely on George's shoulder. He lost a lot of sleep over the state's money problems but awoke each day with renewed confidence that he could lead his people out of the economic wilderness.

In his opening address to the 1984 legislature, George called for "the three R's of state government: reform, reduction, revenue." He said Oklahoma must simultaneously strip the fat from the state budget while raising taxes to finance programs the people needed and wanted.[21]

Two weeks into the session, the House of Representatives passed legislation cutting the state budget for the remaining six months of the fiscal year by $150 million. Representative Steve Lewis of Shawnee, chairman of the House Appropriations and Budget Committee, said the bill would allow state government to operate "scaled down, but not disrupted."[22] More than half of the budget reduction, $83.7 million, came from education. During impassioned debate, Representative Cleta Deatherage of Norman was near tears as she urged House members to reject the cut and look for ways to raise revenue. The proposed cuts in education were described as "suicide" by Representative Penny Williams of Tulsa. House Minority Leader Frank Davis of Guthrie said the budget cut bill would prevent any tax increases.[23]

The Senate followed the lead of the House and approved the $150 million spending cut measure. On January 30, George signed the bill into law. He said, "It is appropriate that the first bill to come to my desk this year is an effort to reduce the cost of government." George thanked legislators for quick action but urged them to take up the next step, obtaining more revenue. House Democrats had proposed a temporary one-cent sales tax. However, George said that alone would not be enough. George believed that it was imperative that the gasoline tax also be hiked.[24]

One of George's strongest backers for a tax increase was Representative Deatherage who formed a group of 15 legislators, Legislators Organized to Vote for Education (LOVE), to inform the citizenry of the importance of a tax increase to education. Seventy percent of the state's general fund went to education which would be severely impacted if a tax increase did not come, soon.[24]

As the legislature began sifting through a hopper full of tax increase and reform bills, George appointed Oklahoma City businessman, and later governor, David Walters, to head a 100-member Commission for the Reform of State Government. The group was charged with looking at the more than 200 state agencies with an eye toward savings and consolidation.

As George's blue-ribbon panel met, House Speaker Jim Barker named a 15-member select committee to study changes in state government. Representative Robert Henry of Shawnee, later Oklahoma Attorney General, dean of the Oklahoma City University Law School, and a Judge of the United States Tenth Circuit Court of Appeals, but then a member of the House Special Committee on Long Range Planning and Reform, said the committee was courting "big thinkers, people who have a larger view of the state and of the future" to join in the House committee's efforts. Ultimately, a dozen civic leaders and economic experts were added to the House committee. Public hearings were held throughout the state.

In March, 1984, George made his second appointment of a woman to the Oklahoma Supreme Court. The new justice, considered a long shot when the appointment process began, was Yvonne Kauger, an art gallery owner and president of Oklahoma City's Lyric Theater. Kauger, a native of Colony, Oklahoma, had served a dozen years as a judicial assistant to Supreme Court Justice Ralph B. Hodges. Kauger, who had been a basketball player in her youth at Colony, called her father, Don, after her appointment and said, "Daddy, I can still hit the long shot."[26]

To show her appreciation for the appointment to the state's highest court, Justice Kauger has sent George flowers each year since 1984 on the anniversary of her appointment.

In May, the Supreme Court heard arguments in a lawsuit that involved George and Donna's use of the state mansion fund, an annual $33,500 appropriation made to the sitting governor to run his official household. The litigation was brought by two professional journalism associations, the Oklahoma Chapter of the Society of Professional Journalism, Sigma Delta Chi, and the Oklahoma City News Broadcasters Association.

The groups wanted the high court to vacate the 1983 opinion of Oklahoma Attorney General Mike Turpen that the mansion account records may be kept secret. Turpen argued that the legislature had authorized unitemized expenditures from the mansion fund "to protect the governor and the integrity of that executive office from every political pundit, gadfly, and opponent who may seek to second guess the governor's good faith determination that an expense was properly connected with the occupancy of the mansion."[27]

The Supreme Court issued an opinion on May 29, declaring that the mansion account did not constitute a public record and therefore was not subject to audit by the Oklahoma examiner and inspector.

The court case involving the mansion was the second time in three years the issue had surfaced in state media. Auditor and Inspector Tom Daxon, while running against George in the 1982 gubernatorial campaign, had charged that George used money from the mansion account for tennis club dues, clothing, luggage, and parties. After the election, George asked Daxon to conduct an audit of the account. However, when Daxon filed his official report in January, 1983, he made no criticism of the fund nor recommendations for changing its use.[28]

On April 18, 1984, the state legislature completed action on George's three-part tax package, voting additional taxes on 3.2 beer, cigarettes, and alcohol, so-called "sin" taxes. Earlier, a temporary one penny state sales tax and a 2.42-cents-per-gallon hike in the state's gasoline tax were enacted. The extra penny sales tax was scheduled to expire on December 31, 1985. The gasoline tax was raised to nine-cents-per-gallon, still among the lowest state gasoline taxes in the nation.

House Speaker Jim Barker left his sick bed, recovering from a heart attack, early to help pass the tax package which was projected to raise $268 million for the ailing state budget. It was the largest tax increase in Oklahoma history.

Chuck Ervin, a veteran State Capitol reporter for the *Tulsa World,* calling the tax-increase package an impressive victory for George, wrote, "It probably wasn't the kind of victory Nigh envisioned two years ago when he ran for re-election on a no-new-tax platform. But the financial dilemma that forced Nigh to abandon this anti-tax stance probably also produced his most impressive performance in the nearly six years he has been Oklahoma's chief executive."[29]

Speaker Barker and Senate President Pro Tempore Marvin York had to beat back rebellious members, headed by a coalition of Republicans and rural Democrats, to pass the tax bills. George, on the other hand, called on business contacts around the state to put the heat on lawmakers to vote for the bills.

George was convinced that Oklahomans preferred more adequately funded services than lower taxes. The former history teacher stated publicly and firmly that he did not enter public service "to preside over the fall of the Oklahoma empire."

George went from one crisis to another. In May, a prison overcrowding emergency was declared, forcing George to release 66 inmates earlier than normal. The convicts were released first from community treatment centers and minimum security prisons. A new "cap" law, passed by the legislature the previous month, required early release of inmates when the prison population reached 95 percent of capacity.

Horse Racing and Liquor By the Wink

Don't send me any legislation that is not enforceable.
George Nigh to the Oklahoma legislature

Two huge, controvsersial, and emotion-packed issues crested in Oklahoma during George's two full terms as governor from 1979 to 1987. One was pari-mutuel betting. The other was liquor by the drink.

George's first brush with pari-mutuel horse race betting was in December, 1980, when the Oklahoma Horsemen's Association presented petitions containing 115,446 signers to Secretary of State Jeannette Edmondson calling for a statewide election on the issue. Betting on horse races had been previously rejected by 64,000 votes in an August 27, 1974, election on SQ-498.

Adopting former Governor Edmondson's position on the repeal vote, George declined to take sides on the issue declaring, "I feel the people who circulate petitions have the right to a reasonably speedy decision." After the Oklahoma Supreme Court verified the petitions contained at least eight percent of voters who voted in the previous general election, SQ-553 was added to the September 21, 1982, primary runoff ballot.

Pari-mutuel betting became a minor issue in the 1982 governor's race. Republican contenders Neal McCaleb and Tom Daxon both opposed legalized gambling. George refused to take a position, saying he would leave the question to the people. George's views were criticized by *The Daily Oklahoman*, which editorialized, "Each candidate owes it to the people to tell them where he stands on this issue... The people are entitled to know where the next governor stands on legalized pari-mutuel betting, particularly, since he will have the major hand in the licensing process. George Nigh should get down off that political fence."[1]

SQ-553 technically permitted counties to vote on pari-mutuel betting. It also set up a seven-member state racing commission, appointed by the governor and confirmed by the state senate, and instructed the legislature to collect a twelve to eighteen percent tax on betting tickets.

Leading the fight against legalized betting were Baptist, Methodist, and Pentecostal church leaders who called upon their ministers to urge congregations to vote against the proposition and work for its defeat. Dr. Joe Ingram, executive director of the Baptist General Convention of Oklahoma, prepared a one-minute statement to be read from the pulpits of the state's 1,430 Baptist churches with 700,000 members. Dr. Ingram said, "The basic issue is not horse racing, it is gambling. And because gambling is the issue, then it would be bad for the state economically, morally, and spiritually."[2]

Dr. Boyce Bowden, director of communications for the Oklahoma Conference of the United Methodist Church, urged 600 Methodist churches to remind people about the election and encourage them to pray. Assemblies of God District Superintendent James Dodd flatly called for the 500 churches of his fellowship to urge members to vote against SQ-553.[3]

The Daily Oklahoman warned about perils of betting on horse races, "Proponents argue that its approval would enhance horse racing as a sport, thus bringing jobs into Oklahoma and producing tax revenues that could be put to good use." The newspaper editorial continued, "The voters must decide, however, whether any such presumed benefits would outweigh the drawbacks sure to result from officially sanctioned gambling at racetracks in this state. Oklahoma already has enough crooks without opening the doors to unsavory elements from outside."[4]

On the other side of the question, Mike Williams, spokesman for the Oklahoma Horsemen's Association, predicted that the $400,000 his group had spent promoting SQ-553 would pay off. Part of the proposition's attractiveness to voters was Williams' claim that Oklahoma's general fund would receive $3.5 million during horse racing's first season in Oklahoma.[5]

When the votes were counted on the night of September 21, horsemen were ecstatic. Fifty eight percent of the nearly 800,000 voters who went to the polls approved pari-mutuel betting on a county option basis. Oklahoma became the 32nd state to legalize gambling on horse races. The issue carried in 54 of the state's 77 counties, including Oklahoma County, where it passed by a 31,000 vote margin.

With voter approval of legalizing betting on horse races, George pledged to make Oklahoma a model state for the sport. The next step was for individual counties to present petitions containing ten percent of the county's registered voters to call a special election to approve pari-mutuel race tracks in that county. The legislature was mandated to formulate legislation to establish the racing commission and decide how much tax to collect on betting tickets.

The legislature battled over George's nominees to the seven-member Oklahoma Horse Racing Commisison (OHRC). Much of the controversy surrounded George's appointment of his best friend, Paul Carris of McAlester.

Carris at first rejected apointment because he knew nothing about horse racing. But George convinced him to take the post with a simple statement, "This issue is so important that I want to send a signal. I want my closest friend on the commission, someone who has instant and complete access to me, a direct line to me. That's the only way I can assure the people of Oklahoma that the right thing will be done."

Carris' nomination prompted a less-than-complimentary report in *The Daily Oklahoman* by State Capitol reporter Mike Hammer. The article questioned George's selection of such a close friend to serve in the controversial position. However, McAlester mayor, and later district judge, Steve Taylor defended Carris, saying, "I don't think he would ever allow a conflict of interest to occur. I don't know of any man who has more credentials as a civic leader. He's a good man, an honest man."[6] In retrospect, most observers believed Carris served admirably on the commission. Each year a "Paul Carris Memorial Race" is run at Remington Park in Oklahoma City.

Because of the newness and the importance of horse racing in Oklahoma, George spent an unusual amount of time in selecting members to the OHRC. He knew very little about prospective appointee Delores Mitchell of Sallisaw. However, George was swayed to her corner when he received a letter from her minister. The letter read, "We strongly oppose betting on horse racing but we would feel more comfortable about it if Delores were on the commission." Mrs. Mitchell served longer than anyone in history on the horce racing commisison and later became president of an international horce racing organization.

Other members of the first horse racing commission were T.J. Henry of Lawton, Sheldon Detrick of Tulsa, Kenneth Russworm of Watonga, and Everett Lowrance of Claremore. The commission, on George's recommendation, hired Jack V. Boyd as the first executive director of the OHRC. Boyd was a retired state government official who was highly respected for his administrative abilities. The fact that Boyd knew nothing about horse racing did not matter to George because he knew Boyd possessed critical skills necessary to oversee the daily operations of the OHRC and gave credibility.

The greatest appointment battle came with George's selection of Allen E. Coles, president of the Oklahoma Horsemen's Association, as chairman of the commission. *The Daily Oklahoman* insinuated that the choice was shady because Coles had been "implicated, but never indicted," in the scandal during the administration of Governor David Hall.[7] George stood fast and Coles' nomination to chair the horse racing commission narrowly passed the state senate.

At least 12 entities proposed building racetracks in 1983. A planned track in Okmulgee would have cost $136 million and hoped to draw 23,000 fans each day. A proposed track in Love County hoped to attract as many as 17,000 fans daily. Entertainer Roy Clark, a regular on the television show *Hee Haw,* announced plans for a $150 million complex to be built 19 miles from Tulsa, called Cimarron Park Racing Resort. Very few of the original plans were completed.

The OHRC weeded out the several proposals and settled on a five-track circuit. But George, and the racing commission, endured a barrage of criticism during the lengthy process. Remington Park, in

Oklahoma City, was chosen as the major track in the state. Other tracks approved were Lincoln County Fair at Midway Downs in Stroud; Rogers County Fair at Will Rogers Downs in Claremore; the Tulsa State Fair at Fair Meadows in Tulsa; and Blue Ribbon Downs at Sallisaw, which already existed before the onslaught of new applications.

George was not spared ridicule during the years of often-heated debate over where to locate race tracks in the state. Disgruntled Love County racetrack backers distributed tee-shirts at a racing commisison meeting in Oklahoma City that bore the words, "IMPEACH GOVERNOR NIGH—WITH HIS RACING COMMISSION—HE HELD BACK OKLAHOMA THREE YEARS." Repeating his pledge not to influence the location of horse racing tracks, George showed his good nature by wearing the blue and white tee-shirt handed out by the people from Love County. George said, "I am not intimidated whatsoever by people being disappointed in the Commission."[8]

George kept racetrack promoters at arm's length. When a group requested to meet with the governor, he would refuse, saying that only the Horce Racing Commission had authority to grant licenses.

Publicly, and privately, George stayed out of the racing commission's business. He told commissioners at a Poteau workshop in August, 1985, "I have tried to make sure not to send any signal indicating what you should or should not be doing in regards to racing applications. That's why I appointed you and that's your job. I'd rather you take longer and be right than move faster and be wrong."[9] George was willing to take responsibility for his appointments to the commission but did not want to tell them what to do.

When the racing commission agreed to have only one major racing facility in the state, Edward G. DeBartolo, owner of the successful Louisiana Downs in Bossier City, Louisiana, and other race tracks in Ohio and Illinois, stepped forward with an application. Three other entities filed applications, but all dropped plans, or either had plans denied by the racing commission. DeBartolo was far ahead of his competition in winning racing commission approval to operate the state's only major pari-mutuel racing facility.

The Oklahoma House of Representatives considered a resolution to overturn the racing commission's decision to approve only one major race track. Pushing the measure was State Representative Kenneth Converse of Tishomingo, upset over denial of Love County's application for a track. When Converse called upon the legislature to make members of the Oklahoma Horse Racing Commision subject to a vote of the people, rather than gubernatorial appointment, George called the idea "asinine."[10]

Former Nigh aide Larry Brawner and David Vance, the DeBartolo pick to run Remington Park, were in the news almost daily as the OHRC considered the DeBartolo family application. About possible legislative action to allow more than one major track, Brawner said, "We applied under certain rules and the rules at the time were for one track. If the legislature or anybody else were to change that rule after the fact. . . it would be very damaging."[11]

When *The Daily Oklahoman* demanded DeBartolo reveal all personal financial information, DeBartolo refused. He called George and said the deal was off and he would not be investing in Oklahoma. George took matters into his own hands.

In early January, 1986, George made a personal call, "an economic development" visit, on DeBartolo during George's trip to Florida for the OSU Gator Bowl and OU Orange Bowl football games. During a 90-minute meeting at a restaurant in Tampa, Florida, George assured DeBartolo that Oklahomans wanted a class race track and were in support of DeBartolo's application to build the $78 million Remington Park. George pointed out to DeBartolo that he had no authority and would not try to persuade members of the OHRC who were scheduled to take final action later that month on DeBartolo's applicaton.[12]

George's visit with DeBartolo drew harsh criticism from Representative Converse who charged that George had "sold out the people of Oklahoma who voted racing in."[13]

On January 16, the Remington Park-DeBartolo proposal was accepted. George personally intervened in discussions between the OHRC and the DeBartolo interests to iron out last-minute differences in the terms of the license issued by the OHRC. Later DeBartolo said, "George Nigh is the reason I am in Oklahoma."[14]

The construction of Remington Park was still uncertain when George accompanied Oklahoma City Mayor Andy Coats and chamber of commerce officials to meet with DeBartolo in Ohio in March, 1986. The purpose of the trip was to convince DeBartolo to accept OHRC license requirements and proceed with construction. Also on the Ohio trip were DeBartolo spokesman, Larry Brawner; Ron Rosser, chairman of the Oklahoma City Zoological Trust, owner of the property where the race track was to be built; Senator Marvin York of Oklahoma City; Nigh chief of staff Dean Gandy; David Walters, chairman of the Oklahoma Human Services Commission, who also was a mediator between the Zoological Society and the DeBartolos; and Dr. William Talley, II, president of the Omniplex Board of Trustees.

DeBartolo accepted the OHRC's license in March, 1986, and began plans for breaking ground on a 420-acre site north of the Oklahoma City Zoo.

Remington Park opened in 1988 with an opening day crowd of 11,128 fans. The 1998 average attendance plummeted to 2,517 per day. Midway Downs was never able to attract good horses or large crowds and closed after two seasons.

Will Rogers Downs and Blue Ribbon Downs eventually sought protection from creditors under federal bankruptcy statutes. Fair Meadows, which hosted the Tulsa County and Tulsa State fairs, declined after 1995.[15]

The second major area of controversy swirled around Oklahoma's liquor laws. In 1984, Oklahoma was the only state that still did not allow its citizens to legally buy intoxicating liquor by the drink. Prohibition had been overturned by voters in 1959 but alcohol had to be purchased by the bottle in retail liquor stores. Owners then had to carry the bottles to a so-called "bottle club," where drinkers could become members. Operators could then serve the person from his or her own bottle.

Oklahoma voters had a long history of rejecting the sale of liquor by the drink. The first defeat of local option for sale of liquor came in 1910, just three years after statehood. Voters specifically rejected liquor by the drink in elections in 1959, 1972, and 1976.

Led by metropolitan chamber of commerce leaders, proponents of liquor by the drink supported a 1979 petition drive to call still another election. However, the Oklahoma Supreme Court ruled that petition unconstitutional.

In reality, Oklahomans' bought their liquor "by the wink." The state Alcoholic Beverage Control Board (ABC) had only 20 agents to cover the entire state and maximum punishment under the law was confiscation of the liquor and a $250 fine, hardly a severe deterrent. After one much-publicized raid in Oklahoma City, the club was serving liquor by the drink within 20 minutes.[16]

The thriving business of the state's 1,500 "bottle clubs" frustrated ABC Board director Richard Crisp so much that he resigned in 1982, saying his conscience would not allow him to "be part of further hypocrisy." Crisp oversaw 2,500 arrests and the seizure of 80,000 bottles of liquor during his term as head of the ABC Board.[17]

George was also frustrated with the hodge-podge Oklahoma liquor laws. He once described the unenforcable laws as analogous to "a camel—a horse put together by committee."

In early 1983, Oklahomans for Responsible Liquor Control successfully circulated a petition containing the names of 227,043 citizens, its purpose to submit SQ-563 to the voters. George set the election on the constitutional amendment which would allow counties the option of voting for or against liquor by the drink, for September 18, 1984. The amendment also did away with the ABC Board and authorized the legislature to set up a new agency to administer liquor laws.[18]

The open saloon proposal was widely supported by civic leaders wanting change. *The Daily Oklahoman* recognized the hypocrisy of existing law, writing, "Only a fool, of course, would assert that the law is honored except in the breach or that liquor does not flow freely in some establishments thinly disguised as club operations."

Opposition to liquor by the drink came primarily from the same church groups that opposed pari-mutuel gambling. Opponents claimed liquor by the drink would increase drunken driving and create law enforcement problems. Baptist and Church of Christ members formed the nucleus of the campaign, in an organization called Oklahoma is OK.

More than 800,000 Oklahomans voted in the September 18, 1984 election, a record turnout in a primary runoff. By a vote of 425,803 to 396,923, citizens reversed the bottle law. Huge victory margins in Oklahoma and Tulsa counties overshadowed the incredible fact that 60 of the state's 77 counties turned the liquor by the drink proposition down. Oklahoma thus became the last state in the nation to open up drinking to on-premises consumption.

Another decade would pass before a majority of the state's counties would vote themselves "wet." By 1999, 40 counties allowed liquor by the drink, leaving the remaining 37 counties to require patrons of private clubs to be served liquor only from their privately owned bottles.[20]

The 1985 session of the Oklahoma legislature was dominated by the state's declining revenues and liquor legislation. Shortly after voters approved county-option liquor by the drink, legislative leaders began forming committees to draft legislation to decide what kind of drinking, liquor taxes, and law enforcement to allow in the state.

In the state senate, newly-elected President Pro Tempore Rodger Randle of Tulsa appointed Senator Bob Cullison of Skiatook to head a panel of senators to draft legislation. House Speaker Jim Barker, whose home county of Muskogee rejected SQ-563, selected a 15-member committee.

Facing the legislature were several perplexing questions. Legislators had to decide what the words "on-premises consumption" in the constitutional amendment meant. Would consumption be limited to taverns and cocktail lounges or would liquor by the drink be permitted in restaurants and hotels and motels where food was served?

The rate of taxation on drinks was a hot topic. Speaker Barker predicted a 10 percent tax on 225 million drinks a year could bring in $45 million in new money. Because of the financial crisis in the state budget, lawmakers gleefully looked at new alcohol taxes as a source of raising income.

Legislators also had to determine how enforcement and regulation in a wet county would differ from a dry county and what specific requirements must be met for obtaining a license to sell liquor by the drink.

On March 14, 1985, after weeks of legislative wrangling, George signed into law House Bill 1118, a compromise measure establishing the Alcohol Beverage Laws Enforcement Commission (ABLE) and mandated that ABLE adopt rules and regulations for implementation of liquor by the drink within 60 days.

A Bully Pulpit

You elected me President and I will use this "bully pulpit" to tell Americans what I believe in.

President Theodore Roosevelt

Most people feel that a governor's or president's performance is best judged by the legislation enacted during their administration. However, George recognized the importance of Teddy Roosevelt's theory that major accomplishments are achieved by a chief executive's ability to call public attention to specific issues of concern. Some of the issues are public, others are private.

Through the power of the position of the office, George was able to make a difference. He operated by the terms of his own pledge to address the special needs of special people. His record is rampant with examples that range from at-home care for senior citizens to veterans' centers. Donna's participation, as first lady, had the same effect on programs for the developmentally disabled, especially in the establishment of group homes.

George considered each of the state's 77 counties to be a special interest group in itself. He instructed boards and commissions to make certain all of Oklahoma benefited from state policies and programs. He pushed through the legislature a bill authorizing funding of additional relay transmission towers for the Oklahoma Educational Television Authority (OETA). The new towers allowed citizens of every county to view OETA programs. A new vocational-technical school was established at Woodward, extending vo-tech education to northwest Oklahoma.

Oklahoma Department of Transportation officials were asked to provide George with a list of every state highway project that had been promised by previous administrations but never funded. They included Governor Gary's pledge in the 1950s to four-lane US-69 from border to border and Governor Edmondson's promise in 1958 to four-lane US-75 from Bartlesville to Tulsa.

George's awareness of the unfunded projects came after he was not invited to a ceremony dedicating a new stretch of US-70 in southern Oklahoma that he personally had directed the Department of Transportation to complete. When he asked the Ardmore Chamber of Commerce official why former Governor Gary, out of office for two decades, was the principal speaker at the dedication, the official replied, "You may have built it but Governor Gary promised it."[1]

George sent for a documented list of gubernatorial road promises. The complete list was honored during George's eight years as governor. When George left office in January, 1987, he was able to assure incoming Governor Bellmon that there were no unfulfilled promises left made by any predecessor and that he could start anew.

George and his staff had an uncanny ability, or maybe a lot of luck, in picking thousands of quality members to serve on the more than 300 state boards and commissions. The original state constitution allowed a governor to serve only one term and intentionally staggered terms on boards and commission, most with seven-year terms, in an effort to prevent a governor from taking control. Originally, a governor would be at the end of his third year, a lame duck, before he could appoint the majority of any board or commission and most people were then interested in who might be the next governor.

George's election to a second term changed all that. With one exception, in eight years in office, George appointed every member of every board that a governor appoints. That lone exception was a commission where George had appointed eight of the nine members.

A major source of pride in George's administrations was the quality and performance of his appointees. Not one board or commission member was a source of public ridicule or humiliation.

George also was proud of state agency directors he appointed or retained from the Boren administration. An example is Abe Hesser, originally appointed as executive director of the Oklahoma Tourism and Recreation Department by Governor Boren. Hesser was challenged by George's ability to work one-on-one with his agency heads. Hesser recalled, "He kept you on your toes with new ideas and friendly persuasion that offered encouragement and guidance. It was easy to be loyal to George because he was loyal to you." Hesser said also it was fun to work for George, "He always liked to have fun and often asked me 'Are you having fun in your job?' His 'You Done Good' award was one of the most cherished by his staff and colleagues."[2]

Often George was asked, "How far would you go to promote Oklahoma?" In the preceding chapter appears the story of George making a personal call on Edward DeBartolo in Tampa, Florida, to convince him to invest in Remington Park in Oklahoma City. An equally interesting story is how the Hitachi plant located in Norman.

Hitachi wanted to locate a large manufacturing facility near the Norman campus, a source of highly-educated workers. However, Hitachi would not commit until University of Oklahoma officials guaranteed the availability of university-owned land in south Norman. George lobbied invidual members of the OU Board of Regents to get the commitment.

When anti-Japanese letters to the editor appeared in local newsapers, Hitachi officials were understandably upset and flatly stated, "We're not coming to Oklahoma." George secretly flew to Tokyo to meet with top Hitachi brass to assure them that Oklahomans, as a whole, were not prejudiced, and that Oklahoma wanted the Hitachi plant in Norman. George's clandestine journey paid off. Within days, Hitachi announced the selection of Norman as the site of their newest American plant.

When George was criticized for the secret trip to Tokyo, he said, "As governor, sometimes negotiations must be completed in private. This was one of those times."

How far would George go with his bully pulpit? At least to Tokyo and Tampa, if it was good for Oklahoma.

On the Road Again

I'll go anywhere to promote Oklahoma.
George Nigh

George often traveled outside Oklahoma's borders to promote Oklahoma and its interests. When the United States Department of Transportation denied federal funds for improvement of the Broadway Extension, a major freeway in north Oklahoma City, George went to Washington, D.C., to find out why. He was told by federal officials that the project did not meet federal guidelines. When George asked to see a copy of the guidelines, he was informed the guidelines were not in writing and if they were he probably would not want to see them.

George could not believe it and left the bureaucrat's office with a warning. He said, "I'm going back to Oklahoma and wait for a list of the requirements you say we don't meet. If I don't get that list, I'm personally calling President Carter to tell him of our conversation and then I'm holding the biggest news conference you ever heard of." After a few days, the Oklahoma Department of Transportation received a letter from its federal counterpart indicating that Oklahoma's application had been reviewed and found to be in compliance with all federal regulations and requirements. To this day, no one knows what they were.[1]

George headed the Oklahoma delegation to the Democratic National Convention in San Francisco, California, in July, 1984, but it was Donna who drew the most attention of the press. Her remarkable resemblance to vice presidential candidate, Congresswoman Geraldine Ferraro of New York, turned many heads on San Francisco streets. Both women had the same hair color, styled the same way. Even their skin tone was the same.

In late July and August, 1984, George vigorously supported the passage of a constitutional amendment dealing with water. SQ-581 sought to amend the state constitution to allow the Oklahoma Water Resources Board (OWRB) to issue up to $250 million in bonds, loan the bond proceeds to local communities for water projects, and use $25 million in previously appropriated state money as collateral for loans. Jim Barnett, OWRB executive director, estimated that 131 com-

Donna Nigh was confused with Congresswoman Geraldine Ferraro, the Democratic vice-presidential nominee in 1984. While in San Francisco for the Democratic National Convention, George and Donna attended a reception hosted by First Lady Rosalyn Carter for women delegates. As Donna entered the hall with security by her side, the crowd began applauding, thinking Donna was Ferraro. It was only when Mrs. Carter recognized Donna that the delegates became aware of the identity mistake. Courtesy Jim Argo.

George, left, is greeted at the McAlester airport by District Judge Steven Taylor, center, and old friend Paul Carris in 1984. On most trips to McAlester, Taylor and Carris were the "unofficial" official greeters in George's hometown. In 1985, Carris was remarried in the backyard of the governor's mansion with George as his best man. Taylor, who had been appointed to the bench the previous year by George, performed the ceremony. Taylor rewrote the wedding ceremony to end with the words, "By the power vested in me by the governor of Oklahoma, I hereby declare you to be husband and wife."

munities in the state had expressed interest in borrowing from the water fund to upgrade sewer systems and water treatment and distribution systems.

George was anxious to convince voters of the merit of the state question because a similar plan had been defeated by more than 8,000 votes two years before.

On August 7, George was the keynote speaker at a rally of about 300 water plan supporters at Oklahoma City's Lincoln Plaza. The rally was sponsored by Glenn Sullivan, chairman of the Oklahoma Water Coalition, a group formed to support state water questions and water legislation.

George told the rally that Oklahoma had plenty of water but cities and towns could not afford to transport the water to their citizens. In exhorting rally-goers to campaign hard for the state question, George said, "Water, water everywhere and not a drop to drink."

He also warned that failure of the state question would harm tourism and recreation, economic development, community development, and agriculture. George said the money made available by passage of the state question was not a handout but a helpful hand from state government to needy cities and towns.[2]

With the backing of George's full political muscle, SQ-581 won approval of 65 percent of the state's voters in the August 28 election. George placed his personal reputation and the full power of his office behind the measure which passed by a stunning margin. George, however, refused to take personal credit for the victory, saying, "It was a bipartisan, unified effort that allayed the fears of the voters."[3]

George led a trade mission to Japan in early September, 1984. George, Oklahoma City Mayor Andy Coats, and Oklahoma City Chamber of Commerce President Ed Cook were entertained at a private dinner by the president of the Keidanren, Japan's prestigious group of the officers of its 200 largest corporations.[4]

"We're sowing seeds for investment," George told a reporter, as he prepared to meet with the presidents of Honda Motor Company and Hitachi. The Hitachi meeting and the efforts of Lieutenant Governor Spencer Bernard became catalysts for international business development in Oklahoma.

George continued the water theme into September when he led a flotilla of boats, comprising the Oklahoma Navy, from the Port of Catoosa near Tulsa toward New Orleans, Louisiana, where Oklahoma would be honored with a special day at the World's Fair. George and Donna occupied a 50-foot cabin cruiser, dubbed the "Ship of State," at the front of the 30-boat flotilla. Each boat was festooned with state banners and decals declaring it a vessel of the Oklahoma Navy, symbolized by a cowboy astride a sea horse.

The theme of the World's Fair was "Rivers and Waterways of the World." The Oklahoma delegation was the only one to arrive by water. The Oklahoma Navy was put together by Carlos Langston of Grand

Lake, Bob Hodder of Oklahoma City, and Oklahoma Tourism and Recreation Director Abe Hesser.

The flotilla stopped at Greenville, Mississippi, on October 1 for a reception with Mississippi officials. After passing Vicksburg and Natchez, the Oklahomans met with Louisiana Governor Edwin Edwards at the governor's mansion in Baton Rouge. On Oklahoma Day, October 5, George and hundreds of Oklahoma guests saw a 25-minute rendition of the musical *Oklahoma!* and a brief performance by Native Americans from Anadarko.

George was recognized by his fellow governors as a leader in the international effort. In an exchange program, he and six other governors spent a week in Austria. George and Donna took a side trip to Liechtenstein, one of the smallest countries in the world, on an economic development trip. George had previously participated at the dedication of the Hilti International Western Hemisphere headquar-

Donna and George were hosted by Arkansas Governor Bill Clinton, on the way to the World's Fair in New Orleans in 1984. The Nighs led a group of Oklahomans to Louisiana as part of a world-class flotilla.

ters in Tulsa. George was scheduled to be the featured speaker at a state dinner at a grand old hotel. When he and Donna arrived, they were surprised to see the flag of Japan flying. The Oklahoma flag was nowhere in sight.

After George completed his speech, he asked his host, Mr. Hilti, why the Japanese flag was posted. He did not know but went to ask the hotel manager. He returned red-faced and embarrassed. He explained, "There's been a communication problem. They thought you were the governor of Yokohama!" [5]

George's staff rubbed salt into the wound when they welcomed their boss and the first lady back to Oklahoma, dressed in kimonos and holding Japanese flags. A further insult was Press Secretary John Reid's submission of the story to *Reader's Digest* for a cash award.

More Money Problems and the Lottery

A leader too far out in front of the troops will get shot in the rear.
Anonymous

George landed in the hotseat of controversy when he used his annual address to the state legislature in January, 1985, to propose submitting to a vote of the people the creation of a state lottery. Oklahoma was very much in need of additional sources of state revenue and George followed the lead of 21 other states that were raising record funds from lotteries. George told legislators, "The ship of state is aground financially. We need to hustle, hit the ground running, we need to prime the pump."[1]

When George announced his support of the plan to present a state lottery question to voters, he found himself at odds with his own minister and personal friend, Reverend Wendell Estep, pastor of the Council Road Baptist Church in Oklahoma City.

Estep was kind in expressing his difference with George, recognizing there should be room for differences of opinion between friends, and even fellow Baptists. However, other Southern Baptists attacked George, one leader suggesting that a lottery violated 20 percent of the Ten Commandments "because it's gambling and the root of gambling is stealing and coveting." George responded, "What's the church supposed to be? Not a showcase for saints, but a hospital for sinners. What I support is giving the people the right to vote."[2]

When one religious leader said a lottery was evil and promoted immorality, George bristled, and said, "I don't consider the lottery evil. Anyone, certainly, has the right to disagree, but if I thought it was evil I wouldn't advocate it."[3]

The first battlefield for the lottery question was in the state senate. George personally lobbied for passage of the bill that would submit the issue to a public vote. On January 21, with George knowing that he did not have the votes to pass the bill, he asked Senator Bill Dawson of Seminole to delay a final vote. George was concerned that a loss could hurt his chances of passing other legislation.

"The people of Oklahoma are very much in support of a lottery," George told reporters, citing a recent poll that showed 59 percent of those polled supporting a lottery. The Bailey Poll showed 72 percent would support a lottery if all the money was used for education. George predicted a lottery could collect $70 million a year for the state's general fund. George proposed that 70 percent of lottery revenues be used for education with the balance to be spent on economic development.[4]

In the end, the state senate refused to give Oklahoma voters the opportunity to choose whether or not state government could benefit from a lottery. George had no regrets for supporting the ballot opportunity. He said, "I don't think you go wrong trying to advocate what the people want. If it hurt my political image, I don't care. I'm not concerned about my political image, I'm governor and I am concerned about trying to get this state moving... If [after the lottery defeat] I am a better governor, I am thankful for that. However, I don't think that the state is a better state."[5]

With the possibility of using a lottery to raise new state revenue gone, George and the first session of the 40th legislature looked elsewhere for the means to balance the budget. The State Equalization Board had certified anticipated revenue to be about $125 million short. George looked at various ways to address the problem, including extending the temporary sales tax that was to expire on December 31, 1985. A one-year extension could, budget officials said, reduce the budget shortfall by $100 million.

The slow economic recovery added to the revenue problem. Even though some economic indicators were beginning to show promise, the general direction was mixed at best. Business leaders were concerned that the legislature might increase corporate taxes and pass other anti-business measures that would send the wrong signal to companies outside Oklahoma that were considering relocating in the state.[6]

Legislators generally resisted many government reform ideas proposed by George's Commission on Reform of State Government. The blue-ribbon panel had endorsed 250 specific proposals to make state government run more smoothly and efficiently. Some of the recommendations were controversial, obviously the result of a consensus of

George, a veteran himself, takes time out of his hectic schedule every year to play dominoes at one of Oklahoma's veterans centers.

Above: Comedian Bob Hope was honored by Oklahomans in 1986. Left to right, former Oklahoma Congressman, and later United States Ambassador to Mexico, James Jones of Tulsa; actor George Lindsay, famous for his role on *The Andy Griffith Show;* entertainer Roy Clark of Tulsa; Hope, and George. Courtesy Bob McCormack.

the commission members' beliefs, but not politically feasible. However, George openly supported the commission's work and asked the legislature to work toward passage of the vast majority of the recommendations.

The establishment of a cabinet system in the executive branch was the reform panel's most important recommendation, so said commission chairman Walter Allison, a Bartlesville banker. Other recommendations included having the governor and lieutenant governor run as a team; the auditor and inspector be elected, a change later made; and other elective offices, including that of attorney general, become appointive, chosen by the governor.

George and the State Capitol Press Corps. During the bad economic times in George's second term, George asked reporters at a news conference, "Why do you keep blaming me personally for the plunging economy?" Reporter Jenifer Reynolds responded, "Because you took all the credit when it was going up." George said, "That's right!" and went on to the next question.

A clear consensus among members of the reform commission was that the well-being of both current and future generations of Oklahomans depended primarily on whether the state could achieve a reasonable degree of sustained economic development. To reach that level, the commission report proposed a right to work law, repeal of the "Little Davis-Bacon Act" that inflated the cost of public construction projects, and a constitutional amendment to allow Oklahoma to offer limited tax-exemption incentives to industry.

House Speaker Jim Barker and Senate President Pro Tempore Rodger Randle said there were too many reform proposals. Both contended the legislature would not have time to tackle more than a half-dozen reform recommendations because of the preoccupation with budget matters. *The Daily Oklahoman* said the legislative leaders' opposition was more than just a lack of time. An editorial said, "Legislative chieftains are moving now to set the stage for deep-sixing the reform proposals... Committee members didn't pull any punches in the areas targeted for reform measures aimed at improving efficiency and reducing costs, stepping on legislative toes by including many of their 'sacred cows.'"[7]

The legislature quickly passed bills submitting three state questions for the people to consider in an April 30th special election. George actively supported the questions that would give a five-year ad valorem tax exemption to any new or expanding industry, set a limit of state liability in case of a lawsuit, and change the balanced budget formula to allow the legislature to have access to additional funds for appropriation.

On April 1, George announced three co-chairmen of the "Yes All Three" effort to pass the proposed constitutional amendments. The co-chairmen were Don Paulsen, president of the Fife Corporation in Oklahoma City; Pat Henry, co-owner of Gibson's Stores in Lawton; and Doug Fox, president of Tribune-Swab Fox Company of Tulsa. Lynne Stewart was hired to coordinate the "Yes All Three" campaign.

George blocked off his calendar for much of April to head a bipartisan effort to pass the three state questions. He was fully supported by Speaker Barker of Muskogee, Senator Randle of Tulsa, Senate

George threw the full weight of the governor's office behind three proposed constitutional amendments in 1985. Voters approved the state questions. Courtesy *The Daily Oklahoman.*

Minority Leader Tim Leonard of Beaver, and House Minority Leader Frank Davis of Guthrie, a true bi-partisan effort.

"I'm ecstatic!" George said when informed that voters had overwhelmingly approved all three state questions on April 30. For nearly three hours, as returns rolled in from around the state, George and Donna paced the floor in a room at the Skirvin Hotel. He sipped black coffee and chatted with reporters and legislators who were jubilant that SQ-587 had passed, freeing up $143 million of new money for appropriation, a much-needed boost for the sagging state budget.

During the month of May, George and legislative leaders sought middle ground on varying tax increase proposals. George announced on May 24 a revised state revenue package that provided for a modest tax increase to strengthen education funding, including a $2,000 average teacher salary hike. Demands for an increase in education funding were front-page news when 10,000 members of the Oklahoma

Education Association attended a rally on the south steps of the State Capitol.

George proposed making permanent the one-cent sales tax enacted in 1984, set to expire at the end of 1985. He also exhorted legislators to eliminate the corporate franchise tax; place a tax on smokeless tobacco; increase the excise tax on automobiles, airplanes, and boats to three percent; and equalize the registration fees for automobiles and farm pickups.[8]

The state senate took a revolutionary approach to raising revenue by proposing to increase the existing 3-cent state sales tax to 7.25 cents and eliminate corporate and individual state income taxes.

After late-night meetings with participants hovering around calculators, George and legislative leaders hammered out a tax agreement in early June, 1985. The $415 million tax bill raised the sales tax, permanently, to 3.25 cents; hiked gasoline, vehicle, and excise taxes; and made the corporate income tax progressive. The measure also raised the price of pickup truck and recreational vehicle license tags, placed a tax on smokeless tobacco, and extended the premium tax charged out of state insurance companies doing business in Oklahoma.[9]

The tax increase package, House Bill 1219, was called by some the "largest tax increase in state history." George refuted that label because much of the tax increase was just a continuation of the already existing temporary additional one-cent sales tax hike and a replacement of part of the 17 tax reductions that had previously been passed in his administration.

Calling it "the responsible thing to do," George signed the tax bill at a west Oklahoma City hotel where he was waiting to speak. George said, "Cutting taxes is fun. Raising taxes is no fun. It is not a pleasant task..But this state is in desperate need of more adequate funding particularly in the areas of education and economic development." George mused that no one remembered the 17 tax cuts during his first full term as governor.

In the closing days of the 1985 session, with the tax increase bill approved, legislators passed other significant legislation. House Bill 1380 required drivers and front seat passengers of passenger cars to wear seat belts. Another bill raised salaries of state workers by 8 percent and hiked salaries of the state's top judges by 15 percent. Senate patronage in the appointment of tag agents was ended. Legislation changing the prevailing wage law and providing financial disclosure rules for elected and appointed officials was approved.

As anyone can imagine, all was not smooth. During debate on the prevailing wage bill, House Republicans Dale Patrick and George Osburne squared off in a fistfight after Patrick broke ranks and voted with Democrats on the bill.

George, by executive order, carried out one of the recommendations of his reform panel when he created a special Ethics Commission. George appointed Ray Anthony of Oklahoma City to chair the 38-member commission which was asked to make recommendations on how to monitor and control ethics among elected officials in Oklahoma.

George reached a milestone in his administration on July 8, 1985, when the Oklahoma Transportation Commission approved a contract for another portion of Oklahoma City's Central Expressway, pushing the total of road work awarded while George was governor above the $1 billion mark.

Road construction during George's first six and one-half years equaled the amount spent during the previous 16 years and four administrations. Transportation commissioner Stanton L. Young thanked George for supporting the Oklahoma City expressway, saying, "You will be known as the road-buildingest governor in history."[10] The Oklahoma Contractors Association honored George at its annual meeting and bestowed that title upon him.

George led the state effort in 1985 to designate an official state holiday to honor slain civil rights leader Dr. Martin Luther King, Jr. It was a bold step for George. Roosevelt Milton, an Oklahoma City leader of the National Association for the Advancement of Colored People (NAACP), said the holiday designation would not have happened without George's influence. Milton said, "It took a real statesman for that to happen in Oklahoma."[11]

George took part in planting a tree on the State Capitol grounds to honor King and asked the state highway commission to name a state highway in Tulsa in memory of the Alabama minister who changed the face of the struggle for civil rights in America.

In 1985 George had the opportunity to appoint yet another member of the Oklahoma Supreme Court. He chose Hardy Summers, a respected and successful Muskogee lawyer. No Oklahoma governor has appointed more justices to the Supreme Court than George.

In the summer of 1985, George had to make a decision whether or not to run against incumbent United States Senator Don Nickles in 1986. Many Oklahoma Democrats and the Democratic Senate Campaign Committee urged George to make the race. However, he and Donna decided to forego the race and become private citizens when the gubernatorial term ended in January, 1987.

George held a press conference on August 26 to announce his intentions. He told a packed room that he had spent his entire adult life in politics, that he had reached his goal set in junior high school to be governor of his home state. He reaffirmed his decision made many years before to limit his service to within the boundaries of Oklahoma. He said, "I do not now have and have never had the Potomac fever. I appreciate people who serve in the United States Senate and Congress, but for me, serving as governor of Oklahoma is the highest compliment that could be paid me."[12]

For the first time in 36 years George stood before reporters and broadcasters announcing he would not be a candidate for something. It was a strange feeling. However, George said he would have an active retirement, "I'll just be 59 years old. I plan to continue to work for Oklahoma. If anywhere along the line I can help, I'll be available."[13]

It was a pleasant surprise when the *Tulsa Tribune,* having never endorsed George, called his announcement "a poignant and interesting moment in Oklahoma history." An editorial entitled "A Farewell to Politics" lauded George's accomplishments, "The dean of Oklahoma's political elite, he has been in the ring longer than any other high-ranking elected official... His contributions to Oklahoma in 35 years of service are considerable. And few politicians of either party have enjoyed a higher level of friendship and general public good will... He has proved that in Oklahoma politics, nice guys don't always finish last."[14]

George and Donna astride a camel in the Gobi Desert in Gansu Province, China. Oklahoma and Gansu became sister states in a successful effort to expand Oklahoma markets internationally.

The *Tulsa World,* whose editors had stuck their necks out on behalf of George in previous races, said, "Oklahoma has lost a champion, our best promoter."[15] Three weeks after his retirement from state government announcement, George and Donna began a 17-day, world industrial promotions tour that included some of the remotest areas of the People's Republic of China. Also on the schedule were Japan, Hong Kong, Thailand, India, and England.

In announcing the trade mission, George emphasized that Oklahoma businesses had signed over $250 million in contracts with Chinese firms during the previous year. Oklahoma was establishing a sister-state relationship with the Chinese state of Gansu, arranging for cultural exchanges, including, with the help of director Steve Wiley, a permanent Gansu exhibit at the Oklahoma City Zoo.

In a telephone news conference from Lanzhou, China, on September 25, George reported that negotiations to expand Oklahoma manufacturers' markets into China were going well. He expressed hope that oil drilling operations in China would result in Oklahoma companies selling drilling equipment to the Chinese.

Oil technology and oil equipment sales were also on George's mind as he and 12 Oklahomans doing business in India met with Indian leaders in the cities of Madras and Delhi. The Indian minister of petroleum told George that India intended to spend $1 billion during the next five years in oil and gas exploration. While in India, George participated in dedication ceremonies for a new Indo-United States joint business venture between Carburettors, India and Facet Industries of Tulsa and spoke to the Indo-American Chamber of Commerce in Delhi.[16] He also arranged a meeting with Halliburton representatives from Duncan and the minister of petroleum. The meeting resulted in a substantial contract for Halliburton.

In London, England, George and the Oklahoma delegation met with representatives of one of England's major banks and the London Chamber of Commerce and Industries, pitching Oklahoma as a logical site for British businesses expanding in America.

Back home in Oklahoma, George reflected on 1985 as "turning the corner to a brighter economy." He was pleased with industrial development efforts that landed commitments by companies to build or expand in Oklahoma. Included in the list of job-producing plums for the state were Telex in Tulsa, Wortz Crackers in Poteau, Skaggs-Albertson in Ponca City, a Hardee's distribution center in Ardmore, and Hitachi in Norman.

Acknowledging that 1985 had been a trying year for all Oklahomans, George said, "Things have gone from bad to worse yet I see the light at the end of the tunnel. We can't have a negative attitude. We should look for the positive and be aggressive in the promotion of Oklahoma."[17]

Final Year as Governor

Only through the passage of time can you prove a point.
George Nigh

Dismal state revenue news greeted George as he began his final year as governor of Oklahoma. The new State Budget Director Vic Thompson estimated the legislature would have $197 million less to appropriate in the 1986 session than the previous year. Thompson's projection meant state spending would be cut eight to nine percent for the fiscal year that began July 1, 1986.

To lessen the blow of a substantial cut in the next year's budget, George directed state agencies to cut 4.5 percent from the remainder of the fiscal year 1985 budget and reduce spending by the same amount in the new fiscal year.

Because Oklahoma's public schools received more than 60 percent of the general fund appropriation, education was hardest hit by the cutback directive. State School Superintendent John Folks said poor and growing school districts would be most adversely affected because it was virtually impossible for them to make such drastic cuts. Local districts were mandated by the legislature to give teachers a $2,000 per year average salary increase. Therefore, any cuts had to come from programs in the state's 613 school districts.

"We should spend our time trying to work together in a cooperative spirit," was the theme of George's state of the state message on January 11, 1986. He mentioned the strife between the House and the

Senate that had delayed progress on reform programs the previous session. George asked legislators to look for innovative ways to cut unnecessary spending and save education from the nine percent cutback mandated by falling oil prices.[1]

George surprised many listeners by calling for an early special election on right to work. Other states had passed right to work legislation which prohibited mandatory union membership as a condition of employment, even in plants organized into collective bargaining units.

George believed a special election was necessary so that neither Democrats nor Republicans could capitalize on the highly emotional issue of right to work in statewide elections scheduled for later in the year. Right to work had been voted down by Oklahomans in 1964 but remained a hot topic almost every legislative session. To George, right to work was an issue for the people to decide, not an issue to stall the legislative process. George said, "It is the type of issue that is so major that only the people can resolve it."[2]

George noted that several politicians of both parties asked him to seek a special election "for the sake of allowing the normal issues to

George congratulates McAlester bankers Clark and Wanda Bass on their selection as Independent Bankers of the Year in Oklahoma.

George and McAlester District Judge Steven Taylor pose underneath the sign designating the portion of US-69 that runs through McAlester the "George Nigh Expressway." Taylor led efforts to name the stretch of road for George. The first thing ever named for George in the McAlester area was years before when Krebs Mayor Bill Pritchard, owner of Pete's Place, named the "George Nigh Bridge" over a small gulley on a jogging trail in a Krebs city park.

prevail in the regular elections." "I want the special election to keep right to work from affecting the ordinary political process," he said.[3]

When the legislature scuttled George's idea to call for an election on right to work, *The Daily Oklahoman* opined, "As for right to work... they refused to enact a statute or even submit the question to voters. Unions won but the public lost."

The economic news turned from bad to terrible when the State Equalization Board met in early February. Oil was selling on the open market for $18 a barrel, and earlier projections of only a $197 million shortfall in revenue became instantly and tragically outdated.

Faced with a true budget crisis, with a projected shortfall of $467 million for the next fiscal year, George, on February 1, ordered a general hiring freeze of state employees, a purchasing freeze by state agencies, and a freeze on out of state travel by state employees. George called for a "soft freeze" not a "hard freeze." Certain positions, especially in health and safety-related agencies, should be made regardless of budgetary restraints. George retained final decision-making power over the limits of the freeze, telling a press conference, "Obviously, if the guard on the prison tower retires, we must have a replacement."[5]

The approval of exceptions to the hiring freeze prompted Representative Frank Harbin of McAlester, chairman of a special House committee, to tell reporter Paul English, "When you have 476 people authorized for hire within a two-week period, it's hard to convince the public... that we have a hiring freeze in place."[6] However, Jim Thomas, director of the Office of Personnel Management, believed the freeze was working. New state hires fell 21 percent from January to February, 1986.[7]

Previous revenue estimates had required George to ask state agencies to slash budgets by nine percent. Based on new estimates, George told agency directors they might be looking at 17 percent reductions. He said, "I would be less than candid if I didn't say that furloughs for state workers will have to be considered."[8]

Earlier promises that no new taxes would be on the table in the 1986 legislative session went out the window as the dismal reality of plummeting oil prices set in. George said, "All bets are off." [9]

As the designated representative of the governors of energy producing states, George met in the Oval Office of the White House with President Ronald Reagan in April, 1986, to request federal help to prevent the steady decline of oil production and falling state revenues. Courtesy The White House.

George and legislative leaders felt helpless in the face of the collapse of world oil prices that was creating political clamor, not only in Oklahoma but throughout the Southwest. The Oklahoma state senate passed a tongue-in-cheek resolution requesting the Oklahoma legislature meet for one day in Washington, D.C., to dramatize the state's problem.

George and Texas Governor Mark White summoned the governors of seven oil producing states to an emergency meeting in Dallas, Texas, to develop a plan for federal intervention to help bail out the states most severely affected. There was general agreement among the seven governors that Congress had the power to create incentives for the domestic oil and gas industry by decontrolling natural gas, repealing the windfall profits tax passed in the boom years of the 1970s, eliminating the law that barred new utility plants and industrial boilers from using natural gas, and scrapping tax proposals that would reduce deductions for intangible drilling costs.[10]

On April 22, 1986, George and Wyoming Governor Ed Herschler met with President Ronald Reagan in the Oval Office of the White House to discuss the crisis. George felt a heavy burden trying to represent so many governors and so many producers in the private sector on such a critical issue. He told the President that the problem was not affecting only the producing states, but that it was a matter of national security if domestic oil and gas production ceased.

Realizing that Reagan was a strong proponent of national preparedness, George reminded the President that America could build a thousand more airplanes but needed fuel to fly them. George expressed his frustration that, politically, cheap energy was more important to many national politicians than critical sources of fuel supply.

Reagan listened carefully as George explained that only 865 oil and gas rigs were in operation, compared to 881 rigs in Oklahoma alone five years before. The President was surprised to learn that 140 refineries had closed and stripper wells were capped by the thousands as low prices made them economically unfeasible.

After the meeting, George was pleased with Reagan's support for natural gas deregulation, and elimination of the windfall profits tax, and other measures to save stripper wells from abandonment. The only recommendation that came out of the governors' summit in Dallas that Reagan did not endorse was the passage of a temporary variable federal tax on imported oil. George said, "I'll take six out of seven any day."[11]

In the energy crisis fight, George had the full support of Oklahoma's two United States Senators, David Boren and Don Nickles, and Congressman Mickey Edwards, all of whom had introduced legislation to accomplish some of the objectives stated by George and governors of other oil producing states.

Back home, George urged the legislature to revisit major reforms suggested by his reform commission the previous year. A cornerstone of the panel's recommendations was the establishment of a state ethics commission. George believed that a perception existed among citizens that no one was in charge of enforcing the dozens of laws on conflict of interest, personal and campaign financial disclosure, and lobbying. The only solution, George said, was to have an independent Oklahoma Ethics Commission to prevent self-enrichment, at the expense of the public in the discharge of official duties by state employees.[12]

The Oklahoma House of Representatives balked at George's push for a full-time ethics commission. The House Rules Committee voted down a bill to create the commission after Representative A.C. Holden of Dewey asked, "Do you really believe that there's enough unethical things going on in this state to justify a full-time state ethics commission?" House Speaker Jim Barker blamed his lack of support for an ethics commission on the fact that no one from his district had asked him to push the idea.[13]

George personally appeared before a state senate committee considering an ethics commission bill. As George lobbied individual legislators, citizens began to write their lawmakers, backing George's idea for a full-time ethics commission to serve as protection against unethical behavior.

Finally, both houses of the legislature passed House Bill 2054 creating a free-standing Oklahoma Ethics Commission that could review the action of not only elected officials but state employees and private members of boards and commissions. At the bill-signing ceremony in the Blue Room of the State Capitol, George said, "I don't know of any bill that I have ever had the opportunity to sign that gives me more pleasure."[14]

Susan Witt Conyers, a law student and veteran aide to three different gubernatorial legal counselors, David Hudson, Bob Renbarger, and Brenda Collins Vincent, was selected as the acting executive director of the Ethics Commission, the state's newest agency.

Conyers, a native of Okarche, Oklahoma, was just 25 years old and was shocked when George said, "You're the right person for the job." Conyers remembered, "He never asked me if I wanted the job. He said I was worthy of his trust that everyone who dealt with the Ethics Commission was treated fairly and with respect."[15]

Conyers, later a judge of the Oklahoma Workers' Compensation Court, is an example of the hundreds of young people who have been influenced, inspired, directed, and prodded along their way by George. Conyers recalled, "I am glad he took the time to give me, to give all of us, an opportunity to be more than we ever thought possible."[16]

The 1986 legislative session may have been the most productive during George's eight years as governor. A tax increase was avoided. Workers' compensation reform was enacted after George revealed that problems in the workers' compensation system was the source of a negative review given Oklahoma in a Price-Waterhouse study of companies looking at Oklahoma as a potential expansion site. A significant part of the 1986 workers' compensation reform was the creation of a medical fee schedule to curtail the rising costs of providing medical care to the tens of thousands of Oklahoma workers injured on the job each year.

The session, described by George as "the toughest of my career," was lauded by Dean Schirf, director of governmental relations for the Oklahoma City Chamber of Commerce. Schirf wrote, "This session comes the closest to making some real reform in areas that the state needs it most, including workers' compensation, tort liability lawsuit control, the passage of a venture capital bill, sweeping changes for the banking and thrift institutions, and the corporation act patterned after the Delaware law."[17]

"The most sweeping change in state government structure since the constitution itself," was the way George described House Bill 1944 when he signed it into law on June 6. The major reform legislation created 15 cabinet-level departments in state government, an attempt to coordinate the 260-plus agencies, boards, and commissions. George said, "Oklahomans are constantly asking why state government is not run more like a business. With the hundreds of agencies, boards, and commissions, this has literally been impossible. At long last we have an opportunity to organize state government into a manageable system."[18]

George often asked, "How can you expect a governor to govern when you have 300 agencies reporting directly to him? There is not enough time in the day to manage the state effectively."

George praised two state senators, Democrat Rodger Randle of Tulsa and Republican Helen Cole of Moore, as "the impetus" behind the cabinet-level structure reorganization legislation.

A major part of George's proposal for reorganization of state government was the creation of an Oklahoma Department of Commerce, combining functions of several agencies and commissions. The legislature passed legislation accomplishing the reorganization.

Legislators turned thumbs down on George's idea to combine all of the state law enforcement agencies. George wanted the Oklahoma State Bureau of Investigation, the Bureau of Narcotics, the Department of Public Safety, the Department of Corrections, and the Oklahoma Military Department placed under a cabinet level person to coordinate a single investigation, communications, and training program.

Within a month after the legislature adjourned, George appointed 15 cabinet secretaries from existing state agency directors. Members of Oklahoma's first cabinet were: Jack Craig, Secretary of Agriculture; Robert Empie, Secretary of Business and Professional Regulation; Francis Tuttle, Secretary of Commerce; Delmas Ford, Secretary of

Government Operations; Dr. Joan Leavitt, Secretary of Health and Environmental Services; Robert Fulton, Secretary of Human Services; Abe Hesser, Secretary of Tourism, Cultural, and Historical Resources; Tom Heggy, Secretary of Law Enforcement; Major General Robert Morgan, Secretary of Military and Veterans Affairs; Jim Barnett, Secretary of Natural Resources; Jim Thomas, Secretary of Personnel and Employee Benefits; and V.O. Bradley, Secretary of Transportation. Higher education, common education, DHS, and vo-tech education remained as separate departments.

George appointed Sylvia A. Lewis of Oklahoma City to the Board of Regents for the University of Oklahoma. Lewis, retired director of the Langston University Urban Center, was the first black to ever serve as an OU regent. George was proud of his record of appointing minorities to state boards and commissions. However, in announcing Lewis' appointment, George said, "I'm looking forward to the day when the next governor makes major appointments and will not have to call a press conference to point out that this is a first."[19]

It was a sentimental journey for George in early July, 1986, as he wandered around the crowd of political candidates lined up to file for office in the State Capitol office of the State Election Board. It was the first time in 36 years he had not filed for office. George quipped, "I worked the crowd as I came in, shook a few hands, had withdrawal pains. It's kind of different. I couldn't stand being away." When reporter John Greiner asked George how it felt to not be a candidate, George answered, "I feel like other people who have been in a job and suddenly are not there. I'm looking forward to more family time."[20]

George led a 50-member economic development team to London in September, 1986, on an official trade mission. The mission's primary objective was the solicitation of foreign investment capital and the recruitment of new industry. George and Oklahoma private business representatives briefed 350 British corporate and government officials about Oklahoma and its attributes as a foreign investment. In addition, Secretary of Tourism Abe Hesser conducted tourism seminars. The entire delegation made personal calls on industrial and financial prospects and attended several receptions and dinners.

The London trade mission was put together by Oklahoma's

European trade representative, the Morgan Grenfell & Company, Limited, a top British merchant bank.

George addressed a special seminar for 50 European travel agents at the American Embassy in London. Ray Ackerman, chairman of Ackerman McQueen Advertising, the state's tourism advertising agency, convinced editors of two leading British magazines to feature Oklahoma and its horse racing industry in future issues.

Media events were a big part of the London trip. George was interviewed live on BBC radio and gave special interviews with several leading financial magazines. Oklahoma was the subject of a four-page financial survey distributed by *The Financial Times* throughout western Europe.[21]

George poses with staff members during his last month in the governor's office, January, 1987. It was their last hurrah! George considered his staff a part of his extended family.

Gov. Clinton and his wife, Hillary, with their daughter.

GOV. BILL CLINTON
ARKANSAS

Christmas dinner at the mansion is served in our formal dining room. My wife, Hillary, our daughter, and I sit down to dinner with our parents and a few close family friends.

Liza Ashley, the governor's mansion cook of 31 years, prepares a dinner of turkey, corn-bread and white-bread dressing, giblet gravy, sweet potatoes with marshmallows and nuts, a vegetable casserole [below], fresh cranberry mold, fruit salad, cranberry nut bread, pumpkin pie, and ambrosia cake.

Savory Vegetable Bake

1 9-ounce package frozen French-style green beans
1 large onion, chopped
1 tablespoon butter or margarine
1 10¾-ounce can condensed cream of mushroom soup
1 10-ounce package frozen peas, thawed
1 8-ounce can sliced water chestnuts, drained
1 5-ounce can evaporated milk
½ cup soft bread crumbs (⅔ slice)
2 teaspoons butter or margarine, melted
½ cup shredded sharp cheddar cheese (2 ounces)

Cook frozen beans according to package directions; drain. In a saucepan cover and cook onion in 1 tablespoon butter over medium heat, stirring occasionally, until onion is tender. Stir in the beans, soup, peas, water chestnuts, and milk. Transfer to a 1½-quart casserole. Toss bread crumbs with melted butter; sprinkle over vegetable mixture. Bake in a 350° oven for 35 minutes. Sprinkle with cheese; bake 5 minutes more. Serves 6 to 8.

Gov. Nigh and his wife, Donna.

GOV. GEORGE NIGH
OKLAHOMA

We're the 15th family to reside in the historic governor's mansion in Oklahoma City, and Christmas is a very special time here for my wife, Donna, and me. Our grown children come home to visit.

We hold an annual public holiday open house during early December, when about 3,000 Oklahomans tour the house and grounds.

And, instead of mailing greeting cards, for the past seven years Donna and I have hosted a holiday show on our local public television network. It features a variety of talent, primarily musical, from across Oklahoma.

Traditionally, we have Christmas at the mansion, with a few close friends and family in for a Christmas dinner. It's a quiet time for us, because we are a close-knit family.

There's always a big decorated tree at the foot of the winding staircase in the foyer, and the fireplace in the main dining room is decorated with a wreath and pine boughs.

Our dinner includes sausage casserole, zucchini casserole, pineapple sheet cake, caramel brownies, and cider punch. And, for holiday brunches, we sometimes feast on a deliciously sweet and gooey coffee bread [below].

Bubble Bread

½ cup firmly packed brown sugar
½ cup chopped pecans
1 4-ounce package regular butterscotch- or chocolate-flavored pudding mix
¼ cup granulated sugar
1 teaspoon ground cinnamon
24 frozen white dinner rolls
½ cup melted butter or margarine

Grease and lightly flour a 10-inch fluted tube pan. In a medium bowl stir together the brown sugar, nuts, dry pudding mix, granulated sugar, and cinnamon. Dip frozen rolls in butter, then roll in the sugar mixture. Layer in prepared pan. Drizzle with any remaining butter and sprinkle with any remaining sugar mixture. Cover loosely; chill in refrigerator overnight. Bake in a 350° oven for 30 minutes or until done. Let stand 10 minutes; invert onto serving plate. To serve, cut into slices. Serves 12. □

Walter Oleksy is a Chicago-based free-lance writer and author of 43 books for adults and children. Molly Culbertson is a food writer and cookbook editor from the Midwest.

24 NOVEMBER 1986 FRIENDLY EXCHANGE

George and Donna, Oklahoma's first family, and Bill and Hillary Clinton, the first family of Arkansas, were featured in a holiday recipe article in *Friendly Exchange*, a magazine published by Farmers Insurance Group, in December, 1986. Courtesy Farmers Insurance Group.

Holding his first lady close, George enjoys a quiet moment during the party celebrating his retirement from the governor's office. On his lapel is a special pin presented him by daughter Georgeann. Courtesy *The Daily Oklahoman.*

As the Nigh administration wound down, George and Donna were honored, on their 23rd wedding anniversary, at an October 19 farewell that began in the afternoon and went into the night. Fifteen hundred friends and supporters jammed the Myriad Convention Center in downtown Oklahoma City to pay tribute to the Nighs' service to Oklahoma.

The afternoon featured no fewer than three performances of the song "Oklahoma!" including a silent, hand-signed rendition by the Deaf Singers Choir of the First Baptist Church of Moore. Tulsa entertainer and Nigh friend Roy Clark headed a long list of Oklahoma performers in a program described by reporter Paul English as "a send-off with a pronounced country accent."[22]

As George reflected on his good fortune, he cried when Clark sang "Yesterday, When I Was Young" He told his friends that he looked forward to resuming private life. He said, "We're grateful for the people who were faces in the crowd, whose names we never heard. Thank you for making our lives possible."

Proceeds from the $100 to $1,000 a plate banquet went to support the Donna Nigh Foundation and the Oklahoma Network for Excellence which announced it had established a George Nigh scholarship.

As would be expected for a "going away" party, the organizers wanted to give the Nighs gifts, a notion contrary to George's 32-year policy of not accepting personal gifts from employees or supporters, even at Christmas. However, the planners decided George's policy should not apply and bought light-hearted gifts, a vacuum sweeper for Donna and a lawn mower for George. George quipped, "Where are the prisoners to go with the mower?" Donna thanked the crowd, "from the bottom of our heart for the wonderful life we've had."[23]

In December, 1986, Russell Perry, publisher of *The Black Chronicle* in Oklahoma City, applauded George for his efforts to appoint minorities to signficant jobs and positions in state government. Perry mentioned George's selection of Sylvia Lewis to the University of Oklahoma Board of Regents; Wayne Chandler as chairman of the Board of Affairs; Erna Winters as senior gubernatorial assistant; James Echols as director of the Commission on Human Rights; and Julia Brown as executive director of the Commission on Ethics and Merit, as a few of the 122 major appointments of blacks to state agency posts and membership on boards and commissions. Perry wrote, "The Nigh mark on Oklahoma history shall be an indelible one and Mr. Nigh can leave state government with the surely comforting satisfaction that he made that mark. . . Because he went about his tasks as governor with a sense of history and a burning desire to alter that history... Nigh... became a true friend of Blacks."[24]

On January 6, 1987, George said his farewell to the Oklahoma legislature. The speech was filled with optimism for the future of Oklahoma. Even George's critics liked the speech. Republican state chairman Tom Cole said, "Despite our partisan differences, I applaud Governor Nigh for the manner in which he conducted himself while in public office. In his personal life, Nigh has been a credit to the office of governor and to the people of Oklahoma."[25]

George made good on his pledge to make the transition between his and Henry Bellmon's administrations "the smoothest in history." George and Donna even moved out of the governor's mansion four weeks early so that Henry and Shirley Bellmon could have some of the rooms repainted and minor repairs completed before they moved in. George encouraged the Bellmons to celebrate their family Christmas at the mansion, even before the inauguration.

George and Donna bought a home on Waverly Drive in Oklahoma City and began preparations to re-enter private life.

On January 12, history repeated itself. Bellmon sat outside George's office, waiting to change places with him for the second time in 24 years. In 1963, a younger Bellmon replaced a younger George as governor of Oklahoma.

George wished Bellmon good luck, saying, "I hope the only thing smoother than the transition is the smoothness of the recovery of Oklahoma."[26] George, the democrat, had nothing but the highest regard for Bellmon, the Republican.

As Henry Bellmon took the oath of office on the south steps of the State Capitol, George's record-setting tenure in the Oklahoma governor's chair ended.

Citizen Nigh

Don't drive through life with your eyes on the rearview mirror.

George Nigh

George was looking for something to do. For his entire adult life, he had bounced out of bed each morning, accepting challenges, leading, governing, being the boss. Donna had predicted it would take George, at age 59, at least a year to discover what he wanted to do in his retirement. Retirement, however, was probably the wrong word to describe George Nigh's years after he left the governor's office.

George had plenty of time to reflect on his four terms as governor. He felt good about his service to Oklahoma. He believed he laid the foundation for diversification of the state's economy, a strong transportation system, and had addressed special needs.

He was leaving public office on a personal high point. He listed as his major accomplishments: elevating programs and salaries in common education, higher education, and vocational-technical education; transferring the former University Hospital to the Department of Human Services, the catalyst to making the University of Oklahoma Health Sciences Center one of the top 10 in the country; de-institutionalization of mental health, mental retardation, and juvenile facilities, leading to widespread community based services; establishment of veterans centers in all geographical areas of the state; improvements in the corrections system; and establishment of an energy research center at the University of Oklahoma and an agricultural research center at Oklahoma State University.[1]

George and Donna missed the amenities of life as governor and first lady, but they enjoyed many benefits of private life. George said, "Can you imagine never going anywhere for eight years without someone else in the car?"[2]

George was sensitive about being accused of making any political deals on future employment before he left office. He purposely delayed any decision on his future until he was a private citizen. He turned down a teaching job at Harvard University in Boston, Massachusetts, and an economic development position in Dallas, Texas. He and Donna definitely wanted to stay in their home state.

Two weeks after his term as governor ended, George was named to the board of directors of the JCPenney Company, Inc., one of the nation's largest retailers. He also served on the boards of Oklahoma City-based Sonic Industries, Inc., the nation's largest chain of drive-in restaurants; First Interstate Bank, later Boatmen's Bank and Bank of America; and on the advisory board of Express Personnel Services, headed by George's good friend Bob Funk.

Attending his first JCPenney board meeting in New York City, George discovered how private life would be. No bodyguards, no aides, no chauffeur-driven limousines. After eight years as governor and sixteen years as lieutenant governor, George had hardly been able to steal a moment alone. The rude awakening at New York's LaGuardia airport began when George, who had flown by commercial air, had to retrieve his own luggage and hail his own cab. He was wrestling luggage, looking at tags, when he was hit on the head by a raincoat held by another traveler looking for his bags. George recognized his fellow traveler as former Vice President and Democratic presidential nominee Walter Mondale, who told George, without formal greeting between the two old friends, "Real life's hell, isn't it?" George last saw Mondale that night standing alone in the rain, hailing a New York cab.

Donna began setting up housekeeping. She reflected on the sudden change, "One day we lived in a mansion. The next day we had no home, no furniture, no cars, no job."[3] She spent her first few weeks as a private citizen making a home and preparing for Georgeann's wedding.

Donna liked the new privacy in her life, telling a reporter, "The nicest part is that I'm beginning to feel in control of my life. I'm not answering to other people so much. I've gotten comfortable saying no—even if the reason is because I just don't want to."[4]

Donna spent substantial time each week working on projects of the Donna Nigh Foundation and the developmentally disabled. She said, "That's part of my life."[5] She also became associated with their friend Stanton Young at Journey House Travel in Oklahoma City.

In March, 1987, George returned to the classroom, named a distinguished statesman in residence at Central State University (CSU), now the University of Central Oklahoma (UCO) in Edmond. Stanton Young and Julian Rothbaum made substantial contributions to the CSU Foundation to privately fund a program for George to lecture CSU history and government students and conduct student forums. He saw the position as an opportunity to encourage young people to be active in government. He also met with business leaders, the goal to link the business community with CSU.

George added a touch of humor to the press conference at which CSU President Dr. Bill Lillard announced his selection as statesman in residence. George said he was not certain about the title because his hero, former President Harry Truman had said, "A statesman is a dead politician."[6]

In September, 1987, CSU announced the establishment of the Nigh Institute of State Government. Dr. Lillard told reporters that the purpose of the Institute was to inform students about state government's impact upon basic needs such as roads to travel, water to drink, jobs for workers, and schools to educate children. Another goal of the Institute was to develop coursework for CSU students and host seminars where students would brush shoulders with leaders in state and federal government.

George moved his office from the *Journal Record* building in downtown Oklahoma City, owned by close friend Dan Hogan, to a permanent location on the fourth floor of the University Center on the Edmond CSU campus. George chose CSU as the repository of many of his records.

The Nigh Institute completed a special energy report to Governor David Walters in April, 1991. The report was presented to Walters at the governor's office. Left to right, Ed Pugh, George's administrative assistant; George; Walters; and Richard Hess, executive director of the Oklahoma Association of Association Executives. Courtesy University of Central Oklahoma.

George and Donna on their 25th wedding anniversary in 1988. On the wall behind them is an enlarged photograph of their wedding portrait in 1963.

After leaving the governor's office, George became a member of the board of directors of Oklahoma City-based Sonic Industries, Inc. Left to right, Cliff Hudson; his wife, Leslie; and George. Hudson later became president and chief executive officer of Sonic, the nation's largest chain of drive-in restaurants. Courtesy Sonic Industries, Inc.

An October 23 reception was held to inaugurate the Nigh Institute. Governor Henry Bellmon, United States Senator David Boren, and Dr. Bill Lillard, and their wives, joined George and Donna as hosts of a $500 per couple banquet to raise initial private funding for the Nigh Institute. At the dinner, it was announced that the George and Donna Nigh Art Collection of Oklahoma Western Artists would be displayed adjacent to the Nigh Institute in the CSU University Center. Jo Ann Adams was the director of the outstanding display of art which included a world-renowned Santa Claus collection from around the globe, a gift of Tom Brittain and Luke Crum.

Also, Governor Bellmon and the legislature made arrangements to transfer state-owned furniture used by George as governor to CSU to create a replica of George's official governor's office.

Before the end of 1987, George and Donna decided their home was just not right for them. The house sold within weeks of putting it on the market and they moved to a home in the Tall Oaks addition in southeast Edmond, where they lived for three years before buying a home in Quail Creek in far northwest Oklahoma City.

In early 1988, Governor Bill Clinton of Arkansas, toying with the idea of running for the Democratic presidential nomination four years later, asked George to recommend him to deliver the keynote address at a major Democratic convention. George contacted Democratic National Chairman Paul G. Kirk, Jr., with his recommendation. After the future president was named the principal speaker for the event, Clinton wrote to George, "Thanks for such a wonderful letter to Paul Kirk. I really appreciate the recommendation... You're a good friend—the best."[7]

Throughout 1988 and 1989, the Nigh Institute of State Government presented special salutes to education and economic development in Oklahoma; Congress; the armed forces; various political leaders; and former Governor J. Howard Edmondson in a "Salute to Oklahoma Series." "A Salute to the Big Red E" was the 1989 recognition of the 30th anniversary of Edmondson's inauguration as governor.

The salute to education featured former Republican Governor and later Secretary of Education Lamar Alexander of Tennessee.

The salute to Congress featured the Oklahoma congressional delegation, the only time the entire congressional delegation has appeard together on an Oklahoma campus. Each congressman and senator addressed his specific area of expertise and interest.

In 1989 George was nominated for membership in the Oklahoma Hall of Fame. The nomination came from former House Speaker Carl Albert, in the past one of the most powerful men in the nation's capital. The letter from Albert to the Hall of Fame selection committee of the Oklahoma Heritage Association was a glance at George's life. Speaker Albert wrote, "I have known George Nigh all of his life. I was a senior at McAlester High School when George was born. He was one of the outstanding boys in our community. His father owned a grocery store here. We traded with him and George used to deliver groceries to our home."

Albert continued, "I doubt that we have ever had a public official who was better liked or more highly respected. The fact he was re-elected governor after having served a term, the first ever to obtain that honor seems to me to be evidence that the people of Oklahoma considered him a very competent, very fine person, morally as well as politically. He knows as much about Oklahoma and its history as anybody I have ever known."[8]

Based upon the recommendation of Albert, and others, George was inducted into the Oklahoma Hall of Fame in November, 1989. He was presented for induction by Arkansas Governor, and later President, Bill Clinton, who described George as the only Oklahoma political candidate who ever asked each Oklahoman personally for his vote.[9]

University President

George changed the face of UCO from that sleepy little college north of Oklahoma City to a great metropolitan university.

Carl Reherman

George had not completed his service to Oklahoma. Rumors began to surface in 1990 that he was a leading contender to replace Dr. Bill Lillard as president of the University of Central Oklahoma (UCO), the new name of Central State University.

UCO was established as the Territorial Normal School by the Oklahoma Territory legislature on Christmas Eve, 1890. Its first mission was to educate students who would become teachers. The school was located in Edmond when city fathers donated 40 acres of land. Its first class of 23 students met in the First Methodist Church in the fall of 1891 before moving to the upstairs of an Edmond store building the following year. By 1893, a square brick building dubbed Old North was home to classes.

In 1992, UCO was the state's third largest university with 14,000 students. Dr. Lillard had brought great prestige and growth to the university since 1975.

George was urged by many of his friends and supporters to apply for the UCO presidency. Even though he did not possess the normal academic background for university presidents, he nevertheless was a former teacher, splendid supporter of higher education, master fund raiser, and unequaled promoter of Oklahoma.

George was one of 61 applicants, whittled down to 11 finalists by an advisory search committee. In early March, 1992, the nine-member Board of Regents of Oklahoma Colleges interviewed George and five finalists and met 19 hours over a two-day period. At a second interview, George was asked by one regent if anything would prevent him from taking the job. George told regents that he would accept only if he was selected by a unanimous vote, to avoid any air of partisan politics, and if he was allowed to live in his new home in Oklahoma City. The vote of the regents was unanimous, including Republican Tracy Kelly of Bristow.

To avoid the appearance of any partisan split of the regents, George called Republican State Chairman Clinton Key to determine if the Republican Party would oppose his appointment. Key not only assured George that the party would not have any negative comment, he volunteered to write a letter of recommendation for George.

With the active support of regent Tracy Kelly, and a member of one of Oklahoma's most prominent Republican families, the vote was unanimous.

In announcing their selection on March 17, Regent Mike Brown of Edmond, said, "We now bring to this campus a man who speaks the language of Oklahoma, who understands the issues of higher education, the regional university concept, and the vision of UCO."[1]

Oklahoma Governor David Walters attended the regents meeting where George's selection was announced. Walters said, "I'm excited. . . I think he will do a tremendous job. This proves there is life after the governor's office."[2]

In accepting the presidency of UCO, at the age of 65, George said his newest hero was Colonel Sanders, who founded Kentucky Fried Chicken after he began receiving Social Security checks. In fact, George had been McAlester's youngest teacher, Oklahoma's youngest legislator, the youngest lieutenant governor in the nation, and was now the oldest person ever hired as a university president in Oklahoma.

George at his desk at the University of Central Oklahoma. Courtesy University of Central Oklahoma.

Left to right, Leland Gourley, Vicki Clark Gourley, George, and Donna. Gourley and Nigh became friends during the Edmondson administration. Courtesy Nichols Hills Publishing Company.

Ed and Kaye Cook, left, join George and Donna at one of the many social functions required of a university president. George had worked closely with Cook, the president of the Oklahoma City Chamber of Commerce, and Highway Commissioner Stanton L. Young, on Oklahoma City metropolitan area highway projects, including the Centennial Expressway and Hefner Parkway. Courtesy University of Central Oklahoma.

Former Oklahoma Governor and United States Senator Henry Bellmon, left, with President Bill Clinton, during a visit to the UCO campus in Edmond. Courtesy University of Central Oklahoma.

George poses with a UCO student to celebrate a new enrollment record for the university. Courtesy University of Central Oklahoma.

Most observers were happy with George's selection to head UCO. Some detractors believed his lack of an academic background was a shortcoming. George told them, "If you don't like it because I don't have a doctoral degree, just think how it's gong to affect you when I remind you I don't even have a master's degree."

Bart Binning, president of the UCO faculty senate, said UCO was in dire need of additional classrooms and George's skills as "a politician and adept fund-raiser" were just what UCO needed.[3]

Leland Gourley, publisher of *Friday,* wrote, "George Nigh has the respect, the popularity, and acceptance of a national constituency as well as Oklahoma. He will be one of the greatest things to ever happen to UCO and the cause of higher education in Oklahoma."[4]

George launched a series of meetings with UCO faculty and administrators to develop a team concept for improving the physical plant and the classroom teaching programs of the university. The concept was patterned after the highly successful cabinet approach George used to manage state government.

During the weekend prior to his assuming the presidency on July 1, 1992, George and 42 faculty members and administrative staff were closeted for two days of planning for UCO's future. The Deer Creek Farms location was offered to UCO several times by owner Bill Swisher, president of CMI.

George was described as "a man in a hurry." He knew he would be at UCO only a few years, necessitating quick and compact resolutions to the university's needs.

Assistant UCO Vice President Nick Widener, left, George, and Regent Mike Brown mull over early stages of the UCO master plan unveiled in 1994. Brown called George the equivalent of a 70-year-old Energizer bunny. Courtesy University of Central Oklahoma.

Oklahoman and Ambassador to Great Britain William Crowe, the former Chairman of the Joint Chiefs of Staff, welcomed George, Donna, and a group of Friends of UCO on a trip to London. The group also met with President Bill Clinton and Secretary of Education Richard Riley. The trip was a project of the Nigh Institute under the leadership of its executive director Carl Reherman, front row, left, and his wife Glo, second from left. Courtesy University of Central Oklahoma.

George was given only four directives by regents: establish a greater awareness of the university; develop a stronger tie with Edmond; create a greater multicultural awareness on campus; and establish a mission for the university.

He reassured the faculty that he was not there to tinker with the academic program. He believed academics at UCO were outstanding, but no one knew it. He said, "I want to give you the facilities you need to do your job. I want former students to pull their diplomas out of their drawer and hang it on the wall. I want Edmond and Oklahoma City both to think of this as their local university. And most importantly, I want never to hear again the reference 'Broncho High.' "

Expressing Oklahoma's pride, George presents a Wheaties box to Edmond Olympic gymnast Shannon Miller as Governor Frank Keating, seated left, and Miller's coach, Steve Nunno, look on. Courtesy University of Central Oklahoma.

George and Donna wave to onlookers during a September, 1993, UCO homecoming parade. Courtesy University of Central Oklahoma.

George and Donna spent a night in Lincoln's bedroom at the White House in 1993. They dined with President Bill Clinton and were joined for after-dinner talk by First Lady Hillary Rodham Clinton. Courtesy The White House.

Before George became president of UCO, a building had not been erected on campus since 1964. George decided to push an innovative $45.7 million revenue-bond plan to supplement $7.7 million from a statewide bond issue to build new buildings. UCO alum Tom Thompson assisted George in selling the innovative idea to the Board of Regents, state legislature, and the Bond Oversight Commission.

A two-year $54 million capital-improvements master plan was officially kicked off April 22, 1994. The roar of bulldozers, shouts of construction workers, and red dirt covered the campus for two years. Added classroom space and modernization of existing buildings put UCO on the same level with the state's two biggest universities.

George loved being in the classroom at UCO, just as he began as a history teacher in McAlester 40 years before. Courtesy University of Central Oklahoma.

George worked hard to improve UCO's relations with Edmond. UCO donated land for a new Edmond Area Chamber of Commerce Building. At the groundbreaking were, left to right, George; Admiral John Kirkpatrick, a major benefactor of UCO; Regent Mike Brown; Edmond Mayor Bob Rudkin; Edmond Chamber of Commerce President Brad Thomas; and chamber executive director Wanda Cantrell. Courtesy University of Central Oklahoma.

Governor and Mrs. Frank Keating invited George and Donna to the governor's mansion in 1995 the evening before Reverend Billy Graham addressed a memorial service days after the April 19, 1995, bombing of the Alfred P. Murrah Federal Building in Oklahoma City. Left to right, Dr. Graham, Donna, Ruth Graham, and George.

Roger Webb replaced George as President of the University of Central Oklahoma. In this photo, taken in Hollywood in 1968, Webb, right, joined George and former University of Oklahoma track star, turned movie star, Dennis Weaver, left, and Oklahoma native singing cowboy Jimmy Wakely at a reception to convince movie moguls in Hollywood to shoot their films in Oklahoma. Courtesy University of Central Oklahoma.

George brought national figures to the UCO campus for special programs. Left to right, George; Admiral William Crowe, retired chairman of the United States Joint Chiefs of Staff; and former Governor and United States Senator David L. Boren. Among other national and international leaders honored by Nigh Institute Salutes were former House Speaker Carl Albert, President Bill Clinton, former Tennessee Governor and Secretary of Education Lamar Alexander, former Oklahoma Congressman and United States Ambassador to Mexico James Jones, corporate leaders, such as Stanley Gault, CEO of Goodyear, the entire Oklahoma congressional delegation, and Gilbert Grosevenor of the National Geographic Society. Courtesy University of Central Oklahoma.

Donna, George, and Oklahoma astronaut Shannon Lucid, who was honored at a 1996 dinner at UCO. Lucid was one of the stars of America's space program in the 1980s and 1990s. Courtesy University of Central Oklahoma.

George met frequently with his executive staff at UCO. Left to right, A.K. Rahman, Dr. John Lolley, Lei Rumley, Kati Schmidt, George, Linda Ralkey, Joyce Mounce, Dr. Clyde Jacob, and Dr. Ed Pugh, George's administrative assistant. Courtesy University of Central Oklahoma.

George, left, and Richard Burpee, UCO vice president for development and community relations. When Tinker Air Force Base was a potential target of base-closing efforts, George assigned Burpee to work as the full-time chairman of the "Save Tinker Committee." George believed economic development was important to UCO and could think of no better use of taxpayer money than to save Tinker for the metropolitan area. Courtesy Gordon Dinsmore.

George, Donna, First Lady Hillary Rodham Clinton, and President Bill Clinton visit the new Education Building on the UCO campus in April, 1996. During his visit, Clinton met with members of his President's Committee that funded scholarships to all surviving children of the Oklahoma City bombing of the Murrah Federal Building. George served as national chairman. Courtesy University of Central Oklahoma.

George lectures students at the Downtown Consortium, a joint effort by UCO and four other metropolitan area colleges to offer classes for college credit in downtown Oklahoma City. Courtesy University of Central Oklahoma.

A new 63,000 square-foot central plant provided heating and cooling to university buildings. A new three-story education building with 30 classrooms was constructed. A four-story, 81,000 square-foot addition doubled the size of the university library.

An addition to the Business Building was funded with a $150,000 contribution from 200 Sonic franchises around the nation to honor Troy N. Smith, Sr., the founder of the drive-in chain headquartered in Oklahoma.

In addition, a 56,000 square-foot addition to Howell Hall housed biology and chemistry laboratories. The University Center was expanded via the addition of a 166,000 square-foot building. Additional parking, landscaping, parks, and a Broncho Lake were completed under the master plan.

The Nigh Institute of State Government, directed by former Edmond Mayor and UCO professor Carl Reherman, was expanded in areas of academics, research, and training of future state government leaders. The institute brought a new and dynamic visibility to the university and a close working relationship with the communities of Edmond and Oklahoma City.

George led efforts to fund and construct on the UCO campus a memorial to World War II heroes. He also was active in the globalization and sister university project in Pueblo, Mexico.

By 1994, UCO enrollment had risen to 16,000 students and the university boasted an economic impact of $130 million annually on the Oklahoma City metropolitan area. George hired retired Lieutenant General Richard Burpee as UCO vice president for development and community relations to assess UCO's impact upon the community and to improve ties with local business and government leaders.

Ever a persistent fund raiser, George sought money for UCO from government and private sources. In August, 1994, he announced a $150,000 donation from Edith Gaylord Harper, secretary emeritus of The Oklahoma Publishing Company. The donation was matched by the university and endowed. Annual interest from the $300,000 was designated for use for faculty and staff development under the banner of the Edith Gaylord Harper Endowment Fund.[5]

For three years while George was president of UCO, Burpee piloted major fund raising efforts on behalf of the university. Under Burpee's leadership, millions of dollars were added to the UCO Foundation. The school's first-ever private fund raising campaign surpassed its goal of $4.5 million. Burpee also headed Tinker Task Force 95, increasing visibility of UCO at Tinker Air Force Base in Midwest City. Burpee and George were later honored for their part in keeping Tinker off the list of military bases to be closed.

George's name was mentioned in political circles again in 1995. Delegates at the state Democratic convention chanted "Nigh, Nigh, Nigh!" when party chairman Mike Turpen suggested it was time to retire United States Senator Jim Inhofe. Betty McElderry was elected as the new chairman of Oklahoma Democrats at the 1995 convention and called on George to seriously consider running for Congress in his native Third Congressional District. However, George was content with his job at UCO and he and Donna did not want to move to Washington, D.C. George was honored by suggestions he re-enter the world of politics, but respectfully declined.

George viewed two-year colleges in the Oklahoma City metropolitan area as feeder schools for UCO. He directed administrators to send UCO counselors to the community colleges to make certain students would not lose credit hours by later transferring to UCO. An innovative step in higher education was taken in 1995 when UCO and four other institutions of higher learning opened a downtown

Above: Donna, right, was inducted into the Oklahoma City Public School's Wall of Fame. She was joined by Previous recipients Madalynne and James Norick.

Facing page: George was master of ceremonies at the March 16, 1999, unveiling of a State Capitol mural, *We Belong to the Land,* by artist Jeff Dodd recognizing Oklahoma's agriculture industry. Left to right, Betty Price, Governor Frank Keating, House Speaker Loyd Benson, and George appear with a framed print of the large mural. Courtesy Oklahoma Arts Council.

Oklahoma City "college consortium" to offer college-level classes. George spearheaded a private fund raising drive to renovate classroom and administration space in the First National Center. George worked out the details of the consortium with presidents of the other colleges offering classes for credit at the Downtown Consortium, Dr. Larry Nutter at Rose State College in Midwest City, Dr. Robert Todd at Oklahoma City Community College, Provost Dr. James Hooper at Oklahoma State University-Oklahoma City, and Dr. Larry Devane at Redlands Community College in El Reno.

The Oklahoma Regents for Higher Education applauded the college consortium idea. Chancellor Hans Brisch called the effort "one of the most creative ventures in Oklahoma higher education history."[6]

In early 1996, George announced he would retire from UCO on June 30, 1997, completing five years of service at the university, and a half century of public service. George had told the regents when they hired him he would serve no less than three and no more than five years. In those five years he had fulfilled his mission.

When George retired as UCO president, Dr. Joe Jackson, right, presided over the retirement festivities. Here George, Jackson, and Edmond attorney Max Speegle, left, enjoy refreshments in the new food court in the UCO Student Center. Courtesy University of Central Oklahoma.

On April 5, 1996, President Bill Clinton spoke to a crowd of 10,000 people in front of Old North on the UCO campus. The appearance was almost a year after the April 19, 1995, bombing of the Alfred P. Murrah Federal Building in Oklahoma City. George was named to a scholarship fund committee by the President. George and other members of the Oklahoma City Scholarship Fund Advisory Board met privately with the President and First Lady Hillary Rodham Clinton. The committee was committed to raise funds for the education of the surviving children of victims of the bombing. Through the efforts of the committee, Governor Frank Keating, Lieutenant Governor Mary Fallin, the Federal Government Employees Association, and the Oklahoma City Community Foundation, enough money was raised to guarantee every child a college scholarship or its equivalent.

It was Hall of Fame year for George and Donna in 1997. George was inducted into the halls of fame of the United States Junior Chamber of Commerce (Jaycees), the Oklahoma Vocational-Technical Education Foundation, and Eastern Oklahoma State College. Donna was selected for membership in the Oklahoma Women's Hall of Fame in 1995 and the Oklahoma City Public School Foundation in 1997.

And What Now?

George Nigh is Oklahoma's Energizer Bunny—
He just keeps on going.

Mike Brown, Member of the Board
of Regents for Oklahoma Colleges

At age 70, after leaving UCO, George slowed down somewhat, but did not stop.

He went to a downtown office at least three days a week to push the college consortium he founded. He joined the Board of Directors of Local Oklahoma Bank and served as Director of Community Relations and continued to serve on the Board of Directors of JCPenney Company. With Donna as chairperson, he continued to lead the Donna Nigh Foundation as its president, serving Oklahomans with developmental disabilities.

He remained active as an elder at the Westminster Presbyterian Church in Oklahoma City where Donna served as a deacon.

George and Donna baby-sat for granddaughter Macy on Tuesday nights while Georgeann worked on a master's degree. During the summer grandsons Berry and Chase Mashburn join Macy on "Tuesday Night Out" at Momma Donna and Daddy George's house.

In May, 1999, George addressed Girls State for the 50th consecutive year and played a major role in the centennial celebration of his hometown of McAlester. In May, 1999, he addressed University of Oklahoma Law School graduates, continuing his commitment to making commencement speeches which he had done without interruption for half a century.

Also, he found time to help Donna in her work at Journey House Travel in Oklahoma City.

George and Donna continued their volunteer efforts on behalf of the Juvenile Diabetes Foundation, American Heart Association, American Cancer Society, and other worthwhile charities.

The governor's office, as it was when George was governor, including furniture, paintings, and books, was donated to his alma mater, Eastern Oklahoma State College, to be displayed at the college's McAlester campus. Other memorabilia has been donated to his second alma mater, East Central State University in Ada and to UCO, Edmond.

. . .

"If you had it to do all over again would you do things differently?"

This was a question George once heard asked of Dr. Henry Kissinger as a former United States Secretary of State. George liked and adopted Kissinger's approach to reviewing past decisions. Kissinger told guests at an Oklahoma State University seminar, "Based upon the information I had at the time, I would do nothing differently."

During a half century of laudatory service to the people of Oklahoma, George has had many opportunities, both public and private, to review his actions. He has no regrets.

George lecturing to students at Carl Albert State College at Poteau.

George gave the commencement address to the graduating class of McAlester High School, his alma mater, on May 19, 2000. On the front row behind him is Judge Steven Taylor, who introduced him, and Dr. Lucy Smith, Superintendent of Schools. In the back row are members of the McAlester School Board. Courtesy *McAlester News-Capital Democrat.*

Left to right, Ed Townsend, chairman of Local Oklahoma Bank; Barbara Townsend; Georgeann; Donna; and George at a 1999 fund raiser for the American Juvenile Diabetes Foundation. That charity is close to the hearts of both the Nighs and Townsends because Hillary Townsend and Macy Nigh Whitener are juvenile diabetics.

Daddy George with granddaughter Macy, left, and Georgeann.

George continued his charity work as community relations director for Local Oklahoma Bank. At a fund raising event are, left to right, Kay Murcer, baseball great Bobby Murcer, Mary England, meteorologist Gary England, Donna, and George.

When George retired from the Board of Directors of JCPenney Company in 1999, he and Donna were greeted at a party that resembled a political convention. George was nominated, and elected, to retirement.

George served on the Board of Directors of the JCPenney Company from 1987 to 1999. Left to right, W. R. Howell, the company's chairman and chief executive officer; Judy Howell, his wife; Donna; and George. Howell began sweeping floors at the JCPenney store in Claremore, Oklahoma, and climbed the ladder to head the corporate empire that included 181,000 employees at 1,400 retail stores, and other holdings. Howell graduated from the University of Oklahoma. He and George were friends in Jaycees.

George lectured on Oklahoma history and government to college classes around the state. He was a guest of Southeastern Oklahoma State University President Glen D. Johnson, Jr., right, in Durant. George also appeared before classes at Langston University, Carl Albert Junior College, and East Central Oklahoma State University. Courtesy Southeastern Oklahoma State University.

Lindsay Smith, center, was one of the 1999 recipients of a special scholarship named in honor of George and Donna for their tenure at the University of Central Oklahoma. George presents a certificate to Smith while UCO President Roger Webb looks on. Courtesy University of Central Oklahoma.

George and Donna, representing Local Oklahoma Bank, with Walter Cronkite at an April, 1999, Salvation Army benefit dinner in Tulsa.

One of George's social groups was the "freeloader's birthday lunch." There was only one rule for the group, if a member's birthday was to be celebrated, he had to throw his own party, inviting other members to the affair. Left to right, back row, George, Bill Dickerson, Bob Hodder, John Reid, Dave Dank, Charlie Sarratt. Front row, left to right, Marty Hauan, Earl DeVilbiss, and Ed Kennedy. The "exclusive" group later included Dr. J. Don Harris and Jack Skaggs.

Macy Whitener, front, with friend Hillary Townsend, left, and Miss America 1999, Nicole Johnson, at a dinner at the governor's mansion hosted by Governor Frank and First Lady Cathy Keating to raise awareness for the Juvenile Diabetes Foundation. All three of the beauties have juvenile diabetes.

George and Donna with Dick and Nina Gaugler on a tour of the Greek Islands. Donna served as a tour agent for Journey House Travel in Oklahoma City.

George and Donna with a group of friends dubbed "the rich and famous." Years ago, when trying to decide on somewhere fabulous to go, the group decided to stay at home and pretend they were on vacation. Charlie and Geneva Sarratt asked, "Why don't we just stay at our house and pretend we are rich and famous and somewhere else?" They hired a couple to prepare meals at the Sarratt home in Edmond and spent four days around the pool for their dream vacation. No phone calls were allowed. An annual tradition was born. Left to right, Delmas Ford, Sheryl Thompson, Tom Thompson, Charlie Sarratt, Carol Ford, Geneva Sarratt, Donna, and George.

Another tradition was born one year when George planned a surprise birthday party of four couples for Donna at the Sheraton Hotel in downtown Oklahoma City. When the guests arrived, they noticed a reception being held for retiring Western Electric executive Dewey Lyon. They had no idea who Dewey Lyon was or what he had done but they went through the reception line shaking hands and telling Lyon what a great job he had done and how much they were going to miss him. The theme was repeated each year thereafter, with George posting the "Dewey Lyon Retirement Banquet" sign as the group vacationed in various sites from Cancun, Mexico, to Chickasha and Grand Lake, Oklahoma. Left to right, Bob and Gayle Jones of Oklahoma City, Mutt and Neda Lewis of Duncan, George and Donna, and Kitty and Morris Gunn of Oklahoma City. A highlight of the Grand Lake retirement party was that Dewey Lyon was at the lake that same weekend, saw the sign, wondered what was going on, and crashed their party.

Georgeann, Donna, and George, summer, 1999, at Lake Thunderbird near Norman. George and Donna considered themselves blessed that both children and all five grandchildren lived nearby in Oklahoma.

Mike Mashburn and his family. Left to right, Mike, Chase, Berry, Suzy, Ayla, and Gray. Retirement gave George and Donna more time to enjoy their role as grandparents.

George appeared at the 1999 Girls State convention. It marked the 50th consecutive year that George had spoken to Girls Staters. Courtesy Betty McElderry.

Donna, right, and Richard Clements, of Clements Foods Company, were named to the Oklahoma City Public Schools Wall of Fame. Both were graduates of the public school system in Oklahoma's capital city.

Left: George received the Lifetime Achievement Award from the Jim Thorpe Association, a rarity for a non-athlete. Courtesy Jim Thorpe Association.

Below: Hundreds of Oklahomans gathered at the Marriott Hotel in Oklahoma City in June, 2000, to honor George for 50 years of service to Oklahoma. Several members of George and Donna's families joined the throng of wellwishers. Left to right, Mary Nigh Cargill, Tammy Agnello, George, Donna, Richard Carleton, Linda Klofkorn, and Tricia Carleton. Leland Gourley wrote in *Friday*, "George Nigh deserved the honor. Seldom has any person anywhere in America served so many years with never a hint of scandal, never any personal profit exploitation, and always at an unprecedented level of popularity."

EPILOGUE

Of the hundreds of awards and citations given George or Donna, none are more meaningful than the George and Donna Nigh Public Service Scholarship in 1999. The Oklahoma legislature and Governor Frank Keating approved funding for scholarships to be granted to a student at every institution of higher education in Oklahoma. The students must be Oklahoma residents and participate in public service. The program is administered by the Board of Regents for Higher Education.

The name of the scholarship alone symbolizes the essence of George and Donna Nigh—public service. In announcing the creation of the scholarship, Higher Education Chancellor Hans Brisch said, "We can only hope that the recipients of the George and Donna Nigh Public Service awards will follow in their footsteps and give back to Oklahoma in a meaningful way."

NOTES

Early Days in Little Dixie

1 *With the Colors* (McAlester: J. H. Tuttle, 1920), p. 178.

2 Bob Burke and Von Russell Creel, *Lyle Boren: Rebel Congressman* (Oklahoma City: Western Heritage Books, 1991), p. 31.

3 Interview, William Lewyn "Bill" Nigh, July 2, 1999, Archives, Oklahoma Heritage Association, Oklahoma City, Oklahoma (hereinafter referred to as Heritage Archives), hereinafter cited Bill Nigh interview.

4 Interview, George Nigh, July 13, 1974, Oral History Collection, Oklahoma Historical Society, Oklahoma City, Oklahoma.

5 Interview, George Nigh, June 17, 1999, Heritage Archives, hereinafter cited as George Nigh interview.

6 Martin Hauan, *How to Win Elections Without Hardly Cheatin' At All* (Oklahoma City: Midwest Political Publication, 1983), p. 305.

7 Interview, Irvin E. "Buck" Conner, June 29, 1999, Heritage Archives.

8 Hauan, *How to Win Elections Without Hardly Cheatin' At All*, p. 303.

9 Interview, George and Mary Brown, June 28, 1999, Heritage Archives.

10 George Nigh interview.

11 Ibid.

12 George Nigh speech to Oklahoma Heritage Association, March 26, 1999, Heritage Archives.

13 Ibid.

14 Ibid.

The Younger Nighs

1 George and Mary Brown interview.

2 Bill Nigh interview.

3 Ibid.

Getting Ready

1 George Nigh interview.

2 Ibid.

3 Ibid.

4 *The East Central Story*, privately printed, 1984.

The First Step

1 George Nigh interview.

2 Interview, Fred Turner, July 6, 1999, Heritage Archives.

3 George Nigh interview.

4 Interview, Robert Bartheld, June 28, 1999, Heritage Archives.

5 *McAlester News Capital* (McAlester, Oklahoma), July 5, 1950.

6 George Nigh interview.

7 Danney Goble and W. David Baird. *The Story of Oklahoma* (Norman: University of Oklahoma Press, 1994), p. 439.

8 LeRoy H. Fischer. *Oklahoma's Governors, 1929-1955.* (Oklahoma City: Oklahoma Historical Society, 1983), p. 179.

9 *The Daily Oklahoman* (Oklahoma City, Oklahoma), January 13, 1951.

10 Ibid., June 8, 1997.

Life is Like a Mountain Railroad

1 George Nigh interview.

2 Ibid.

3 *McAlester Democrat* (McAlester, Oklahoma), April 17, 1952.

4 *Pittsburg County Oklahoma* (Wolfe City, Texas: Henington Industries, Inc., 1997), p. 278.

5 *McAlester Democrat,* June 5, 1952.

6 George Nigh interview.

7 Ibid.

8 *McAlester Democrat,* June 12, 1952.

9 Ibid.

A New State Song

1 George Nigh interview.

2 *The Daily Oklahoman,* February 14, 1993.

3 George Nigh interview.

4 Ibid.

5 Ibid.

6 Ibid.

7 *The Journal Record* (Oklahoma City, Oklahoma), April 20, 1991.

8 *The Daily Oklahoman,* February 14, 1993.

9 Ibid.

Aiming Higher

1 George Nigh interview.

2 John Ellis Freeny, *Whuppin' and Spurrin' Through Choctaw Country* (Edmond: privately printed, 1998), p. 52-53.

3 George Nigh interview.

4 Bob Bartheld interview.

5 *Tulsa World* (Tulsa, Oklahoma), January 9, 1979.

6 George Nigh interview.

7 Ibid.

8 Ibid.

9 *McAlester News Capital* June 17, 1958.

10 Ibid.

11 Ibid.

12 George Nigh interview.

13 Hauan, *How to Win Elections Without Hardly Cheatin' At All,* p. 309.

14 *McAlester News Capital,* June 26, 1958.

15 Ibid., June 27, 1958.

16 Ibid., July 8, 1958.

17 George Nigh interview.

A Heartbeat Away

1 *McAlester News Capital,* July 14, 1958.

2 Ibid.

3 George Nigh interview.

4 Hauan, *How to Win Elections Without Hardly Cheatin' At All,* p. 308.

5 George and Mary Brown interview.

6 Ibid, p. 310.

7 Ibid.

8 Ibid.

9 *McAlester News Capital,* July 21, 1958.

10 Ibid., July 23, 1958.

11 Ibid., July 25, 1999

12 Ibid., July 26, 1958.

13 Ibid., July 25, 1958.

14 *The Daily Oklahoman,* July 24, 1958.

15 Ibid.

16 George Nigh interview.

Second in Command

1 Hauan, *How To Win Elections Without Hardly Cheatin' At All,* p. 311.

2 George Nigh interview.

3 Ibid.

4 *The Daily Oklahoman,* January 13, 1960. George Nigh interview.

5 *The Daily Oklahoman,* April 18, 1999.

6 Will Rogers. *The Cowboy Philosopher on Prohibition.* (Stillwater: Oklahoma State University Press, 1975) p. 10.

7 *The Daily Oklahoman,* April 5, 1959.

8 Ibid., April 18, 1999.

9 Ibid.

10 George Nigh interview.

Falling Short of the Mark

1 James C. Milligan and L. David Norris, *The Man on the Second Floor: Raymond Gary* (Oklahoma City: Western Heritage Books), p. 192.

2 Ibid., p. 193.

3 Fischer, *Oklahoma's Governors, 1955-1979,* p. 112.

4 George Nigh interview.

Ibid.

5 Stephen Jones, *Oklahoma Politics.* (Enid, Oklahoma: Haymaker Press, Inc., 1974), p. 228.

6 *The Daily Oklahoman,* April 29, 1962.

7 Irvin E. "Buck" Conner interview.

8 Jones, *Oklahoma Politics,* p. 230.

9 Ibid., p. 233.

10 *The Daily Oklahoman,* April 29, 1962.

11 *Tulsa World,* April 26, 1962.

12 Milligan and Norris, *The Man on the Second Floor: Raymond Gary,* p. 203.

13 George Nigh interview.

14 Ibid.

A Dream Fulfilled

1 George Nigh interview.

2 Ibid.

3 Ibid.

4 *Tulsa World,* May 23, 1976.

5 *The Daily Oklahoman,* January 2, 1963.

6 Hauan, *He Buys Organs for Churches, Pianos for Bawdy Houses.* (Oklahoma City: Midwest Political Publications, 1976), p. 181.

7 Interview, William Christian, August 18, 1999, Heritage Archives.

8 Ibid.

9 George Nigh interview.

10 Ibid.

11George Nigh interview.

12 Hauan, *He Buys Organs for Churches, Pianos for Bawdy Houses,* p. 184.

13 Ibid., p. 185.

14 *The Daily Oklahoman,* January 7, 1963.

15 George Nigh interview.

Nine Days of Nigh

1 Hauan, *He Buys Organs for Churches, Pianos for Bawdy Houses,* p. 187.

2 *The Daily Oklahoman,* January 7, 1963.

3 *McAlester News Capital,* January 7, 1963.

4 Ibid.

5 *The Daily Oklahoman,* January 9, 1963.

6 Ibid.

7 Interview, Richard R. Hefton, March 22, 2000, Heritage Archives.

8 Fred Turner interview.

9 *The Sunday Oklahoman* (Oklahoma City, Oklahoma), January 13, 1963.

10 Fischer, *Oklahoma's Governors, 1955-1979,* pp. 126-127

11 *The Daily Oklahoman,* January 11, 1963.

Donna

1 George Nigh interview.

2 Ibid.

3 *Oklahoma City Times,* September 5, 1963.

4 George Nigh interview

5 Ibid.

6 *Oklahoma Journal,* (Midwest City, Oklahoma), October 7, 1965.

7 Ibid., November 13, 1965.

8 *Tulsa Daily World,* December 8, 1965.

9 *The Daily Oklahoman,* November 6, 1966.

10 George Nigh interview.

11 *The Sunday Oklahoman,* November 13, 1966.

12 December 8, 1965.

13 *The Daily Oklahoman,* November 6, 1966.

14 George Nigh interview.

Return to Public Service

1 George Nigh interview.

2 Ibid.

3 *Oklahoma City Times* (Oklahoma City, Oklahoma), March 15, 1967.

4 *The Daily Oklahoman,* September 20, 1967.

5 Fischer, *Oklahoma Governors, 1955-1979,* p. 131.

6 Ibid., p. 195.

7 *Tulsa Daily World,* September 12, 1968.

8 George Nigh interview.

9 *The Daily Oklahoman,* September 12, 1968.

10 *The Daily Oklahoman,* January 10, 1967.

11 *Tulsa Tribune* (Tulsa, Oklahoma), January 28, 1969.

12 Ibid.

13 *The Daily Oklahoman,* August 16, 1969.

14 Fischer, *Oklahoma's Governors, 1955-1979,* pp. 132-133.

15 *The Daily Oklahoman,* February 2, 1973.

Teaming with a New Governor

1 George Nigh interview.

2 *The Sunday Oklahoman,* November 1, 1970.

3 *Oklahoma Journal,* November 4, 1970.

4 George Nigh interview.

5 *Shawnee News-Star* (Shawnee, Oklahoma), April 18, 1971.

6 *The Daily Oklahoman,* June 5, 1971.

7 Transcript of radio show, Oral History Collection, Archives and Manuscript Division, Oklahoma Historical Society, Oklahoma City, Oklahoma.

8 Interview, Margaret Hall, June 24, 1999, Heritage Archives, hereinafter cited as Margaret Hall interview.

9 Ibid.

10 George Nigh interview.

I Love Oklahoma

1 *Seminole Producer* (Seminole, Oklahoma), September 19, 1972.

2 Edmond Booster (Edmond, Oklahoma), May 18, 1972.

3 *McAlester News-Capital,* July 25, 1972.

4 *The Daily Oklahoman,* August 30, 1972.

5 *Tulsa Tribune,* August 30, 1972.

6 Fischer, *Oklahoma's Governors, 1955-1979,* p. 135.

7 *Yukon Review* (Yukon, Oklahoma), June 14, 1973.

8 *Hughes County Times* (Holdenville, Oklahoma), October 25, 1973.

9 *Tulsa Daily World,* June 7, 1973.

10 *Oklahoma Journal,* February 15, 1974.

11 Ibid.

12 Ibid.

13 Ibid.

14 Ibid.

15 Ibid.

16 *Tulsa Tribune,* April 23, 1974.

The 1974 Campaign

1 Fischer, *Oklahoma's Governor's 1955-1979,* p. 235.

2 *The Daily Oklahoman,* May 23, 1978.

3 *Tulsa Daily World,* November 19, 1974.

4 *Oklahoma Journal,* November 21, 1974.

5 *The Daily Oklahoman,* December 21, 1974.

6 *Oklahoma Journal,* March 16, 1975.

7 Ibid.

8 Ibid., August 1, 1975.

9 *Oklahoma City Times,* August 21, 1975.

10 *Tulsa Daily World,* February 27, 1976.

11 *Guymon Herald* (Guymon, Oklahoma), March 21, 1976.

12 Ibid.

13 *Oklahoma Journal,* March 7, 1976.

14 *Tulsa Daily World,* June 10, 1976.

15 Fischer, *Oklahoma's Governors, 1955-1979,* p. 135.

16 *Oklahoma Journal,* June 2, 1977.

17 Ibid.

18 George Nigh interview.

19 Ibid.

20 Ibid.

Good Guy Nigh

1 George Nigh interview.

2 George Nigh interview; Interview, July 22, 1999 with Robert White, Dean Gandy, and John Reid, Heritage Archives.

3 *Oklahoma Journal,* March 2, 1978.

4 Hauan, *How to Win Elections Without Hardly Cheatin' At All,* p. 314.

5 Ibid, p. 316.

6 Fischer, *Oklahoma's Governors, 1955-1979,* p. 138.

7 Margaret Hall interview.

8 Ibid.

9 Fischer, *Oklahoma's Governors, 1955-1979,* pp. 318-319.

10 George Nigh interview.

11 *The Daily Oklahoman,* August 20, 1978.

12 Ibid.

13 George Nigh interview.

14 Ibid.

15 Hauan, *How to Win Elections Without Hardly Cheatin' At All,* p. 318.

16 *Oklahoma Journal,*

August 20, 1978.

17 Ibid.

18 Ibid.

19 Ibid., August 23, 1978.

20 *The Daily Oklahoman,* August 23, 1978.

21 Ibid.

22 Ibid.

23 Ibid.

24 George Nigh interview.

25 *Oklahoma Journal,* September 16, 1978.

26 Ibid.

27 Hauan, *How to Win Elections Without Hardly Cheatin' at All,* p. 324.

28 Ibid.

29 *Oklahoma Journal,* September 17, 1978.

30 Ibid., September 20, 1978.

31 *The Daily Oklahoman,* September 20, 1978.

32 Ibid.

GOOD GUY VS NICE GUY

1 *The Sunday Oklahoman,* September 2 24, 1978.

3 Ibid.

4 Ibid.

5 Ibid.

6 *The Daily Oklahoman,* September 27, 1978.

7 Hauan, *How To Win Elections Without Hardly Cheatin' At All,* p. 322.

8 Ibid.

9 Glenda Carlile to author, November 18, 1999.

10 Ibid., p. 328; George Nigh interview.

11 *The Daily Oklahoman,* November 3, 1978.

12 George Nigh interview.

13 Ibid.

14 *The Daily Oklahoman,* November 1, 1978.

15 Ibid.

16 George Nigh interview.

17 *The Daily Oklahoman,* November 2, 1978.

18 Ibid.

19 Ibid., November 3, 1978.

20 Ibid.

21 Ibid.

22 Ibid.

23 George Nigh interview.

24 *The Daily Oklahoman,* November 4, 1978.

25 *Oklahoma Observer* (Oklahoma City, Oklahoma), November 25, 1978.

26 *Oklahoma Journal,* November 3, 1978.

27 Ibid.

28 Ibid.

29 Ibid.

30 Ibid.

31 Ibid.

32 *The Daily Oklahoman,* November 5, 1978.

33 Ibid., November 8, 1978.

34 Ibid.

35 George Nigh interview.

36 *The Daily Oklahoman,* August 12, 1991.

37 Ibid., November 9, 1978.

38 Ibid.

39 George Nigh interview.

AT LAST

1 George Nigh interview.

2 *The Daily Oklahoman,* January 4, 1979.

3 Ibid.

4 Ibid., January 9, 1979.

5 Baird and Goble, *The Story of Oklahoma,* pp. 477-478.

6 Hauan, *How To Win Elections Without Hardly Cheatin' At All,* p. 330.

7 *Oklahoma Monthly* Magazine, December, 1978, p. 26.

8 Margaret Hall interview.

9 *The Daily Oklahoman,* June 2, 1979.

10 *Oklahoma Monthly* Magazine, June, 1979.

11 Ibid.

12 *The Daily Oklahoman,* May 1, 1979.

13 Ibid., May 17, 1979.

14 Ibid.

15 Ibid.

16 Ibid.

17 Ibid.

18 Ibid., July 19, 1979.

19 *Oklahoma Monthly*

Magazine, July, 1979.

20 Ibid.

21 Ibid.

22 Ibid.

23 Ibid.

24 Ibid.

25 George Nigh interview.

26 *The Sunday Oklahoman,* December 16, 1979.

The First Family

1 *Oklahoma Today,* (Winter 1980), p. 29.

2 Ibid.

3 *Tulsa Daily World,* December 31, 1978.

4 *Tulsa Tribune,* February 15, 1979.

5 *The Daily Oklahoman,* July 26, 1979.

6 Ibid.

7 *Tulsa Tribune,* February 15, 1979.

8 *The Daily Oklahoman,* July 26, 1979.

9 Interview, Donna Nigh, September 8, 1999, Heritage Archives, hereinafter cited as Donna Nigh interview.

10 Ibid.

11 Ibid.

12 *Tulsa Tribune,* February 15, 1979.

13 *M-R Quarterly,* (Summer, 1983), pp. 10-12.

14 *Friday* (Oklahoma City, Oklahoma), March 13, 1984.

15 *Tulsa World,* October 19, 1985.

16 October 9, 1984 proclamation. Heritage Archives.

17 *The Daily Oklahoman,* September 18, 1985.

18 *Tulsa World,* December 31, 1978.

19 Georgeann Nigh Whitener interview.

20 Ibid.

21 Ibid.

22 Ibid.

23 Ibid.

24 *Stillwater NewsPress* (Stillwater, Oklahoma), October 9, 1983.

25 Georgeann Nigh Whitener interview.

26 Ibid.

27 *The Daily Oklahoman,* September 11, 1981.

28 *Tulsa Tribune,* December 2, 1985.

29 Donna Nigh interview.

Boom Times Continue

1 George Nigh interview.

2 *Tulsa,* (Tulsa, Oklahoma), December, 1980, p. 27.

3 *Oklahoma Observer,* July 25, 1981.

4 George Nigh interview.

5 *The Daily Oklahoman,* June 17, 1980.

6 Ibid.

7 *Oklahoma Business* (Oklahoma City, Oklahoma), January, 1981, p. 26.

8 George Nigh interview.

9 *The Daily Oklahoman,* June 19, 1980.

10 Ibid.

11 Ibid., December 11, 1983.

12 Ibid., July 2, 1980.

13 *The Sunday Oklahoman,* January 4, 1981.

14 *Oklahoma Business,* January, 1981, p. 27.

15 Ibid., p. 28.

16 Ibid, p. 29.

17 Ibid.

18 *The Daily Oklahoman,* December 31, 1981.

19 John Kyle to author, May 12, 2000.

20 *The Daily Oklahoman,* December 12, 1981.

21 Harry Holloway and Frank S. Meyers, *Bad Times for Good Ol' Boys* (Norman: University of Oklahoma Press, 1993), p. 173.

22 Ibid., p. 175.

23 *The Daily Oklahoman,* January 7, 1982.

24 *Forbes* (New York, New York), May 14, 1982, p. 27.

25 Interview, Robert Henry, March 27, 2000, Heritage Archives.

26 *The Daily Oklahoman,* July 28, 1999.

27 Freda Diane Deskin, dissertation, University of Oklahoma, 1993, p. 294.

28 Ibid.

29 *Billboard* (New York, New York), July 17, 1982, p. 7.

30 Ibid.

31 *Friday,* August 12, 1982.

32 *Billboard,* p. 27.

33 Ibid., p. 28.

34 Ibid, p. 29.

35 Ibid.

36 *The Daily Oklahoman,* December 31, 1981.

Runing for Re-Election

1 *The Sunday Oklahoman,* March 7, 1982.

2 *Oklahoma Observer,* November 10, 1981.

3 Press Release, March 5, 1982, Heritage Archives.

4 *The Daily Oklahoman,* July 11, 1982.

5 Ibid., January 8, 1982.

6 Ibid., June 20, 1982.

7 Ibid., August 25, 1982.

8 Ibid.

9 Ibid., September 12, 1982.

10 Ibid.

11 Ibid., October 3, 1982.

12 Nigh brochure, Heritage Archives.

13 Ibid.

14 *Elk City Daily News* (Elk City, Oklahoma), August 20, 1982.

15 *The Daily Oklahoman,* October 17, 1982.

16 Henry Bellmon, with Pat Bellmon, *The Life and Times of Henry Bellmon* (Tulsa: Council Oak Books, 1992), p. 318.

17 Ibid.

18 *The Daily Oklahoman,* October 26, 1982.

19 Ibid, October 31, 1982.

20 George Nigh interview.

21 Donna Nigh interview.

22 *The Daily Oklahoman,* November 1, 1982.

23 Newspaper clippings from Nigh campaign scrapbook. Heritage Archives.

24 George Nigh interview.

25 *The Daily Oklahoman,* November 3, 1982.

26 Ibid., November 4, 1982.

27 Ibid.

Penn Square and Beyond

1 *The Daily Oklahoman,* January 11, 1983.

2 *Tulsa World,* January 17, 1983.

3 Phillip L. Zweig, *Belly Up: The Collapse of the Penn Square Bank* (New York: Crown Publishers, Inc., 1985), p. 211.

4 Baird and Goble, *The Story of Oklahoma,* p. 479.

5 *The Daily Oklahoman,* January 11, 1983.

6 Ibid., January 2, 1983.

7 Ibid., October 16, 1999.

8 Ibid., April 7, 1983.

9 *The Daily Oklahoman,* September 24, 1983.

10 Zweig, *Belly Up,* p. 434.

11 *U.S. News and World Report,* May 23, 1983.

12 *The Daily Oklahoman,* November 6, 1983.

13 Ibid., November 22, 1983.

14 Ibid., November 29, 1983.

15 *Tulsa Daily World,* November 29, 1983.

16 *The Daily Oklahoman,* December 1, 1983.

17 Ibid., December 2, 1983.

18 Ibid., December 1, 1983.

19 Ibid.

20 Baird and Goble, *The Story of Oklahoma*, pp. 479-480.

21 *The Daily Oklahoman,* January 5, 1984.

22 Ibid., January 18, 1984.

23 Ibid.

24 Ibid., January 31, 1984.

25 Ibid., January 14, 1984.

26 *The Daily Oklahoman,* March 15, 1984.

27 Ibid., April 17, 1984.

28 Ibid., January 8, 1983.

29 *Tulsa World,* April 22, 1984.

Horse Racing and Liquor by the Wink

1 *The Daily Oklahoman,* July 2, 1982.

2 Ibid., September 19, 1982.

3 Ibid.

4 *The Daily Oklahoman,* August 29, 1982.

5 Ibid., September 19, 1982.

6 Ibid., February 7, 1983.

7 Ibid., May 8, 1983.

8 Press conference highlights, August 22, 1985. Heritage Archives.

9 *The Daily Oklahoman,* August 8, 1985.

10 Ibid., December 20, 1985.

11 Ibid., January 8, 1986.

12 Ibid., January 9, 1986.

13 Ibid.

14 George Nigh interview.

15 *The Daily Oklahoman,* July 16, 1999.

16 Ibid.

17 Ibid.

18 George Nigh interview.

19 *The Daily Oklahoman,* December 7, 1982.

20 Ibid., April 18. 1999.

A Bully Pulpit

1 George Nigh interview.

2 Abe Hesser to author, August 27, 1999, Heritage Archives.

On the Road Again

1 George Nigh interview.

2 *The Daily Oklahoman,* August 8, 1984.

3 Ibid., August 29, 1984.

4 *The Journal Record,* September 12, 1984.

5 *Oklahoma Character* (Oklahoma City, Oklahoma), July, 1983.

More Money Problems and the Lottery

1 *The Daily Oklahoman,* January 8, 1985.

2 Ibid., January 20, 1985.

3 Ibid.

4 January 21, 1985 press conference highlights, Heritage Archives.

5 January 22, 1985 press conference highlights, Heritage Archives.

6 *Oklahoma,* January 3, 1985, p. 1.

7 *The Daily Oklahoman,* November 4, 1984.

8 May 24, 1985 press release, Heritage Archives.

9 *The Daily Oklahoman,* June 22, 1985.

10 Ibid., July 9, 1985.

11 Interview, Roosevelt Milton, September 15, 1999, Heritage Archives.

12 Press release statement, August 26, 1985, Heritage Archives.

13 Ibid.

14 *Tulsa Tribune,* August 27, 1985.

15 *Tulsa World,* August 27, 1985.

16 Press conference highlights, October 2, 1985, Heritage Archives.

17 Press conference highlights, December 11, 1985, Heritage Archives.

Final Years as Governor

1 *The Daily Oklahoman,* January 12, 1986.

2 Ibid.

3 Ibid.

4 Ibid., June 12, 1986.

5 February 11, 1986 press conference highlights, Heritage Archives.

6 *The Daily Oklahoman,* March 26, 1986.

7 Ibid.

8 February 11, 1986 press conference highlights, Heritage Archives.

9 Ibid.

10 *The New York Times* (New York, New York), April 15, 1986.

11 April 22, 1986 press conference highlights, Heritage Archives.

12 *The Daily Oklahoman,* February 23, 1986.

13 Ibid.

14 June 13, 1986 press conference highlights.

15 Interview, Susan Witt Conyers, May 16, 2000,

Heritage Archives.

16 Ibid.

17 *Oklahoma,* July 3, 1986, p. 3.

18 June 6, 1986 press conference highlights, Heritage Archives.

19 April 24, 1986 press conference highlights, Heritage Archives.

20 *The Daily Oklahoman,* July 8, 1986.

21 *Oklahoma Business,* November, 1986, pp. 17-21.

22 *The Daily Oklahoman,* October 20, 1986.

23 Ibid.

24 *The Black Chronicle* (Oklahoma City, Oklahoma), December 11, 1986.

25 *The Daily Oklahoman,* January 7, 1987.

26 Ibid., January 13, 1987.

BIBLIOGRAPHY

PRINTED MATERIAL

Newspapers

Christian Science Monitor
Boston, Massachussetts

Denver Post
Denver, Colorado

Los Angeles Times
Los Angeles, California

New York Times
New York, New York

Oklahoma Journal
Midwest City, Oklahoma

Oklahoma City Times
Oklahoma City, Oklahoma

The Daily Oklahoman
Oklahoma City, Oklahoma

Tulsa Daily World
Tulsa, Oklahoma

Tulsa Tribune
Tulsa, Oklahoma

Magazines

Billboard
Los Angeles, California

Life
New York, New York

Look
New York, New York

Oklahoma Today
Oklahoma City, Oklahoma

Books

Albert, Carl with Danney Goble. *Little Giant.* Norman: University of Oklahoma Press, 1990.

An Anthology of Oklahoma Poetry, 1776-1976. Oklahoma City: Metro Press, 1976.

Baird, W. David and Danney Goble. *The Story of Oklahoma.* Norman: University of Oklahoma Press, 1994.

Bellmon, Henry with Pat Bellmon. *The Life and Times of Henry Bellmon.* Tulsa: Council Oak Publishing Company, Inc., 1992.

Carter, Joseph H. *Never Met A Man I Didn't Like.* New York: Avon Books, 1991.

Creel, Von Russell and Bob Burke. *Mike Monroney: Oklahoma Liberal.* Edmond, UCO Press, 1997.

Dale, Edward Everett. *The West Wind Blows.* Oklahoma City: Oklahoma Historical Society, 1984.

Debo, Angie. *Oklahoma, foot loose and fancy free.* Norman: University of Oklahoma Press, 1949.

Ellison, Ralph. *Going To The Territory.* New York: Random House, 1986.

Fischer, Leroy H.

Oklahoma Governors, 1955-1979. Oklahoma City: Oklahoma Historical Society, 1985.

Franks, Kenny A. *You're Doin' Fine Oklahoma!* Oklahoma City: Oklahoma Historical Society, 1983.

Freeny, John Ellis. *Whuppin' and Spurrin' Through Choctaw Country.* Edmond:

Privately printed, 1998.

Goble, Danney. *Progessive Oklahoma: The Making of a New Kind of State.* Norman: University of Oklahoma Press, 1981.

________ with James R. Scales. *Oklahoma Politics: A History.* Norman: University of Oklahoma Press, 1982.

Hauan, Martin. *He buys organs for churches, pianos for bawdy houses.* Oklahoma City: Midwest Political Publications, 1976.

________ *How To Win Elections Without Hardly Cheatin' At All.* Oklahoma City: Midwest Political Publications, Inc., 1983.

Holloway, Harry with Frank S. Meyers. *Bad Times for Good Ol' Boys.* Norman: University of Oklahoma Press, 1993.

Jones, Stephen. *Oklahoma Politics in State and Nation.* Enid: The Haymaker Press, Inc., 1974.

Kennedy, John F. *Profiles in Courage.* New York: Harper and Row, 1955.

Kerr, Robert S. *Land, Wood and Water.* New York: Fleet Publishing Corporation, 1960.

Kirkpatrick, Samuel, David R. Morgan, and Thomas G. Kielhorn. *The Oklahoma Voter.* Norman: University of Oklahoma Press, 1977.

Milligan, James C. and L. David Norris. *The Man on the Second Floor: Raymond Gary.* Oklahoma City: Western Heritage Books, 1988.

Murray, William H. *Memoirs of Governor Murray and True History of Oklahoma.* Boston: Meadow Publishing Company, 1945.

Rogers, Will. *The Cowboy Philosopher on Prohibition.* Stillwater: Oklahoma State University Press, 1975.

Roosevelt, Franklin D. *Looking Forward.* London: William Heineman Ltd., 1933.

Stewart, Roy P. *Country Boy Hornbook.* Oklahoma City: Oklahoma Publishing Company, 1968.

Truman, Harry S. *Mr. Citizen.* New York: Bernard Geis Associates, 1953.

Wooldrige, Clyde E. *Wilburton: I.T. and OK.* Privately printed, 1976.

Zweig, Phillip L. *Belly Up, The Collapse of the Penn Square Bank.* New York: Crown Publishers, Inc., 1985.

INDEX

D